The Truth about Muhammad

The Truth about
Muhammad

Founder of the World's Most Intolerant Religion

❖

ROBERT SPENCER

Since 1947
**REGNERY
PUBLISHING, INC.**
An Eagle Publishing Company • Washington, DC

Library of Congress Cataloging-in-Publication Data
 Spencer, Robert, 1962-
   The truth about Muhammad : founder of the world's most intolerant religion / Robert Spencer.
       p. cm.
   Includes bibliographical references and index.
   ISBN-13: 978-1-59698-028-0
   ISBN-10: 1-59698-028-1
   1. Muhammad, Prophet, d. 632. 2. Islam—History. 3. Islam—Controversial literature. I. Title.
   BT1170.S657 2006
   297.6'3–dc22

                                                            2006027740

Published in the United States by
Regnery Publishing, Inc.
One Massachusetts Avenue, NW
Washington, DC 20001
www.regnery.com

Distributed to the trade by
National Book Network
Lanham, MD 20706

Manufactured in the United States of America

10 9 8 7 6 5 4 3 2 1

Books are available in quantity for promotional or premium use. Write to Director of Special Sales, Regnery Publishing, Inc., One Massachusetts Avenue NW, Washington, DC 20001, for information on discounts and terms or call (202) 216-0600.

TO THOSE WHO PERSEVERE
IN THE FACE OF TYRANNY

Contents

Islamic tolerance?
A kinder, gentler Muhammad
The veneration of Muhammad
Imitating Muhammad today
Frightening reality
What is to be done

Chronology of Muhammad's life

(All dates are approximate)

570   Muhammad is born in Mecca

595   Muhammad marries Khadija, who later becomes the first Muslim

610   Muhammad receives what he comes to believe is his first visitation from the angel Gabriel and revelation from Allah

613   Muhammad begins preaching Islam publicly in Mecca

615   Friction with the Quraysh causes some Muslims to leave Arabia for Abyssinia

619   Khadija dies

619   The Satanic verses incident

620   The Night Journey: Muhammad reports that he has been carried to Paradise and has met the other prophets

622   The Hijra: Muhammad and the Muslims flee to Medina

622   Muhammad consummates his marriage to the nine-year-old Aisha

624   The Nakhla raid and the beginning of violence in the name of Islam

624   The Battle of Badr: the Muslims overcome great odds to defeat the pagan Meccans

624   Muhammad and the Muslims besiege the Jewish Qaynuqa tribe and exile them from Medina

625   The Battle of Uhud: the pagan Meccans defeat the Muslims

625   Siege and exile from Medina of the Jewish Nadir tribe

Names and places

Abdullah bin Jahsh: the Muslim warrior who carried out the first Muslim raid (at Nakhla) on Muhammad's orders

Abdullah bin Salam: a Jewish rabbi who became an early convert to Islam

Abdullah bin Ubayy: a leader of the "Hypocrites," insincere Muslims who opposed Muhammad

Abu 'Afak: A poet who mocked Muhammad in his verses and was assassinated on Muhammad's orders

Abu Bakr: One of Muhammad's earliest companions and his successor as leader of the Muslims (caliph)

Abu Jahl: A leader of the pagan Quraysh who opposed Muhammad

Abu Lahab: Muhammad's uncle, who opposed him and was cursed in the Qur'an (111:1-5)

Abu Sufyan: A leader of the pagan Quraysh who opposed Muhammad, but who later converted to Islam

Aisha: Muhammad's favorite wife; he married her when she was six and consummated the marriage when she was nine

Al-'Aqaba: A city where the early Muslims pledged fealty to Muhammad

Al-Lat: One of the goddesses worshipped by the pagan Quraysh

Al-'Uzza: One of the goddesses worshipped by the pagan Quraysh

Ali: Muhammad's son-in-law, whom Shi'ite Muslims regard as his rightful successor; he reigned briefly as the fourth caliph, after Abu Bakr, Umar, and Uthman

Asma bint Marwan: A poetess who mocked Muhammad in her verses and was assassinated on Muhammad's orders

Badr: An Arabian town about 80 miles from Medina where the Muslims won their first great military victory, against the Quraysh in 624

Bahira: A Syrian Christian monk who, according to Islamic tradition, recognized the boy Muhammad as a prophet

Bukhari: Ninth-century collector of traditions about Muhammad that Muslims generally consider reliable

Buraq: The winged horse with a human head that is supposed to have carried Muhammad from Mecca to Jerusalem and thence to Paradise on his Night Journey

Chosroes: The Persian emperor in Muhammad's day, whom Muhammad called to Islam

Gabriel: The angel who is supposed to have delivered Allah's revelations to Muhammad

Ghatafan: The pagan Arabian tribe that, along with the Quraysh, laid siege to Medina in the Battle of the Trench

Hafsa: One of Muhammad's wives

Heraclius: The Byzantine emperor in Muhammad's day, whom Muhammad called to Islam

Hudaybiyya: A town about nine miles from Mecca where Muhammad concluded a treaty with the Quraysh

Hunayn: A dry riverbed near Mecca where Muhammad defeated the last large-scale resistance to him in Arabia

Ibn Ishaq: Muhammad's first biographer (704–773)

Ibn Sa'd: An early compiler of biographical traditions about Muhammad (d. 845)

Jerusalem: The city from which Muhammad is supposed to have ascended to Paradise on his Night Journey

Ka'b bin Al-Ashraf: A Jewish poet who mocked Muhammad in his verses and was assassinated on Muhammad's orders

Ka'bah: A shrine and place of pilgrimage in Mecca that Muhammad emptied of its idols and transformed into a site for Islamic pilgrimage

Khadija: Muhammad's first wife and first convert

Khalid bin al-Walid: A renowned Muslim warrior

Khaybar: An oasis near Medina which Muhammad attacked, exiling the Jews who inhabited it

Kinana ibn Rabi: A Jewish leader at Khaybar who was tortured and killed on Muhammad's orders for refusing to disclose the location of treasure

Manat: One of the goddesses worshipped by the pagan Quraysh

Mary the Copt: Muhammad's concubine and mother of his son Ibrahim, who died in infancy

Mecca: Muhammad's birthplace; a principal city for trade and pilgrimage in pre-Islamic Arabia

Medina: An Arabian city north of Mecca, in which Muhammad first became a political and military leader after his flight there (Hijra)

Muhammad: the prophet of Islam (570–632)

Muhammad bin Maslama: An early Muslim who carried out several assassinations on Muhammad's orders

Nadir: A Jewish tribe of Medina; Muhammad besieged and exiled them

Nakhla: An Arabian town where the Muslims carried out their first military raid against the Quraysh

Qaynuqa: A Jewish tribe of Medina; Muhammad besieged and exiled them

Quraysh: The pagan Arabs of Mecca; Muhammad belonged to this tribe, but they rejected his prophetic message

Qurayzah: A Jewish tribe of Medina; Muhammad supervised their massacre after they betrayed an alliance with the Muslims

Sa'd bin Mu'adh: The Muslim warrior who pronounced sentence, with Muhammad's permission, against the Qurayzah tribe

Safiyya bint Huyayy: Wife of Kinana ibn Rabi; Muhammad took her as his own wife after killing Kinana

Tabuk: A northwestern Arabian city to which Muhammad led an expedition against the Byzantines

Ta'if: A city south of Mecca that initially rejected Muhammad and was later conquered by the Muslims

Uhud: A mountain near Mecca where the Quraysh defeated the Muslims after the Battle of Badr

Umar: One of Muhammad's earliest companions and the successor of Abu Bakr as leader of the Muslims (caliph)

Waraqa: Khadija's uncle and a Christian priest; he is supposed to have confirmed Muhammad's prophetic status

Zayd bin Haritha: Muhammad's adopted son and the first husband of Zaynab bint Jahsh

Zaynab bint Jahsh: Muhammad's daughter-in-law, whom he subsequently married by what he represented as a command of Allah

CHAPTER ONE

Why a biography
of Muhammad
is relevant today

◈ How the "Islam is peace" mantra still controls American policy
◈ Muslim presentations of Muhammad: are they talking about
the same man?
◈ Why it matters what Muhammad was like
◈ Why this book is dangerous

Is Islam a religion of peace? Why it matters

FIVE YEARS INTO THE WAR ON TERROR, IT IS STILL COMMONPLACE
to hear Islam called a religion of peace. It is now also common to hear that
term used derisively or ironically, in light of continued acts of violence
committed in the name of Islam. A tiny minority of extremists has supposedly hijacked the religion, but jihadist Muslims won elections in the
Palestinian Authority and elsewhere. The new, American-backed Iraqi
and Afghan constitutions have enshrined sharia, Islamic law, (which
includes the death penalty for Christian converts), as the highest law of

1

the land. And the vast majority of peaceful Muslims show no signs of resisting or condemning the global Islamic jihad that is being fought in their name.

Mounting evidence that jihadist violence is actually quite popular among Muslims worldwide has not made Western officials reconsider their views of Islam. On April 10, 2006, President George Bush took questions from graduate students at the Paul H. Nitze School of Advanced International Studies at Johns Hopkins University in Washington, D.C. One student prefaced a question with a series of assertions about Muhammad, the Prophet of Islam:

> Morning, Mr. President. I have a more general question about the United States' work to democratize the rest of the world. Many have viewed the United States' effort to democratize the world—especially nations in the Middle East—as an imposition or invasion on their sovereign rights. Considering that it was, in fact, the Prophet Muhammed who established the first known constitution in the world—I'm referring to the constitution he wrote for the city of Medina—and that his life and the principles outlined in his constitution, such as the championing of the welfare of women, children and the poor, living as an equal among his people, dissolving disputes between the warring clans in Arabia, giving any man or woman in parliament the right to vote, and guaranteeing respect for all religions, ironically parallel those principles that we hold most precious in our own Constitution, I'm wondering how might your recently formed Iraq Study Group under the U.S. Institute for Peace explore these striking similarities to forge a new relationship with Iraqis and educate Americans about the democratic principles inherent in Islam?

The president responded generously, taking for granted the veracity of this portrait of Muhammad:

I'm not saying to countries, you've got to look like us or act like us, but I am saying, you know, give your people a chance to be free. And I think it's necessary for America to take the lead on this issue. I think it is—I think it is vital for our future that we encourage liberty, and in this case, the Middle East. And as you said, it doesn't necessarily run contrary to what the Prophet Muhammad said.[1]

Dueling Muhammads

It is exceedingly curious that so few Muslim countries, in which Muhammad is generally revered, encourage liberty and democracy and grant women legal equity. Yet the idea of Muhammad as a champion of these values was not original to the president's questioner. The Muslim writer Farida Khanam portrays him as meek, mild, and full of love and compassion:

His heart was filled with intense love for all humankind irrespective of caste, creed, or color. Once he advised his Companions to regard all people as their brothers and sisters. He added: "You are all Adam's offspring and Adam was born of clay."

All this tells us what kind of awareness Muhammad wanted to instill in humans. His mission was to bring people abreast of the reality that all people—despite that they come from different countries and are seemingly different from one another in regards to their color, language, dress, and culture—are interconnected. Hence a proper relationship can only be established between all humans if they were to regard one another as sisters and brothers. Only then will proper feelings of love and respect prevail throughout the world.[2]

Islamic apologists and contemporary academics have echoed the same ideas. Muhammad "was, by all accounts," says Islamic scholar Carl Ernst, "a charismatic person known for his integrity."[3] Safi-ur-Rahman al-Mubarakpuri, whose biography of Muhammad, *Ar-Raheeq Al-Makhtum (The Sealed Nectar)*, won first prize in an international Muhammad biography competition held in Mecca in 1979, wrote that "the Prophet combined both perfection of creation and perfection of manners....The Prophet is the most just, the most decent, the most truthful at speech, and the honestest [sic] of all."[4]

In a similar vein, Ibrahim Hooper of the Council on American-Islamic Relations, an organization that says it wants "to enhance understanding of Islam, encourage dialogue, protect civil liberties, and empower American Muslims," urged Muslims during the Muhammad cartoon riots, which erupted internationally in early 2006, to imitate the Prophet's example:[5]

> You do not do evil to those who do evil to you, but you deal with them with forgiveness and kindness (Sahih Al-Bukhari). That description of Islam's Prophet Muhammad is a summary of how he reacted to personal attacks and abuse. Islamic traditions include a number of instances of the Prophet having the opportunity to strike back at those who attacked him, but refraining from doing so....As Muslims, we need to take a step back and ask ourselves, "What would the Prophet Muhammad do?"[6]

But the international riots and murders committed over these cartoons—universally explained by the perpetrators as revenge for the alleged insult to Muhammad—suggested that Hooper's view was by no means universally accepted among Muslims.

Some Muslims even invoked Muhammad's example in exactly the opposite direction of Hooper's plea for restraint. Sheikh Omar Bakri Mohammed, an open supporter of Osama bin Laden who preached jihad in Britain for many years before finally leaving the country in the wake of the July 7, 2005, jihad bombings in London, declared that Muhammad himself would want the cartoonists dead: "The insult has been established now by everybody, Muslim and non-Muslim, and everybody condemns the cartoonist and condemns the cartoon. However, in Islam, God said, *and the messenger Mohammed said*, whoever insults a prophet, he must be punished and executed. This man should be put on trial and if it is proven to be executed" (emphasis added).[7] The English jihadist group Al-Ghurabaa, the successor to Bakri's Al-Muhajiroun organization, published a similar statement, referring to incidents in Muhammad's life to justify its position:

> At the time of the Messenger Muhammad (saw)[8] there were individuals like these who dishonoured and insulted him upon whom the Islamic judgement was executed. Such people were not tolerated in the past and throughout the history of Islam were dealt with according to the Shariah [Islamic law]. Shortly after these incidents the people began to realize that insulting the Messenger of Allah (saw) was not something to be taken lightly and doing so could get you killed, a concept that many seem to have forgotten today.[9]

In April 2006, the Mujahadeen Council, led by Abu Musab al-Zarqawi, then leader of al Qaeda in Iraq, announced that it had murdered a Christian in Mosul because "this impure crusader offended our noble prophet Mohammed."[10] Mukhlas, a perpetrator of the 2002 Bali jihadist bombings, sounded a similar note:

> You who still have a shred of faith in your hearts, have you forgotten that to kill infidels and the enemies of Islam is a deed that has a reward above no other. . . . Aren't you aware that the model for us all, the Prophet Mohammed and the four rightful caliphs, undertook to murder infidels as one of their primary activities, and that the Prophet waged jihad operations 77 times in the first 10 years as head of the Muslim community in Medina?[11]

Most Western scholars of Islam would assert that Mukhlas does not understand his religion and mischaracterizes its prophet. Karen Armstrong, in her hagiographical *Muhammad: A Biography of the Prophet,* notes that the September 11 hijackers "had Muhammad in mind, when they boarded the doomed aircraft. 'Be optimistic,' they were told in the documents that were allegedly found in their luggage, 'the Prophet was always optimistic.'" However, Armstrong continues, "the very idea that Muhammad would have found anything to be optimistic about in the carnage committed in his name on September 11 is an obscenity, because, as I try to show in these pages, Muhammad spent most of his life trying to stop that kind of indiscriminate slaughter.... Muhammad eventually abjured violence and pursued a daring, inspired policy of non-violence that was worthy of Gandhi."[12]

Why Muhammad matters

So what was Muhammad really like? The question becomes more pressing every day—for if he was indeed a man of peace, one may reasonably hope that his example would become the linchpin of reform efforts in the Islamic world that would eventually roll back the influence of jihad terrorists. If he really championed democracy and equality of the sexes, one could profitably invoke his example among Muslims, who revere him as the highest example of human behavior, to work for these ideals in the Islamic world. But if the jihad terrorists are correct in invoking his example to justify their deeds, then Islamic reformers will need to initiate a respectful but searching re-evaluation of the place Muhammad occupies within Islam—a vastly more difficult undertaking.

Western non-Muslims need to know the answer so that we can plan public policy accordingly. The common distinction drawn between "Islam" and "Islamism," which is accepted without question by the vast majority of public policy analysts, opinion-makers, lawmakers, and diplomats, rests on the idea that there is a core, a kernel, or perhaps an original form of Islam that did not teach warfare against non-Muslims; "Islamism" is widely reputed to be a Muslim imitation of fascism and communism that has little or nothing to do with the actual teachings of Islam. When seven-

teen Muslims were arrested in Canada in June 2006 on suspicion of plotting jihad terror attacks against the Canadian Parliament building and
other landmarks, the *Ottawa Citizen* hastened to reassert liberal pieties:

> In 2001, they brought their war against the West to two great
> American cities. Next were Spain and England. In Holland,
> they butchered a filmmaker on the street. Australians got theirs
> in Bali. It's surprising it took them so long to turn to Canada.
>
> Let's be clear about who we mean by "they." We mean
> Islamists. Not Muslims, but Islamists. A Muslim is one who
> practices Islam, a great religion. An Islamist is one for whom
> Islam is not just a religion, but a political ideology.
>
> Islamists seek to establish pure Islamic societies governed
> according to the harshest interpretation of Islam. Islamism has
> apocalyptic echoes of another millennial ideology, fascism
> (think of the Thousand Year Reich). Islamism is totalitarian,
> utopian, violent—and like fascism it is expansionist.[13]

Likewise, after the 2005 jihadist bombings in London, British prime minister Tony Blair declared: "We know that these people act in the name of
Islam but we also know that the vast and overwhelming majority of Muslims both here and abroad are decent and law-abiding people who abhor
this kind of terrorism every bit as much as we do."[14]

Britain, like the states of continental Europe, has staked a great deal on
this assumption—most notably, its immigration policies. Of course, even if
the jihadists are right about Muhammad that does not mean that all or even
most Muslims will not be law-abiding and opposed to terrorism. In Islam,
as in every religious tradition, there is a spectrum of belief, knowledge, and
fervor. One cannot be sure from anyone's self-identification as a Muslim
how much he knows about the Qur'an and the life of Muhammad. This is
true particularly because Islam is an essentially Arabic religion; Muslims
must learn the daily prayers and the Qur'an in Arabic, which is the language of Allah. To pray to him in another tongue is unacceptable. Since

most Muslims today are not native Arabic speakers, and the Qur'an is in difficult, classical, seventh-century Arabic (and most English translations are in equally difficult ersatz King James Bible-like language), many Muslims, even those who are quite serious about their faith, have only a dim awareness of what these texts actually say.

Difficulties aside, the texts can be read and understood. And if peaceful Muslims can mount no comeback when jihadists point to Muhammad's example to justify violence, their ranks will always remain vulnerable to recruitment from jihadists who present themselves as the exponents of "pure Islam," faithfully following Muhammad's example.

The Qur'an and Islamic tradition are clear that the Prophet is the supreme example of behavior for Muslims to follow. His importance to hundreds of millions of Muslims worldwide is rooted in the Qur'an, the Muslim holy book. In brief, he is "an excellent model of conduct" (Qur'an 33:21). He demonstrates "an exalted standard of character" (68:4), and indeed, "he who obeys the Messenger [Muhammad], obeys Allah" (4:80). The Qur'an frequently tells Muslims to obey Allah and Muhammad: while the Muslim holy book takes for granted that Muhammad is fallible (cf. 48:2; 80:1-12), it also instructs Muslims repeatedly to obey Muhammad (3:32; 3:132; 4:13; 4:59; 4:69; 5:92; 8:1; 8:20; 8:46; 9:71; 24:47; 24:51; 24:52; 24:54; 24:56; 33:33; 47:33; 49:14; 58:13; 64:12).

Any devout Muslim will take this seriously. Muqtedar Khan of the Center for the Study of Islam and Democracy explains:

> No religious leader has as much influence on his followers as does Muhammad (Peace be upon him) the last Prophet of Islam....And Muhammad as the final messenger of God enjoys preeminence when it comes to revelation—the Qur'an—and traditions. So much so that the words, deeds and silences (that which he saw and did not forbid) of Muhammad became an independent source of Islamic law. Muslims, as a part of religious observance, not only obey, but also seek to emulate and imitate their Prophet in every aspect

of life. Thus Muhammad is the medium as well as a source of the divine law.[15]

As both reform-minded Muslims and bloodthirsty jihadists invoke his example to justify their actions, the question of which group is likely to prevail in the future, and which will guide an Islamic world that is in the grip of a religious revival and increasingly hostile toward America and the West, will largely be determined by Muhammad—by what he was really like according to Islamic texts.

By examining the Islamic texts and what they say about the religion's founding prophet, we can learn something of Muhammad, even if there has not been a scholarly "quest for the historical Muhammad" the way there has been, and still is, a great quest for the historical Jesus. The true identity, words, and deeds of the Prophet of Islam are topics that have only been lightly explored by scholars, largely owing to the paucity of early, reliable sources, and the entrenched Islamic resistance to any questioning of accepted Islamic beliefs, even if that questioning is based on non-polemical, scholarly principles. While historical critics of the Bible have operated freely and wielded tremendous influence in the Christian and post-Christian West, in the Islamic world such studies are virtually nonexistent. The few scholars who work in this field, such as Christoph Luxenberg, receive death threats and publish under pseudonyms.

But ultimately the quest for the historical Muhammad, while fascinating and important, is not what will determine the course the Islamic world will take in the coming decades. For any such investigations are extremely unlikely to gain any significant audience in the Islamic world. What is certain to be influential, however, is the figure of Muhammad as he appears in the Qur'an and other accepted Islamic sources—especially the Hadith, the traditions of the Prophet that have largely determined the bases of Islamic practice and piety.

This battle is already raging. Members of jihad groups are already claiming the Qur'an and Hadith as their allies in their efforts to win over cultural Muslims. Muslim hardliners have made deep inroads into peaceful Muslim communities by preaching violent Islam as the "pure Islam" and calling Muslims back to what they present as the full observance of their religion. And that full observance involves warfare against non-Muslims in order to establish the hegemony of the Islamic social order.[16] This recruitment centers not only upon the Qur'an and other key Islamic texts, but also on the figure of Muhammad.

Polite fictions are useless

Many policymakers and pundits do not want to pursue such a line of investigation because its conclusions could be frightening. If the terrorists have not "hijacked" a peaceful religion, if they have not perverted Islam's substance, then what? Do you want to see a global war? Do you want to see the United States having to take on the fifty-seven states of the Organization of the Islamic Conference simultaneously? One prominent conservative political analyst even asserted that although the idea that Islam is a religion of peace "seems a polite fiction, it is an important one. Influential Muslims believe it to be true, and it is crucial that they prevail in the Muslim struggle for self-definition. Rather than scorning them, we should be doing what we can to support the likes of King Abdullah of Jordan, who has launched an anti-terror initiative, and Iraq's Ayatollah Sistani, who has been consistent in condemning terrorism. Whatever the theological niceties of Islam, religious cultures take on different colorations across time. Some people wondered whether Christianity was a religion of peace three hundred years ago when rival Christian princes were warring over questions of faith."[17]

The difference is that no Christian could credibly argue that Jesus, the prince of peace, taught violence, or anything that contradicted his precepts that those who live by the sword shall die by the sword, that men should turn the other cheek, and that they should render unto Caesar the things that are Caesar's. But if Muhammad taught violence, if Muhammad taught a doctrine of required holy war against infidels, if Muhammad conflated religion and government it will change mujahedin around the world not one bit to pretend otherwise; they will continue to invoke what they believe to be his authentic teachings in order to justify their actions. The fact that truths are difficult is no reason to choose unreality and "polite fictions."

If Muhammad's own life and teachings are the source of jihad violence, identifying that truth will not compel Islamic states to fight America. But it will allow for clear-minded policymaking, make possible honest reform within Islam, and have the advantage of being based on the facts.

The purpose of this book

This is not a comprehensive biography of the Prophet of Islam, although it does provide a general outline of the trajectory of his career. Above all, it is an examination of some aspects of his life that non-Muslims find problematic, and that are used by Muslims today to justify violent actions or other behavior not in accord with Western notions of human rights and the dignity of the human person. Western readers will learn why moderate Muslims—on whom Western governments and law enforcement officials are placing so much hope—appear so weak and marginalized compared to jihadist movements in the Islamic world. And they will learn why Muslims find Muhammad's example so compelling, and why that example can be used to justify such widely divergent actions.

Along the way, I will show how popular views of Muhammad and Islam have been shaped in the English-speaking world and the West in general, and reveal some of the biases of those who did the shaping.

Why I did not want to write this book

In early 2006, Muslim rage erupted worldwide over the famous Danish cartoons of the Prophet Muhammad. The cartoons themselves were much less offensive than what is routinely printed in every American newspaper about presidents, presidential candidates, and other pols. There were twelve in all; nine were entirely innocuous, while three made a connection between Islam and violence. Although the idea of riots over cartoons seemed ridiculous to most non-Muslims, the "crisis" provoked diplomatic responses, official United Nations discussions, international boycotts, and the threatening of utterly innocent businesspeople and embassy personnel. Just a few examples from the height of the cartoon crisis:

- Gaza: In late January, gunmen seized an EU office, demanding apologies from Denmark and Norway (where another publication later reprinted the cartoons).[18] The following day, demonstrators chanted "War on Denmark, death to Denmark" as they burned Danish flags. Said Islamic Jihad leader Nafez Azzam: "We feel great rage at the continued attacks on Islam and the Prophet of Islam and we demand that the Danish government make a clear and public apology for the wrongful crime."[19]
- Arab interior ministers, meeting in Tunis, declared: "We ask the Danish authorities to take the necessary measures to punish those responsible for this harm and to take action to avoid a repeat."[20]
- Libya and Saudi Arabia recalled their ambassadors from Copenhagen.
- In Saudi Arabia, an angry mob beat two employees of the Danish corporation Arla Foods.
- Throughout the Islamic world, Arla Foods was subjected to a crippling boycott—a boycott that was endorsed by Muslim officials worldwide.[21]
- Iraqi foreign minister Hoshiyar Zebari complained to the Danish ambassador to Baghdad, when Danish troops were put on alert there after a fatwa concerning the cartoons was issued.[22]

These incidents followed diplomatic protests from the Muslim World League, the Organization of the Islamic Conference, and other organizations; protests in Kashmir; death threats emanating from Pakistan; and more.[23] Even Bill Clinton got into the act, decrying "these totally outrageous cartoons against Islam" and huffing self-righteously: "So now what are we going to do?...Replace the anti-Semitic prejudice with anti-Islamic prejudice?"[24] Of course not, but his question was beside the point. The cartoons were not a manifestation of anti-Islamic prejudice: criticism of Muhammad or even of Islam is not and should not be considered equivalent to anti-Semitism. Islam is not a race; the problems with it are not the product of fear-mongering and fiction, but of ideology and facts—facts that have been stressed repeatedly by Muslims around the world, when they commit violence in the name of Islam and justify that violence by its teachings. Noting, as some of the cartoons do, that there is a connection between the teachings of Muhammad and Islamic violence is simply an awareness of what has been repeatedly asserted by Osama bin Laden, Ayman al-Zawahiri, Abu Musab al-Zarqawi, Omar Bakri, Abu Hamza, Abu Bakar Bashir, and so many other jihadists. Do all these men and so many, many others misunderstand and misrepresent the teachings of Muhammad and Islam? This question, as crucial as it is, is irrelevant to an ethical evaluation of the cartoons. The fact is, these and other jihad terrorists claim Muhammad's example and words as their inspiration. Some of the cartoons call attention to that fact.

Ultimately, then, the cartoon controversy is a question of freedom of speech. As it grew into an international cause célèbre, the cartoon controversy indicated the gulf between the Islamic world and the post-Christian West in matters of freedom of speech and expression. And it may yet turn out that as the West continues to pay homage to its idols of tolerance, multiculturalism, and pluralism, it will give up those hard-won freedoms voluntarily. Freedom of speech encompasses precisely the freedom to annoy, to ridicule, and to offend. If it doesn't, it is hollow: inoffensive speech doesn't need the protection of a constitutional amendment. The instant that any person or ideology is considered off-limits for critical examination and even ridicule, freedom of speech has been replaced by an ideological straitjacket. Westerners seem to grasp this easily when it comes to affronts to Christianity, even when they are as sharp-edged and offensive as Andres

Serrano's *Piss Christ* or Chris Ofili's dung- and pornography-encrusted
Holy Virgin Mary. But the same clarity of thought doesn't seem to carry
over to an Islamic context.

Yet that is where it is needed the most. The cartoon controversy,
insignificant and even silly as it may have been in its origins, grew to be an
increasingly serious challenge to Western notions of pluralism and freedom
of speech. The newspaper that originally printed the cartoons, *Jyllands-
Posten*, and Danish prime minister Anders Fogh Rasmussen generally limited themselves to saying essentially that they were sorry if Muslims took
offense, and that none was intended. But calls from Muslims to go farther
and "punish those responsible," as the Arab interior ministers demanded, or
to treat the cartoons as a human rights violation, as a Belgian imam
demanded, continued. Even the European Union castigated the Danes for
mishandling the controversy, apparently oblivious to the fact that to place
Muhammad and Islam beyond criticism and even beyond lampooning
would be just as dangerous for a free society as the idea that the "Beloved
Leader" of North Korea or dialectical materialism is above criticism.
Indeed, it would be death for a free society.

The Organization of the Islamic Conference had decided at a meeting
in Mecca in December 2005 to use the cartoons as an abject lesson in the
perils of Western secularism. Muslim cartoon rage was not spontaneous,
but it spread quickly all across the Muslim world.[25] At least 139 people
were killed and 823 were injured in the international cartoon riots, and the
cartoonists now live under death threats.[26]

Death to "blasphemers"

Nor was cartoon rage unique. In September 2004, Dutch filmmaker Theo
van Gogh's film *Submission* aired on Dutch TV. The brainchild of an ex-
Muslim member of the Dutch Parliament, Ayaan Hirsi Ali, *Submission*
decried the mistreatment of Muslim women—and even featured images of
battered women wearing see-through robes that exposed their breasts, with
verses from the Qur'an written on their bodies. On November 2, 2004, van

Gogh was shot dead on an Amsterdam street by Muhammad Bouyeri, a Muslim who, after shooting van Gogh several times, stabbed him repeatedly, slit his throat with a butcher knife, and left a note on the body containing verses from the Qur'an and threats to other Dutch public figures who opposed the flood of Muslim immigrants into the Netherlands.[27]

This kind of murder has ample precedent in the Islamic world. In 1947, Islamic radicals murdered Iranian lawyer Ahmad Kasravi in court, where he was defending himself against charges that he had attacked Islam. Four years later, members of the same radical Muslim group, Fadayan-e Islam, assassinated Iranian prime minister Haji-Ali Razmara after a group of Muslim clerics issued a fatwa calling for his death. In 1992, the Egyptian writer Faraj Foda was murdered by Muslims enraged at his "apostasy" from Islam—another offense for which traditional Islamic law prescribes the death penalty. Foda's countryman, the Nobel Prize–winning novelist Naguib Mahfouz, was stabbed in 1994 after accusations of blasphemy. Under Pakistan's blasphemy laws, many non-Muslims have been arrested, tortured, and sentenced to die on the slimmest of evidence. And of course, there is the Ayatollah Khomeini's notorious death fatwa against the novelist Salman Rushdie.

Van Gogh no doubt intended *Submission* to be provocative and even insulting. The great-grandson of Vincent van Gogh's brother, he was a well-known and controversial gadfly on the Dutch scene; in the past, he had criticized Jews and Christians with enough vehemence to elicit formal complaints. Even Hirsi Ali acknowledged that "the criticism of van Gogh was legitimate. But when someone has to die for his world view, what he may have done wrong is no longer the issue. That's when we have to stand up for our basic rights. Otherwise we are just reinforcing the killer and conceding that there was a good reason to kill this person."[28]

Defending freedom of speech

The free world should have stood resolutely with Denmark, ready to defend freedom of expression. But it did not. After the murder of van Gogh, the free world should have defended free speech. But it did not. Against Islamic intolerance and violence, the West should have promoted its own Judeo-Christian heritage, with its emphasis on the dignity of the human person, from which Western freedoms of speech and conscience flow. But it did not.

Undefended, we will lose our rights to free speech and thought.

That is why I determined, after a great deal of hesitation and uncertainty, that I must write this book. I am fully aware of the risks involved. But the question of Muhammad—of who he was, what he did, and what he believed—is key to understanding today's global conflict with the jihadists, and what we must do about it.

The subject matter is provocative—possibly lethally so.

But I will report on what Muslim sources—sources regarded as reliable by most Muslims—say about Muhammad. And I will discuss some of the implications. It is not necessary—and it is not my intention—to insult Muhammad, to deride him, to lampoon or mock him, or to write anything except a scrupulously accurate account of what he said and did about some key issues. But in these areas tempers run hot very quickly.

Still, that is why this book had to be written. Freedom of inquiry and speech, the quest for truth, should not be cowed into silence by violent intimidation or the acceptance of half-truths and propaganda meant to appease freedom's enemies.

One thing is certain: if no one is willing to take such risks, freedom of speech will swiftly become a relic of history.

General notes

In writing this book I have relied exclusively upon Islamic sources for the life of Muhammad: the earliest biographical material in the Islamic tradition, which I will detail in chapter three, as well as the English translations of the Qur'an made by the Muslims Abdullah Yusuf Ali and Mohammed Marmaduke Pickthall. (Qu'ranic verse numeration is not standard; therefore, if you are using a translation other than Ali's or Pickthall's, please be aware that a verse I am citing may be several verses away from the location I specify for it.) There is in this material some divergence in the way names are transliterated from the Arabic, so that occasionally someone's name will be spelled one way by me and by one source but in another way by another source; I apologize for the confusion this causes, and have tried to keep it to a minimum.

Similarly, I have in all cases referred to the deity of Islam as "Allah," while the English translation of the earliest Muslim biography of Muhammad refers to the same deity as "God"—as I'll illustrate in my quotations from that biography in this book. Of course, the word "Allah" does not belong exclusively to Islam; it predates Islam, and Arabic-speaking Christians and Jews use the word Allah for God. The Qur'an, of course, claims that the deity of Jews and Christians is the same as that of the Muslims (29:46). However, since traditional Islam rejects such Christian doctrines as the Trinity, the divinity of Christ, and others, and classifies Judaism along with Christianity as a renegade perversion of Islam, it seems prudent to me, as well as to many English-speaking Muslims, to continue to use the Arabic word "Allah" to refer to the Islamic deity in English. I hope that this will not cause further confusion.

CHAPTER TWO

In search of the historic Muhammad

- ◈ Why the Qur'an cannot be understood independently of the Hadith
- ◈ Sorting fact from fiction in the Hadith—and why this is largely impossible
- ◈ The best early sources for details of Muhammad's life
- ◈ Why historical fact and Muslim belief about Muhammad are *not* synonymous

What can we really know about Muhammad?

MOST WESTERN NON-MUSLIMS KNOW VIRTUALLY NOTHING ABOUT the Prophet of Islam. While even in the post-Christian West the broad outline of the story of Jesus Christ is still generally familiar, and many people would be able to recount the tale of Gautama Buddha attaining enlightenment while sitting under a bo tree, the figure of Muhammad has for most non-Muslims remained peculiarly indistinct and devoid of content.

Muslims would say that non-Muslims are ignorant about Muhammad by their own choice, and not for want of information. Islamic spokesmen generally maintain that we can know a great deal about Muhammad.

Muqtedar Khan of the Center for the Study of Islam and Democracy enunciated a commonplace assumption when he said: "An extraordinary aspect of Muhammad's life is that he lived in the full light of history. There are detailed accounts of his life available to us. No comparable religious figure's life and times have been so well recorded as Muhammad's."[1] It was the French scholar Ernest Renan who first wrote in 1851 that Muhammad lived "in the full light of history."

The Qur'an

The Qur'an contains a good deal of detail about particular incidents in the Prophet's life, but no continuous narrative—and the incidents it does relate are often told obliquely or incompletely, as if the audience knows the outline of the story already. Allah, according to the traditional Muslim view, dictated every word of the Qur'an to the Prophet Muhammad through the Angel Gabriel. The Qur'an is, according to Islamic tradition, a perfect copy of an eternal book—the *umm al-kitab*, or Mother of the Book—that has existed forever with Allah. It was delivered piecemeal through Gabriel to Muhammad during his twenty-three-year prophetic career.

Allah himself is the only speaker throughout virtually all of the Qur'an. (Occasionally Muhammad seems to have lapsed a bit on this point: sura 48:27, for example, contains the words "if Allah wills"—an odd locution for Allah himself to be using.) Most often he addresses Muhammad directly, frequently telling him what to say about various matters. Allah legislates for the Muslims through Muhammad, giving him instructions on what laws to lay down: "They ask thee concerning women's courses. Say: They are a hurt and a pollution: so keep away from women in their courses, and do not approach them until they are clean. But when they have purified themselves, ye may approach them in any manner, time, or place ordained for you by Allah. For Allah loves those who turn to Him constantly and He loves those who keep themselves pure and clean" (2:222).

But often the matter at hand is not so straightforward: reading the Qur'an is in many places like walking in on a conversation between two people with whom one is only slightly acquainted. When Islamic apologists say terrorists quote the Qur'an on jihad "out of context," they neglect to mention that the Qur'an itself often offers little context. Frequently it makes reference to people and events without bothering to explain what's going on. For example—and I ask the reader's indulgence as we enter the Qur'an and its exegesis, which can seem a little confusing—the first five verses of the Qur'an's sixty-sixth sura say this:

> O Prophet! Why holdest thou to be forbidden that which Allah has made lawful to thee? Thou seekest to please thy consorts. But Allah is Oft-Forgiving, Most Merciful. Allah has already ordained for you, (O men), the dissolution of your oaths (in some cases): and Allah is your Protector, and He is Full of Knowledge and Wisdom. When the Prophet disclosed a matter in confidence to one of his consorts, and she then divulged it (to another), and Allah made it known to him, he confirmed part thereof and repudiated a part. Then when he told her thereof, she said, "Who told thee this?" He said, "He told me Who knows and is well-acquainted (with all things)." If ye two turn in repentance to Him, your hearts are indeed so inclined; but if ye back up each other against him, truly Allah is his Protector, and Gabriel, and (every) righteous one among those who believe—and furthermore, the angels—will back (him) up. It may be, if he divorced you (all), that Allah will give him in exchange consorts better than you, who submit (their wills), who believe, who are devout, who turn to Allah in repentance, who worship (in humility), who travel (for Faith) and fast, previously married or virgins.

It is impossible to tell from this passage what the Prophet has held forbidden that Allah has made lawful for him, or how he tried to please his consorts, or under what circumstances Allah permits oaths to be broken, or what secret the consort told that Allah later told Muhammad, or even which two consorts are being admonished, warned to repent and not to band together against Muhammad, and threatened with divorce. The entire passage—and there are many like it in the Qur'an—is completely opaque to anyone who was not directly involved in the proceedings.

But Islamic tradition fills in the story—and does so in the context of an early Muslim, Abdullah bin 'Abbas, asking the Caliph Umar, a companion of the Prophet and his second successor as leader of the Muslim community (*umma*), about this Qur'anic passage. During the Hajj—the pilgrimage to Mecca—Abdullah met Umar and posed the question: "O Chief of the believers! Who were the two ladies from among the wives of the Prophet to whom Allah said: 'If you two return in repentance (66.4)'?"

Umar replied, "I am astonished at your question, O Ibn 'Abbas. They were Aisha and Hafsa." According to Umar, Hafsa, one of Muhammad's wives, had been angering the Prophet by talking back to him. So when Umar learned that Muhammad had divorced all his wives, he was not surprised; he exclaimed: "Hafsa is a ruined loser! I expected that would happen some day."

Umar goes to Muhammad, who initially declines to receive him and then relents. "I greeted him and while still standing, I said: 'Have you divorced your wives?' He raised his eyes to me and replied in the negative." Umar then complains that his wife has grown disobedient, under the influence of some of recent female Muslim converts. At that, says Umar, "the Prophet smiled." And he smiled again when Umar related that he had told Hafsa not to talk back to Muhammad; Muhammad's wife Aisha, he told her, could get away with it only because she was prettier and Muhammad loved her more.

Umar explains to Abdullah that "the Prophet did not go to his wives because of the secret which Hafsa had disclosed to Aisha, and he said that he would not go to his wives for one month as he was angry with them when Allah admonished him (for his oath that he would not approach Maria). When twenty-nine days had passed, the Prophet went to Aisha first of all."[2]

But Umar does not reveal Hafsa's secret. According to some authorities, it was that Hafsa had caught Muhammad in bed with his concubine, Mary the Copt, on the day he was supposed to spend with Hafsa. Muhammad promised to stay away from Mary and asked Hafsa to keep the matter a secret, but Hafsa told Aisha. Then Allah stepped in with the revelation of the threat of divorce that we now find in sura 66, freeing Muhammad from his oath to stay away from Mary.[3] But another tradition explains the matter quite differently. Aisha explains:

> The Prophet used to stay for a long while with Zainab bint Jahsh [another one of his wives] and drink honey at her house. So Hafsa and I decided that if the Prophet came to any one of us, she should say to him, "I detect the smell of Maghafir (a nasty smelling gum) in you. Have you eaten Maghafir?" So the Prophet visited one of them and she said to him similarly. The Prophet said, "Never mind, I have taken some honey at the house of Zainab bint Jahsh, but I shall never drink of it any-more." So there was revealed: "O Prophet ! Why do you ban (for you) that which Allah has made lawful for you. . . . If your two (wives of Prophet) turn in repentance to Allah," (66.1-4) addressing Aisha and Hafsa. "When the Prophet disclosed a matter in confidence to some of his wives," (66.3) namely his saying: but I have taken some honey.[4]

In this scenario the revelation of sura 66 concerns only his wives' jealousy (or perhaps Muhammad's bad breath) and his oath to stop drinking honey. In this case what the Prophet has held forbidden that Allah has made lawful for him would be honey. That is, Muhammad tried to please his consorts by promising to give up honey, and Allah is allowing him to break this oath and threatening the errant wives with divorce.

In another hadith, Umar takes oblique credit for inspiring part of this particular revelation: "Once the wives of the Prophet made a united front against the Prophet and I said to them, 'It may be if he (the Prophet) divorced you, (all) that his Lord (Allah) will give him instead of you wives better than you.' So this Verse [(V. 66.5) the same as I had said] was revealed."[5]

Leaving aside the question of the nature of a divine revelation concerning either the Prophet's oral hygiene or the squabbles and jealousy of his wives, it clear that neither of the traditional Islamic explanations for the cryptic, allusive statements in sura 66 could possibly be reconstructed from the Qur'an alone.

The Hadith

Perhaps reacting to the fragmentary quality of the Qur'anic narrative, early Muslims elaborated two principal sources to provide context for the Qur'an: *tafsir* (commentary on the Qur'an) and *hadith*, traditions of the Prophet Muhammad. And a significant amount (although by no means all) of the hadith is itself tafsir. It gives the *asbab an-nazool*, or circumstances of revelation (as we have just seen for sura 66:1-5), for various Qur'anic verses—which can have important implications for how the verse is to be applied in the modern age. One hadith, for example, recounts the occasion on which Muhammad was reciting a Qur'anic verse which scolds Muslims who take no part in jihad: "Those of the believers who sit still ... are not on an equality with those who strive in the way of Allah with their wealth and lives. Allah hath conferred on those who strive with their wealth and lives a rank above the sedentary. Unto each Allah hath promised good, but He hath bestowed on those who strive a great reward above the sedentary" (4:95).

At that point in Muhammad's recitation, a blind man spoke up: "O Allah's Messenger! If I had power, I would surely take part in Jihad." Whereupon "Allah sent down the revelation to His Messenger" of another segment of the verse, removing the Prophet's blind friend from this condemnation: "other than those who have a (disabling) hurt."[6]

The *sunnah*, or model, of the Prophet, which is largely comprised of the Hadith, is second only to the Qur'an in authority for most Muslims and contains a huge amount of information about Muhammad. It is from the Sunnah that most of the laws that distinguish Islamic society from other societies have been elaborated. The Sunnah is so important in Islamic thought that according to Islamic scholar Ahmad Von Denffer, "there is agreement among Muslim scholars that the contents of the *sunna* are [in addition to the Qur'an] also from Allah. Hence they have described it as also being the result of some form of inspiration."[7]

From the vantage point of fourteen hundred years later it is virtually impossible to tell with any certainty what is authentic in this mass of information and what isn't. Muslims themselves acknowledge that there are a great many forged *ahadith* (the plural form of hadith), which were written to give the Prophet's sanction to the views or practices of a particular party in the early Muslim community. This makes the question of what the historical Muhammad actually said and did well-nigh insoluble. But it does not mean that the Hadith has no relevance for Muslims. Reacting to the confusion caused by the proliferation of forged ahadith, relatively early in the history of Islam several Muslims assembled collections of accounts of the Prophet's words and deeds that they considered more or less definitive and authentic.[8] In the ninth century several Islamic scholars ranged through the Muslim world collecting traditions about Muhammad and then attempting to winnow the true ones from the false. The imam Muhammad Ibn Ismail al-Bukhari (810–870), who compiled the most respected and authoritative hadith collection (known as *Sahih Bukhari*), is said to have gathered 300,000 ahadith. These he examined carefully, trying to trace each back through a discernable chain of transmission (*isnad*) to the Prophet himself. Ultimately he chose and published around two thousand separate ahadith as authentic; repetitions bring the number of ahadith in his collection to over seven thousand.

Sahih Bukhari alone fills nine volumes in a deluxe English-Arabic edition published in Saudi Arabia. Besides providing the context of an enormous number of verses of the Qur'an, it gives the reader insights into Muhammad's private life, and his wisdom and example on a huge range of topics, including ablutions, characteristics of prayer and actions while praying, funerals, the obligatory charity tax (*zakat*), the obligatory pilgrimage to Mecca (*hajj*), fasting, good manners, sales and trade, loans, mortgaging, wills and testaments, marriage, divorce, laws of inheritance, jihad and the subjugation and punishment of unbelievers, blood money, and much more—even the interpretation of dreams.

Sahih Bukhari is just one of six collections, all lengthy, that Muslims generally regard as trustworthy. Among these *Sahih Sittah*, or reliable collections, is another that bears the designation *sahih*—meaning reliable. This is *Sahih Muslim*, which was compiled by Muslim ibn al-Hajjaj al-Qushayri (821–875). The others are considered lesser authorities after Bukhari and Muslim, but still enjoy great respect: *Sunan Abu-Dawud* by Abu Dawud as-Sijistani (d. 888); *Sunan Ibn Majah* by Muhammad ibn Majah (d. 896), *Sunan At-Tirmidhi* by Abi 'Eesaa Muhammad At-Tirmidhi (824–893), and *Sunan An-Nasai* by Ahmad ibn Shu'ayb an-Nasai (d. 915).

Also highly regarded, although not numbered among the *Sahih Sittah*, are several other collections, notably one known as *Muwatta Imam Malik* (or simply *Muwatta Malik)*. Malik bin Anas bin Malik bin Abu Amir Al-Asbahi (715–801), or Imam Malik, lived closest in time to the life of Muhammad of all the collectors of ahadith—and he was born more than eighty years after the death of the Prophet.

In Islam the study of hadith is a complex and absorbing science. Scholars grade individual traditions according to such designations as "sound," "good," "weak," "forged," and many others. If a tradition appears in Bukhari or Muslim, Muslim scholars accord it a great presumption of reliability, and if it's in both, its authenticity is virtually assured—at least from a traditional Muslim perspective. And this is not just the view of Muslim scholars but of everyday Muslims: Bukhari and Muslim are regarded as preeminent sources. One Islamic Internet resource, while assuring readers that "nothing on this site violates the fixed principles of Islamic law," sums up the prevailing opinion of Muslims succinctly: "Sahih Bukhari is distinguished with it's [sic] strong reliability"; regarding *Sahih Muslim*, it adds: "Out of 300,000 Hadiths which were evaluated by Muslim, only 4,000 approximately—divided into forty-two books—were extracted for inclusion into his collection based on stringent acceptance criteria."[9]

Bukhari and Muslim, and to a lesser degree the other collections of *Sahih Sittah*, remain the gold standard for ahadith. The English translator of *Sahih Muslim*, Abdul Hamid Siddiqi, explains that the hadiths "which are recognized as absolutely authentic are included in these two excellent compilations," and that "even of these two, Bukhari's occupies a higher position in comparison to Muslim's."[10]

The Sira

Then there is the *sira*, or biography of Muhammad. With the Hadith and Qur'an, it makes up the Sunnah. The first full-length biography of the Prophet of Islam did not appear until 150 years after his death. The Prophet's first biographer was Muhammad Ibn Ishaq Ibn Yasar, generally known as Ibn Ishaq (704–773). While many biographical nuggets are contained in other sources, not least the Qur'an, Ibn Ishaq's *Sirat Rasul Allah (Biography of the Prophet of Allah)* was the first attempt to provide a continuous narrative of Muhammad's life.

Unfortunately, the original form of this book is lost to history. It exists only in a later revised and shortened (although still quite lengthy) version by Ibn Hisham, who died in 834, sixty years after Ibn Ishaq, and in fragments quoted by other early Muslim writers, including another historian, Muhammad Ibn Jarir at-Tabari (839–923). Ibn Hisham explains that in his version he omits, among other material from Ibn Ishaq's biography, "things which it is disgraceful to discuss; matters which would distress certain people; and such reports as al-Bakka'i told me he could not accept as trustworthy."[11] Some of these "disgraceful" matters may have induced Malik ibn Anas (715–801), himself the compiler of a respected hadith collection, *Muwatta*, to call Ibn Ishaq "an antichrist" and to complain that the biographer "reports traditions on the authority of the Jews." Malik and Ibn Ishaq later reconciled, and numerous other early Muslim authorities attest to the biographer's reliability. One Muslim who knew him for many years stated that "none of the Medinans suspected him or spoke disparagingly of him"; another contemporary called him "truthful in tradition."[12]

Muslims have generally accepted Ibn Ishaq's work as trustworthy based on the fact that the distaste that some early Muslims like Malik felt for him stemmed not from a belief that his historical material was unreliable, but from his writings on Islamic law. He was suspected of quoting legal traditions with incomplete or inadequate chains of transmitters establishing their authority (although he scrupulously includes such chains for most of his historical accounts). He was further accused of Shi'ite tendencies and other deviations from orthodoxy. But the great Islamic jurist Ahmed ibn Hanbal (780–855) summed up the prevailing view: "in *maghazi* [Muhammad's military campaigns] and such matters what Ibn Ishaq said could be written down; but in legal matters further confirmation was necessary."[13] In other words, he is a good source for history, not for legislation.

However, Ibn Ishaq's life of Muhammad is so unashamedly hagiographical that its accuracy is questionable. The Prophet's biographer was a believing Muslim, anxious to portray Muhammad as a larger-than-life figure. He recounts one incident in which the captive wife of a man Muhammad had ordered killed poisons the Prophet's dinner. According to Ibn Ishaq, the Prophet had some preternatural awareness of the woman's deed; he spat out the poisoned meat, exclaiming, "This bone tells me that it is poisoned."[14] On another occasion his men were digging a large trench for a battle and came upon a huge rock that no one could move. The Prophet spat in some water and sprinkled it on the rock, whereupon the obstacle became "pulverized as though it were soft sand so that it could not resist axe or shovel."[15]

Whatever his overall reliability as a historian, much of Ibn Ishaq's portrait of Muhammad has over the centuries passed into the general consciousness of Muslims. Many incidents in the Prophet's life, including ones that became influential in Islamic history, have no other source; later Muslim historians' accounts often depend solely on Ibn Ishaq. He is read and respected by Muslims today; Muslim bookstores still stock copies of his biography among more modern accounts of the Prophet.[16] Modern Muslim historians praise his accuracy: Lieutenant-General A.I. Akram of the Pakistani Army, in his biography of Khalid bin Waleed—one of the companions of the Prophet Muhammad, known as the "Sword of Allah"— explains that Ibn Hisham's:

abridgement of the last pioneering work, *Seerah Rasoolullah*,
by Muhammad bin Ishaq, is invaluable.... Muhammad bin
Ishaq (who died in 150 or 151AH[17]), is unquestionably the
principal authority on the Seerah (Prophetic biography) and
Maghazi (battles) literature. Every writing after him has
depended on his work, which though lost in its entirety, has
been immortalised in the wonderful, extant abridgement of it,
by Ibn Hisham.... Ibn Ishaq's work is notable for its excellent,
rigorous methodology and its literary style is of the highest standard of elegance and beauty. This is hardly surprising when we
recall that Ibn Ishaq was an accomplished scholar not only in
Arabic language but also in the science of hadith.[18]

Javeed Akhter, author of *The Seven Phases of Prophet Muhammad's Life*,
agrees: "Was Ibn Ishaq trustworthy? He appears to be very careful in his
writings. When in doubt, he frequently precedes a statement by the word
'Za'ama' (he alleged)."[19] In a survey of Muslim historians, Salah Zaimeche
of a Muslim organization known as the Foundation for Science Technology and Civilisation writes this of Ibn Ishaq: "He corrects hadiths, and also
rids his accounts of legends and poetry that are not on the reliable side.
The actions and deeds of the Prophet (PBUH[20]) are scrupulously noted,
and his battles described in great detail."[21]

And in his modern biography of the Prophet (which is distributed by
the Council on American-Islamic Relations, a group that bills itself as a
civil rights organization defending Muslims in America), Islamic apologist
Yahiya Emerick praises Ibn Ishaq's *Sirat Rasul Allah* as "one of the earliest
attempts at presenting a complete biography of Muhammad using a wide
variety of sources."[22]

The contemporary Islamic scholar (and, as Abu Bakr Siraj Ad-Din, convert to Islam) Martin Lings (1909–2005), whose biography *Muhammad:
His Life Based on the Earliest Sources*, is respected by non-Muslims and
Muslims alike (and won Lings awards in Egypt and Pakistan), relies chiefly
on three sources: Ibn Ishaq's biography; a chronicle of the battles of

Muhammad by Muhammad ibn Umar al-Waqidi (d. 823); and the tradi-
tions collected by Muhammad by al-Waqidi's secretary, Muhammad Ibn
Sa'd (d. 845): *Kitab Al-Tabaqat Al-Kabir* (*The Book of The Major Classes*).
Since the latter two are several generations younger than Ibn Ishaq, *Sirat
Rasul Allah* still has pride of place as the principal source for information
about Muhammad. Lings also uses the "The History of the Messengers and
the Kings" (*Ta'rikh ar-Rasul wa 'l-Muluk*) by Tabari, as well as Bukhari,
Muslim, and other sources of hadith.

I will, therefore, rely primarily on those sources as well—chiefly Ibn
Ishaq, since his work is the oldest chronologically, and also on Ibn Sa'd,
who is considered by many Muslim scholars to be more reliable in his
transmission of hadith than al-Waqidi.[23] I will also make extensive use of
Bukhari and Muslim, as well as other hadith collections considered reliable by Muslims—all so as to construct a picture of Muhammad from
Islamic sources, the kind of picture that a pious Muslim might get if he set
out to learn more about the life and sayings of his prophet.

Historical fact and Muslim belief

Using the Qur'an, Hadith, and Sira, what can we ultimately know about
Muhammad? Historical certainty is not easy to ascertain with a text as
sketchy as the Qur'an, as overwhelmed with false information as the
Hadith, and as late as the Sira. And even the Qur'an, in the opinion of
some modern historians, "as we have it is not the work of Muhammad or
the 'Uthmanic redactors . . . but a precipitate of the social and cultural pres-
sures of the first two Islamic centuries."[24] While Islamic apologists generally assert with pride that the Qur'anic text has never been altered and
there are no variants, there are some indications even in Islamic tradition
that this is not actually the case. One early Muslim, Anas ibn Malik,
recounts that after a battle in which many Muslims were killed, that the
Qur'an originally contained a message from the slain Muslims to the living ones: "Then we read a verse in al-Qur'an for a long time which was

either removed or forgotten. (It was): convey to our people from us that we met our Lord Who was pleased with us and we were pleased with Him."[25]

Some Western scholars, meanwhile, such as the pioneering Hadith expert Ignaz Goldziher (1850–1921), as well as John Wansbrough, Patricia Crone, Michael Cook, Christoph Luxenberg, and others, have done ground-breaking work in researching which ahadith reflect what Muhammad really said and did, and which are pious legend—research which often deviates sharply from the received wisdom of Muslim scholars of the Hadith.[26]

From a strictly historical standpoint, it is impossible to state with certainty even that a man named Muhammad actually existed, or if he did, that he did much or any of what is ascribed to him. In all likelihood he did exist—particularly in light of recorded aspects of his life that are acutely embarrassing for Muslims today (and, to varying degrees, throughout history) who are confronted with the difficulty of squaring them with modern sensibilities. It is hard to imagine that a pious hagiographer would have invented Muhammad's marriage to a nine-year-old girl, or his marriage to his ex-daughter-in-law. Muslims have struggled to explain these and other aspects of Muhammad's life for centuries; if an editor or compiler could have simply consigned them to oblivion, he most likely would have. Still, some historians believe that the Muhammad who comes to us in the Qur'an, Hadith, and Sira is a composite figure, constructed later to give Arab imperialism a foundational mythos. Others have questioned also whether the Muhammad of history was really connected with Mecca and Medina, or if the story was given this setting in order to situate it in Arabia's most important centers.

These historical speculations have had virtually no effect on Islamic doctrine or practice. For our purposes it is less important to know what really happened in Muhammad's life than what Muslims have generally accepted as having happened, for the latter still forms the foundation of Muslim belief, practice, and law. It is important to know the Muhammad of history, but perhaps even more important to know the Muhammad who has shaped and continues to shape the lives of so many Muslims world-wide. The popular picture of Muhammad, and the mass of Islamic legisla-tion that is accepted by millions of Muslims today as the veritable law of Allah, has been elaborated from his words and deeds in the Hadith that orthodox Islamic schools of jurisprudence and clerics consider authentic.

It is this picture of Muhammad that inspires Muslims worldwide, whether for good or for ill, and that remains true whatever the actual his-torical accuracy of this material. Millions of Muslims look to the Muham-mad of the Qur'an, Hadith, and Sira for guidance on how to imitate the man that Islamic tradition has dubbed *al-insan al-kamil*, or the Perfect Man. This concept has played a significant role in Islamic mysticism. Scholar Itzchak Weismann, in discussing the mystical thought of Amir 'Abd al-Qadir al-Jaza'iri (1808–1883), who waged jihad against the French in what would become modern Algeria, explains that in some Islamic mys-tical traditions, "the Perfect Man is the ideal of humanity. In the strictest sense only Muhammad has perfectly realized this state, since it is only in him that the Divine names were revealed in complete harmony and per-fection."[27] While some less mystically minded Muslims may find this an excess of reverence, popular devotion to Muhammad among Muslims around the world is scarcely less ardent.

That is why it is all the more imperative today that Westerners become familiar with this singular and fascinating figure.

CHAPTER THREE

Muhammad
becomes a prophet

- The religions and gods of Arabia before Islam
- Muslim traditions: the Jews and Christians were expecting a prophet
- Muhammad's first vision: an angel—or something else?
- Muhammad's fear and suicidal despair
- How Muhammad became convinced he was a prophet

Arabia before Muhammad

MUHAMMAD INTRODUCED ISLAM INTO AN ARABIA THAT WAS A welter of cultures and religions. Muhammad's own tribe, the Quraysh, was pagan. The Quraysh was based in the city of Mecca, which was a center of trade and pilgrimage: travelers from all the surrounding regions passed through it. The Quraysh did a lucrative trade from the pilgrimages to the local shrine, the Ka'bah, which housed numerous pagan idols—chiefly the image of the god Hubal. The local gods of all the area tribes were represented in the shrine, along with other idols identified with trees and stones

33

near the Ka'bah. One of these gods, "Allah," not yet identified with the lone god of Islam, may have been the tribal god of the Quraysh. Others included three goddesses beloved of many of the area tribes, al-Lat, al-'Uzza, and Manat, who would play a significant role in Muhammad's prophetic career.

Because of the central role Mecca played in both the commerce and religion of the surrounding areas, the Quraysh wielded considerable influence; indeed, as we shall see, the Quraysh's rejection of Muhammad provoked his rejection by many other tribes, while its later acceptance of him sparked the other tribes' conversion to Islam as well.

Pagan Arabia was a rough land. Blood feuds were frequent, and the people had grown to be as harsh and unyielding as their desert land. Women were treated as chattel; child marriage (of girls as young as seven or eight) and female infanticide were common, as women were regarded as a financial liability. Later, the Qur'an would inveigh against female infanticide as bringing retribution on the dreadful Day of Judgment:

When the sun ceases to shine;
when the stars fall down and the mountains are blown away;
when camels big with young are left untended,
and the wild beasts are brought together;
when the seas are set alight and men's souls are reunited;
when the infant girl, buried alive, is asked for what crime she was
    slain;
when the records of men's deeds are laid open, and heaven is
    stripped bare;
when Hell burns fiercely and Paradise is brought near:
then each soul shall know what it has done. (81:1–14)

Of child marriage, however, the Qur'an would have quite a different message.

Jews and Christians also inhabited the area. Christians were centered around Najran in southern Arabia, near Yemen—where there had been a

Jewish kingdom in the sixth century, under the rule of Masruq Dhu Nawas. There were also pockets of Christians in other areas of Arabia—mostly from heretical groups that had left the Byzantine Empire to escape persecution and harassment. These included the Gnostics, who held that physical matter was evil and indulged in cosmic speculations that were held to be the province only of an elect group of the initiated. Another Christian presence was the Nestorians, anathematized at the third ecumenical council (held in Ephesus in 431) for refusing to confess the unity of Jesus' Divine Personhood or, consequently, Mary as the Mother of God. The Nestorians made their way out of the Byzantine Empire for Persia, where they were welcomed and began a series of energetic evangelization efforts around the Euphrates area in the sixth century, gaining converts in Arabia.

Late in the sixth century, Numan III, ruler of the northeastern Arabian Lakhmid kingdom, converted to Christianity. In northwestern Arabia, the Ghassanid kingdom was also Christian, with a strong influence from yet another heretical group, the Monophysites, who held that Jesus's human nature had been absorbed into his divine nature, and who were bitter rivals of the Nestorians. The Ghassanids were vassals of the Byzantines, and the Lakhmids of the Persians—and both powers used these Arab states to protect themselves from Bedouin raiders from farther south in Arabia.

There was an even greater Jewish presence in Arabia. Prominent Jewish tribes were centered in Yemen and in the Khaybar oasis, about one hundred miles north of Medina. In Medina itself were three powerful Jewish tribes: the Banu Qaynuqa, Banu Nadir, and Banu Qurayzah. There were also three Jewish clans in Mecca. These Jewish tribes would loom large in the story of Muhammad, whose full name was Muhammad ibn Abdallah ibn Abd al-Muttalib.

Muhammad's early life

According to tradition, Muhammad was born in Mecca on April 20, 570, (or April 26, according to Shi'ites). Tradition holds his father died soon after he was born and his mother died when he was only six; before that, he had been entrusted to a foster mother and nursemaid, as was customary. Islamic tradition later elaborated a number of hagiographical stories befitting his prophetic status. One has his mother, Aminah, saying: "When I delivered him, there emitted a light from my womb which illuminated the palaces of Syria."[1]

Muslims believe that a prophet was awaited in Arabia at the time of Muhammad's birth, and that the Jewish and Christian Scriptures prophesied his coming. Ibn Ishaq recounts that a strange thing happened to Muhammad's foster mother as she was returning him to his mother: "a number of Abyssinian Christians saw him with her when she brought him back after he had been weaned. They looked at him, asked questions about him, and studied him carefully, then they said to her, 'Let us take this boy, and bring him to our king and our country, for he will have a great future. We know all about him.' The person who told me this alleged that she could hardly get him away from them."[2]

Likewise a few years later, Muhammad's uncle Abu Talib, who was by this time his guardian, took him, while on a long journey, to the town of Busra in Syria to visit the Christian monk Bahira. Although Muhammad was still just a boy, "when Bahira saw him he stared at him closely, looking at his body and finding traces of his description (in the Christian books)."[3]

These stories of Christian expectations of the advent of Muhammad conform to the Qur'anic assertion that Jesus himself foretold Muhammad's coming: "And remember, Jesus, the son of Mary, said: 'O Children of Israel! I am the messenger of Allah (sent) to you, confirming the Law (which came) before me, and giving Glad Tidings of a Messenger to come after me, whose name shall be Ahmad'" (61:6). "Ahmad" is a variant of Muhammad; Muslims now identify the Holy Spirit whom Jesus promises to send (John 14:16) with the Prophet of Islam. Muhammad also abetted this idea during his prophetic career, saying, "I am (in response to) the prayer of my ancestor Ibrahim [Abraham], and 'Isa Ibn Maryam [Jesus son of Mary] gave good news about me."[4]

The young Muhammad demonstrated his special bond with Allah in a conversation with the monk Bahira, who invoked the pagan goddesses al-Lat and al-'Uzza. The future Prophet of Islam would have none of it: "Do not ask me by al-Lat and al-'Uzza, for by Allah nothing is more hateful to me than those two." Bahira then proceeded to ask him questions, and Muhammad answered them in accord with what was expected of a future prophet. Bahira "looked at his back and saw the seal of prophethood between his shoulders in the very place described in his book." Bahira then told Abu Talib: "Take your nephew back to his country and guard him carefully against the Jews, for by Allah! If they see him and know about him what I know, they will do him evil; a great future lies before this nephew of yours, so take him home quickly."[5] He added: "Verily the Jews are his enemies, and he is the Prophet of these people; he is an Arab and the Jews are jealous of him wishing that he should have been an Israelite. So guard your brother's son."[6]

This accords with another Islamic fable about Muhammad's birth: a Jew, hearing that he had been born, asked to see the child. When he saw him, according to Ibn Sa'd, and "observed the mole on his back"—said to be a sign of the Prophet who was to come—he "fell into a swoon." When he came to, he explained: "The prophethood has gone from the Israelites and the Scriptures out of their hands. It is written that he will fight with them and will kill their scholars"—a rather revealing statement as an early Muslim view of the mission of Muhammad.[7]

Here sound two recurring themes of Islamic thought: the proposition that the Christians (and Jews) knew Muhammad was coming but rejected him out of willful disobedience to the command of Allah—and that Jews are the most inveterate and crafty enemies of the Muslims. The Qur'an explicitly denounces the Jews, claiming: "As often as they light a fire for war, Allah extinguisheth it. Their effort is for corruption in the land, and Allah loveth not corrupters" (5:64). The Jews are also compared negatively to Christians: "Strongest among men in enmity to the believers wilt thou find the Jews and Pagans; and nearest among them in love to the believers wilt thou find those who say, 'We are Christians': because amongst these are men devoted to learning and men who have renounced the world, and they are not arrogant" (5:82). Although the Qur'an is quite harsh toward Christians in other places (those who consider Jesus to be the Son of God are under the "curse of Allah" in sura 9:30), the character of Bahira was perhaps created with that kind of friendly Christian in mind.

It should be noted, as a matter of history, that there is no record of Christians expecting a prophet in Arabia 540 years after the death of Jesus; nor is there any record of any Christian book with signs marking out an Arabian prophet (unless one includes the time St. Paul spent in Arabia after his conversion and return to Damascus); nor is there any record of any Christian heresy that held such beliefs; and to put Muhammad's life in the context of Christian history, during the transition from the sixth to the seventh centuries, the Church was led by Pope St. Gregory the Great; in short, Christianity was well established and seeking neither new prophets nor new heresies.

Khadija

Muhammad's boyhood was relatively uneventful, but as a young man, according to some Islamic traditions, he had a sense of the great destiny that awaited him: he is supposed to have declined to take up farming with the words, "I have been raised for jihad and I am not raised for tillage."[8] The chain of events that would make him the leader and inspiration of all jihads was set in motion when he met a distant cousin, Khadija bint Khuwaylid, whom Ibn Ishaq calls "a merchant woman of dignity and wealth."[9] Without Khadija, Muhammad might never have become a prophet at all. Fifteen years older than Muhammad, she was a woman of significant accomplishment when they met. She hired him as a traveling salesman to go to Syria and trade her goods. She sent with him a slave boy named Maysara. On their way back to Mecca, in the scorching heat, Maysara saw two angels shielding Muhammad. In Mecca, Maysara told Khadija what he had seen. Khadija was also impressed that Muhammad had doubled her wealth on his journey. She proposed marriage, although she was forty and Muhammad just twenty-five.

Traces of Muhammad's career as a tradesman appear in the Qur'an, which admonishes the unbelievers in language borrowed from the world of commerce: "And they say: If we were to follow the Guidance with thee [that is, Muhammad] we should be torn out of our land. Have We not established for them a sure sanctuary, whereunto the produce of all things is brought (in trade), a provision from Our presence? But most of them know not" (28:57). Indeed, such unbelievers "are they who purchase error at the price of guidance, so their commerce doth not prosper, neither are they guided" (2:16).

Khadija had a cousin, Waraqa bin Naufal bin Asad bin 'Abdul-'Uzza bin Qusai, who was a convert to Christianity from Judaism, a priest who had "studied the scriptures that a prophet would arise among this people."[10] Khadija told him about Maysara's vision and Waraqa was deeply moved: "If this is true, Khadija," said Waraqa, "verily Muhammad is the Prophet of this people. I knew that a prophet of this people was to be expected. His time has come."[11]

Waraqa would later play a vital role in Muhammad's early prophetic career, but not until fifteen years later, after, according to Islamic tradition, numerous pagan soothsayers, Jewish rabbis, and Christian monks perceived Muhammad's prophetic status. According to an early Muslim, Asim bin Umar bin Qatada, in the years before the beginning of Muhammad's ministry, the Jews in the area used to say to the Arabs: "The time of a prophet who is to be sent has now come. We will kill you with his aid." But when Muhammad actually began preaching, Asim continued, "We believed in him but they denied him."[12] The Qur'an laments their perversity: "And when there comes to them a Book from Allah, confirming what is with them [the Torah]—although from of old they had prayed for victory against those without Faith—when there comes to them that which they (should) have recognized, they refuse to believe in it but the curse of Allah is on those without Faith" (2:89).

The repercussions of this rejection would reverberate to our own time.

The first visitation

As an adult, Muhammad was, according to his early follower Ali, "neither excessively tall or extremely short. He was medium height among his friends. His hair was neither curly nor wavy. It was in between.... His face was not swollen or meaty-compact. It was fairly round. His mouth was white. He had black and large eyes with long-haired eyelids. His joints (limbs) and shoulder joints were rather big.... At walking, he lifted his feet off the ground as if he had been walking in a muddy remainder of water."[13] Another said: "When he walked, he inclined as if walking over a height."[14] According to yet another early Muslim, he "had a broad face with reddish (wide) eyes, and lean heels."[15] Still another reported that he had "fleshy palms and fleshy feet" and was "of handsome face. I never saw anyone like him after him."[16] Between his shoulders was the mole that had so impressed Bahira the monk: one Muslim described this "seal of prophet-hood" as "resembling a fist... and round about it there were moles as if they were warts."[17] Later in life, when his hair and beard started to turn grey, he began to dye them with henna, telling his followers: "Verily the best thing with which you can change the colour of hair is al-henna and indigo.... Dye your gray hair but do not resemble the Jews and the Christians," who used black dye.[18] It is not uncommon today for mujahedin to dye their beards with henna in imitation of the Prophet.

Muhammad would declare himself a prophet of Allah—the one true God—when he was about forty years old. At the very beginning, however, he was much less clear than he ultimately became about what was happening to him.

According to an account by Aisha, the young woman who much later would become his favorite wife, Muhammad was chosen as a prophet after devoting himself to long periods of prayer. One night during the month of Ramadan he was rapt in prayer when he had a vision:

> The commencement of the (Divine) Revelation to Allah's Messenger was in the form of good righteous (true) dreams which came true like bright daylight. (And then the love of seclusion was bestowed upon him.) He used to go in seclusion (in the cave of) Hira where he used to worship (Allah alone) continuously for many (days and) nights... till sud-

denly the Truth descended upon him while he was in the cave of Hira.[19]

Muhammad could not at first identify the source of the dreams or "the Truth" that descended upon him. It was not until some time later that he came to believe that he was being visited by the angel Gabriel, sent from Allah. Ibn Sa'd records a Muslim tradition asserting that an angel named Seraphel originally visited Muhammad, and was replaced by Gabriel after three years. He also records the fact that "the learned and those versed in Sirah literature" contradicted this tradition, and maintained that only Gabriel ever appeared to Muhammad.[20] Nevertheless, it is hard to see how anyone would have gotten the idea that another angel was involved with Muhammad if he had been absolutely certain from the first moment that it was Gabriel.

In any case, the angel came to Muhammad and commanded him to read and recite what he read. Muhammad replied, 'I do not know how to read.'"

The spiritual being, however, would brook no objections. He pressed his will upon Muhammad in a terrifying fashion:

> (The Prophet added), "The angel caught me (forcefully) and pressed me so hard that I could not bear it anymore. He then released me and again asked me to read, and I replied, 'I do not know how to read.' Thereupon he caught me again and pressed me a second time till I could not bear it anymore. He then released me and asked me again to read, but again I replied, 'I do not know how to read (or, what shall I read?).' Thereupon he caught me for the third time and pressed me and then released me and said, 'Read! In the Name of your Lord, Who has created (all that exists). Has created man from a clot. Read! And Your Lord is Most Generous ... [unto] ... that which he knew not.' (V. 96:5)"[21]

This is the famous first revelation of the Qur'an, now found as sura 96:1-5. It began what Muhammad represented as a series of messages from Allah;

they would continue off and on for the next twenty-three years—the rest of Muhammad's life. His followers committed them to memory and wrote them on whatever was available; after his death they were collected into the Qur'an.

At the beginning Muhammad regarded his spiritual encounter with considerable agitation. He "suffered much pain and his face turned dust-coloured."[22] He wondered if he had been demonically possessed, and even contemplated suicide:

> I will go to the top of the mountain and throw myself down that I may kill myself and gain rest. So I went forth to do so and then when I was midway on the mountain, I heard a voice from heaven saying: "O Muhammad! Thou art an apostle of God and I am Gabriel." I raised my head towards heaven to see (who was speaking) and lo, Gabriel in the form of a man with feet astride the horizon, saying, "O Muhammad! Thou art the apostle of God and I am Gabriel."[23]

Muhammad returned to Khadija in tremendous distress. According to Aisha: "Then Allah's Messenger returned with that (the Revelation), and his heart severely beating; (and the) muscles between his neck and shoulders were trembling till he came upon Khadija (his wife) and said, 'Cover me!' They covered him, till his fear was over, and after that he said, 'O Khadija! What is wrong with me? I was afraid that something bad might happen to me.' Then he told her all that had happened."[24] And he repeated to her his initial fears: "Woe is me poet or possessed."[25] He meant "poet" in the sense of one who received ecstatic, and possibly demonic, visions.

Khadija appeared to have more confidence in Muhammad than he did in himself.[26] She then went to see Waraqa and told him what Muhammad had told her he had experienced in the cave of Hira. Waraqa exclaimed: "Holy! Holy! Verily by Him in whose hand is Waraqa's soul, if thou has spoken to me the truth, O Khadija, there hath come unto him the greatest

Namus [that is, Gabriel] who came to Moses aforetime, and lo, he is the Prophet of this people. Bid him be of good heart."[27]

Khadija told Muhammad what Waraqa had said, lessening Muhammad's anxiety. According to another account, she went with Muhammad to visit Waraqa:

> ... who, during the [pre-Islamic] Period of Ignorance became a Christian and used to write the writing with Hebrew letters. He would write from the Gospel in Hebrew as much as Allah wished him to write. He was an old man and had lost his eyesight. Khadija said to Waraqa, "Listen to the story of your nephew, O my cousin!" Waraqa asked, "O my nephew! What have you seen?" Allah's Apostle described whatever he had seen. Waraqa said, "This is the same one who keeps the secrets (angel Gabriel) whom Allah had sent to Moses."[28]

Then Waraqa gave the new prophet a warning:

> "I wish I were young and could live up to the time when your people would turn you out." Allah's Messenger asked, "Will they drive me out?" Waraqa replied in the affirmative and said, "Anyone (man) who came with something similar to what you have brought was treated with hostility; and if I should remain alive till the day when you will be turned out then I would support you strongly."[29]

Then Waraqa kissed the new prophet on the forehead and bid him farewell.[30]

As a final test of his prophethood, Khadija asked Muhammad, "O son of my uncle, are you able to tell me about your visitant, when he comes to you?" When Muhammad told her that he could, she devised a sure-fire way to tell if the spirit was good or evil:

So when Gabriel came to him, as he was wont, the apostle said to Khadija, "This is Gabriel who has just come to me." "Get up, O son of my uncle," she said, "and sit by my left thigh." The apostle did so, and she said, "Can you see him?" "Yes," he said. She said, "Then turn round and sit on my right thigh." He did so, and she said, "Can you see him?" When he said that he could she asked him to move and sit in her lap. When he had done this she again asked if he could see him, and when he said yes, she disclosed her form and cast aside her veil while the apostle was sitting in her lap. Then she said, "Can you see him?" And he replied, "No." She said, "O son of my uncle, rejoice and be of good heart, by God he is an angel and not a satan."[31]

When she "disclosed her form," the angel departed.

Muslim hardliners to this day insist upon the veiling of women because of, among other things, this underlying assumption: the sight of an unveiled woman is so distressing, so deeply sinful, that it causes even the angels to flee.

The suicidal despair returns

Without the care of Khadija (who remained Muhammad's only wife until her death) and the affirmation of Waraqa, the world might never have known Islam. Soon after Waraqa identified the being who had appeared to Muhammad, the old man died. The Prophet he had effectively anointed was again plunged into a despair so intense that he again contemplated suicide:

But after a few days Waraqa died and the Divine Revelation was also paused for a while and the Prophet became so sad as we have heard that he intended several times to throw himself from the tops of high mountains and every time he went up the top of a mountain in order to throw himself down, Gabriel would appear before him and say, "O Muhammad! You are indeed Allah's Messenger in truth," whereupon his heart would become quiet and he would calm down and would return home.

This scenario evidently played out again whenever Muhammad had to wait too long for Gabriel to reappear: "And whenever the period of the coming of the Revelation used to become long, he would do as before, but when he used to reach the top of a mountain, Gabriel would appear before him and say to him what he had said before."[32]

In another account, Muhammad reacted to the resumption of the revelations in the same way he reacted to the first one. He explained:

> The Divine Inspiration was delayed for a short period but suddenly, as I was walking, I heard a voice in the sky, and when I looked up towards the sky, to my surprise, I saw the angel who had come to me in the Hira Cave, and he was sitting on a chair in between the sky and the earth. I was so frightened by him that I fell on the ground and came to my family and said (to them), "Cover me! (with a blanket), cover me!"[33]

The spiritual messenger gave him this message:

> O thou wrapped up (in the mantle)! Arise and deliver thy warning! And thy Lord do thou magnify! And thy garments keep free from stain! And all abomination shun! Nor expect, in giving, any increase (for thyself)! But, for thy Lord's (Cause), be patient and constant! (Qur'an 74:1-7)

Muhammad no longer doubted that his visitor was Gabriel—but others did. One of the early Muslims, Jundab bin 'Abdullah, recounts: "Gabriel did not come to the Prophet (for some time) and so one of the Quraish women said, 'His Satan has deserted him.' So came the Divine Revelation:

'By the forenoon (after sunrise) and by the night when it darkens (and stands still). Your Lord (O Muhammad) has neither forsaken you nor hates you.' ([Qur'an] V. 93:1-3)"[34]

As we shall see, Muhammad was often frustrated by skeptics of his preaching, with eventual dire results.

CHAPTER FOUR

Muhammad's revelations and their sources

- ◈ Islamic borrowings from Judaism, Christianity, and Zoroastrianism
- ◈ Muhammad's furious replies to charges that he borrowed material
- ◈ The perks of prophethood: revelations of convenience
- ◈ Negative effects for women and others from these convenient revelations
- ◈ Islamic apologetic attempts to explain away uncomfortable material in Islamic tradition

Borrowings from Judaism

ONE OF THE MOST SEVERE AND LINGERING CHALLENGES TO Muhammad's claim to be a prophet, both during the twenty-three years of his career and throughout the history of Islam, was his apparent dependence on Jewish, Christian, and other sources.

Many observers throughout history have noted the numerous and obvious similarities between Islam and Judaism, including the "pure" monotheism, the line of prophets, the proliferation of laws, the facing toward the holy city for prayer, and more. Muhammad no doubt had extensive contact as a

47

young merchant, as well as later as a fledgling prophet, with the powerful Jewish tribes in and around Mecca. Muhammad respected them and sought their approval of his prophetic mission.

In fact, Muhammad situates himself squarely within the salvation history of the Jews. In the Qur'anic scheme, Muhammad is the last and greatest of a long succession of prophets that includes those in the Biblical line and others. After Satan deceived Adam and Eve into turning away from the truth (in a story imported straight from Genesis, with important modifications and embellishments), Allah sent prophets to call people back to true worship. Several Qur'anic passages list as prophets figures from both the Jewish and Christian Scriptures: "We gave him Isaac and Jacob, all (three) guided, and before him, We guided Noah, and among his progeny, David, Solomon, Job, Joseph, Moses, and Aaron. Thus do We reward those who do good. And Zakariya and John, and Jesus and Elias: all in the ranks of the righteous, and Isma'il and Elisha, and Jonas, and Lot: and to all We gave favour above the nations" (6:84-86). Allah adds Muhammad to this illustrious group: "Lo! We inspire thee as We inspired Noah and the prophets after him, as We inspired Abraham and Ishmael and Isaac and Jacob and the tribes, and Jesus and Job and Jonah and Aaron and Solomon, and as We imparted unto David the Psalms" (4:163).

Along with the Biblical prophets, the Qur'an is full of stories from the Bible. The twelfth sura tells the story of Joseph and his brothers, although it's shorn of its significance for Israel as a nation. Noah's ark appears in sura 10; Jonah and his whale in sura 37. Moses figures prominently throughout the book—notably in a curious series of allegorical tales in sura 18.

One might expect, if Muhammad is trying to present himself as a prophet in the Biblical line, that he would repeat at least some Biblical material. But some of the Qur'an's stories and details about Biblical characters actually come from sources other than the Bible itself—notably, the Talmud.

The Talmudic writings, compiled in the second century A.D., circulated among Arabia's Jews in Muhammad's day, and some of their divergences from or additions to Biblical accounts made it into the Qur'an. In the Qur'anic version of "the story of the two sons of Adam" (Qur'an 5:27), Cain and Abel, Allah sends Cain a raven to show him what to do with his brother's body: "Allah sent a raven, who scratched the ground, to show him how to hide the shame of his brother. 'Woe is me!' said he; 'Was I not even able to be as this raven, and to hide the shame of my brother?' then he became full of regrets" (5:31). The raven does not appear in the Genesis story of Cain and Abel, but it does appear in several Jewish rabbinical documents, including the *Pirqe de-Rabbi Eliezer*, a recreation of Biblical history from creation to the wandering of the Israelites in the wilderness. Islamic apologists point out that the *Pirqe de-Rabbi Eliezer* in its present form dates from the eighth or ninth century, as do several of the other writings in which the raven story appears—so it is possible that the rabbis were borrowing from Muhammad.

However, the next verse of the Qur'an—which is one of the most celebrated and oft-quoted verses in the entire book, at least in Western countries today—makes clearer the direction of the borrowing. Qur'an 5:32 says:

> We ordained for the Children of Israel that if any one slew a person—unless it be for murder or for spreading mischief in the land—it would be as if he slew the whole people: and if any one saved a life, it would be as if he saved the life of the whole people. Then although there came to them Our messengers with clear signs, yet, even after that, many of them continued to commit excesses in the land.

There is no stated reason why this injunction against murder follows the story of Cain and Abel, when Cain's murder of Abel did not endanger a whole people. Nor is the connection clear from the context. But it is clear in the Talmud:

> We find it said in the case of Cain who murdered his brother, "The voice of thy brother's bloods crieth" (Gen. 4:10). It is not

said here blood in the singular, but bloods in the plural, that is,
his own blood and the blood of his seed. Man was created single in order to show that to him who kills a single individual it
shall be reckoned that he has slain the whole race, but to him
who preserves the life of a single individual it is counted that
he hath preserved the whole race.[1]

Here the connection between the killing of Abel and that of the whole
human race comes from the interpretation of the plural word "bloods" in
Genesis 4:10. Shorn of its link to a Bible verse, this connection as it appears
in the Qur'an suggests to numerous readers across the centuries that the
Qur'an's author or compiler was depending on the Jewish source.

Likewise, in the Qur'an, the patriarch Abraham smashes some of the
idols worshipped by his father and his people. Enraged, the people throw
him into a fire, but Allah cools the flames and saves Abraham: "They said,
'Burn him and protect your gods, if ye do (anything at all)!' We said, 'O
Fire! Be thou cool, and (a means of) safety for Abraham!'" (21:68-69).

An account of Abraham being thrown into a fire appears in the
Talmud—*Midrash Genesis Rabbah*, which was compiled in the sixth century A.D.[2]

"Tales of the ancients"

There are many other such echoes in the Qur'an, and the pre-Islamic der-
ivation of these stories was not unknown to many of his hearers. Some of
their sneers are recorded in the Qur'an: "We have heard this (before): if we
wished, we could say (words) like these: these are nothing but tales of the
ancients" (8:31). "Such things have been promised to us and to our fathers
before! They are nothing but tales of the ancients!" (23:83).

Allah responds to this charge directly in the Qur'an: "But the misbeliev-
ers say: 'Naught is this but a lie which he has forged, and others have helped
him at it.' In truth it is they who have put forward an iniquity and a falsehood. And they say: 'Tales of the ancients, which he has caused to be writ-

ten: and they are dictated before him morning and evening.' Say: 'The (Qur'an) was sent down by Him who knows the mystery (that is) in the heavens and the earth: verily He is Oft-Forgiving, Most Merciful'"(25:4-6). Muhammad's detractors make this charge out of the hardness of their hearts: "Of them there are some who (pretend to) listen to thee; but We have thrown veils on their hearts, so they understand it not, and deafness in their ears; if they saw every one of the signs, not they will believe in them; in so much that when they come to thee, they (but) dispute with thee; the Unbelievers say: 'These are nothing but tales of the ancients'" (6:25).

Muhammad reacted with fury to one person who made these charges. In a revelation, Allah pointed out that the man was illegitimate ("base-born") and promised to brand him on the nose (Qur'an 68:10-16).[3]

Muhammad steadfastly professed certainty that any fair-minded reader would find prophecies of his coming in the Scriptures of the People of the Book—that is, the Jews and Christians: "The Unbelievers say: 'No messenger art thou.' Say: 'Enough for a witness between me and you is Allah, and such as have knowledge of the Book'" (Qur'an 13:43). The sincere Jews and Christians would become Muslims: "Those to whom We sent the Book before this, they do believe in this (revelation)" (Qur'an 28:52). Those who did not convert to Islam should be reminded that Muslims, Jews, and Christians all worship the same deity. (Qur'an 29:46).

Allah even tells Muhammad to consult with the Jews and Christians if he doubts the truth of what he has been receiving: "And if thou (Muhammad) art in doubt concerning that which We reveal unto thee, then question those who read the Scripture (that was) before thee. Verily the Truth from thy Lord hath come unto thee. So be not thou of the waverers" (Qur'an 10:94).

It was only the obstinacy of the People of the Book that kept them from recognizing Muhammad and the veracity of the Qur'an. And ultimately that obstinacy would lead Muhammad to turn fiercely against them, and proclaim his new community their superior—and, indeed, the superior of all others as well: "Ye are the best of peoples, evolved for mankind, enjoining what is right, forbidding what is wrong, and believing in Allah. If only the People of the Book had faith, it were best for them: among them are some who have faith, but most of them are perverted transgressors" (Qur'an 3:110).

The conviction that they are the "best of peoples," and a concomitant suspicion of the People of the Book, is common among Muslims world-wide even today. Social inequalities and injustices are blamed on the infidel; and jihadists around the world assert that only strict observance of Islam can keep Muslims "the best of peoples."

Borrowings from Christianity

In some variants of the accounts of Waraqa bin Naufal recognizing Muhammad as a prophet, Waraqa writes the Gospel not in Hebrew, but in Arabic.[4] The purpose of the variants might be to distance Waraqa from the Jews, who, some charged, was teaching Muhammad the Qur'an. Allah himself answers the charges in the Qur'an: "We know indeed that they say, 'It is a man that teaches him.' The tongue of him they wickedly point to is notably foreign, while this is Arabic, pure and clear" (16:103).

That foreigner may also have been someone else; after all, Waraqa wasn't the only learned Jew, Christian, or pagan who had contact with Muhammad. Another was a mysterious and pivotal figure of early Islam, Salman the Persian. The Arabic word translated here as "foreign" in Qur'an 16:103 is *Ajami*, which means Persian or Iranian. The Qur'an's repeated insistence that it is in Arabic may betray an anxiety to head off suspicions of any foreign (or Persian) influence. Then there is an unnamed figure who, according to a hadith, "was a Christian who embraced Islam and read *Surat-al-Baqarah* [sura 2 of the Qur'an] and *Al-Imran* [sura 3], and he used to write (the revelations) for the Prophet." In other words, he used to transcribe Muhammad's Qur'anic recitations. Evidently this experience disabused him of the notion that they were divinely inspired, for "later on he returned to Christianity again and he used to say: 'Muhammad knows nothing but what I have written for him.'" The tradition asserts that this man's sin was so grave that, after he died, the earth itself would not accept his body, and after his people made several attempts to bury him only to find that the earth had spat him out again, they gave up.[5]

That Muhammad's prophetic mission was confirmed by a Christian convert from Judaism has been a source of embarrassment to Muslims, and some Muslim sources have denied that Waraqa was a Christian. Meanwhile, some modern scholars contend that Waraqa actually rejected Muhammad, and that the text of Ibn Hisham's version of the Sira was later corrupted. They point out that there is no account in the voluminous hadith of Waraqa's conversion to Islam or the details of his death—an argument from silence, to be sure, but a curious omission in a corpus that contains the minutest details of Muhammad's activities and the events of the early Muslim community. After all, the conversion of a Christian priest, the cousin of Muhammad and his wife, would have been a momentous event. Nevertheless, there is no doubt that mainstream Islam accepts that Waraqa recognized Muhammad's prophetic status, that Waraqa converted to Islam, and that the Bible—at least in its uncorrupted, original state— predicted the coming of Muhammad.

Even so, the suspicion that Waraqa taught Muhammad significant portions of what Muhammad represented as divine revelation in the Qur'an, has haunted Islam. Across these many centuries there is no way to determine the precise relationship between Muhammad and Waraqa, and no way to tell if his wife's cousin was his source for anything. What, however, is indisputable and interesting is that the Qur'an incorporates Jewish and Christian sources and that some of the "tales of the ancients" that found their way into the Qur'an are not from the canonical gospels but from decidedly heterodox sources—the sorts of sources Muhammad would likely encounter in Arabia, where heretical Christians predominated.

The Jesus of the Qur'an, although not divine, is a powerful miracle worker. He even speaks in His cradle: "He shall preach to men in his cradle and in the prime of manhood, and shall lead a righteous life" (3:46). Mary, knowing this, directs those who doubt her chastity upon seeing the baby Jesus to ask the baby himself: "But she pointed to the babe. They said: 'How can we talk to one who is a child in the cradle?' He said: 'I am indeed a servant of Allah: He hath given me revelation and made me a prophet; and He hath made me blessed wheresoever I be, and hath enjoined on me prayer and charity as long as I live; (He) hath made me kind to my mother, and not overbearing or miserable; so peace is on me the day I was born, the day that I die, and the day that I shall be raised up to life (again)!'" (19:29-33).

In an Arabic Infancy Gospel that dates from the sixth century: "Jesus spoke, and, indeed, when He was lying in His cradle said to Mary His mother: I am Jesus, the Son of God, the Logos, whom thou hast brought forth, as the Angel Gabriel announced to thee; and my Father has sent me for the salvation of the world."[6]

In the same Infancy Gospel is this tale:

> Now, when the Lord Jesus had completed seven years from His birth, on a certain day He was occupied with boys of His own age. For they were playing among clay, from which they were making images of asses, oxen, birds, and other animals; and each one boasting of his skill, was praising his own work. Then the Lord Jesus said to the boys: The images that I have made I will order to walk. The boys asked Him whether then he were the son of the Creator; and the Lord Jesus bade them walk. And they immediately began to leap; and then, when He had given them leave, they again stood still. And He had made figures of birds and sparrows, which flew when He told them to fly, and stood still when He told them to stand, and ate and drank when He handed them food and drink. After the boys had gone away and told this to their parents, their fathers said to them: My sons, take care not to keep company with him again, for he is a wizard: flee from him, therefore, and avoid him, and do not play with him again after this.[7]

And likewise in the Qur'an, where it becomes another indication of the treachery of the Jewish unbelievers:

> Then will Allah say: "O Jesus the son of Mary! Recount My favour to thee and to thy mother. Behold! I strengthened thee with the holy spirit, so that thou didst speak to the people in childhood and in maturity. Behold! I taught thee the Book and Wisdom, the Law and the Gospel and behold! Thou makest out of clay, as it were, the figure of a bird, by My leave, and thou breathest into it and it becometh a bird by My leave, and thou healest those born blind, and the lepers, by My leave. And behold! Thou bringest forth the dead by My leave. And behold! I did restrain the Children of Israel from (violence to) thee when thou didst show them the clear Signs, and the unbelievers among them said: 'This is nothing but evident magic.'" (5:110)

Muhammad's experiences with Christian heretical groups may also explain his view of the crucifixion of Christ. Muslims believe that he was taken up to Heaven alive, never having tasted death; it would have been wrong for Allah to allow one of his prophets to die in shame and humiliation, so Allah substituted someone who looked like him before he was placed on the cross. The Jews thought they were actually killing Jesus, but actually the imposter was crucified: "they slew Him not nor crucified, but it appeared so unto them" (4:157)! This is closely akin to the view of some groups of the heretical Christians known as Gnostics. Gnostics held that physical matter was evil and that therefore Jesus, as the savior of the world, could not have taken on a physical body, and certainly could not have been crucified. God just made it seem as if he was on the Cross—or, according to some Gnostic texts, made Judas to resemble Jesus and put him on the Cross in the Lord's place.

The fact that the Qur'an presents this verse as resolving a point of dispute ("those who differ therein are full of doubts, with no [certain] knowledge, but only conjecture to follow, for of a surety they killed him not") suggests that perhaps Muhammad had encountered squabbling rival groups of Christians, and intended to present his revelation as the final resolution of the matter.

One need not assume that Muhammad actually read the heretical Christian material that seems to have influenced the Qur'an. It's much more likely that he heard this material being recited or taught, since these are clearly not word-for-word borrowings. Sometimes his appropriation of Biblical material suggests that he had only a glancing acquaintance with the stories he was retelling; in the Qur'an's chapter on the birth of Jesus, his mother Mary's relatives address her as "sister of Aaron" (19:28). It would appear, and appeared to some of Muhammad's contemporaries, that Muhammad confused Miriam the sister of Moses and Aaron with Mary the mother of Jesus. The two names are identical in Arabic: *Maryam*. However, when one of his followers was confronted with this by the Christians of Najran, and returned to ask Muhammad about it, the Prophet of Islam had a ready explanation: "The (people of the old age) used to give names (to their persons) after the names of Apostles and pious persons who had gone before them."[8] So Mary the Mother of Jesus was called "sister of Aaron" as an honor, not an error.

The possible confusion does buttress the oft-repeated claim that Muhammad was illiterate. This is a cornerstone of Islamic apologetics, as it apparently makes it all the more miraculous the sublime poetry of the Qur'an—which calls him "the Prophet who can neither read nor write [*al-ommiyya*], whom they will find described in the Torah and the Gospel (which are) with them" (7:157).

From the Muslim perspective, it is immaterial that some of the Qur'an has echoes in earlier sources, whether canonical or non-canonical. Traditional Islamic theology, after all, holds that earlier revelations have been corrupted and altered, and thus need the corrective that the Qur'an provides—but since the original form of the earlier revelations was completely consonant with the Qur'an, it should be no surprise that some earlier books contain Qur'anic foreshadowings.

So for many Muslims, the existence of traces of Qur'anic revelation in earlier books only confirms the Qur'an's role as correcting and superseding all earlier revelations. Muhammad himself spoke forthrightly about Islam replacing Judaism and Christianity, and on one occasion used a parable to explain how.[9]

Other borrowings

The Qur'an's descriptions of Paradise are many and vivid. The blessed will be adorned "with bracelets of gold and pearls" (22:23) and "dressed in fine silk and in rich brocade" (44:53). He will recline "on green cushions and rich carpets of beauty" (55:76), sit on "thrones encrusted with gold and precious stones" (56:15), and share in "dishes and goblets of gold"—on which would be "all that the souls could desire, all that their eyes could delight in," including an "abundance of fruit" (43:71, 73) along with "dates and pomegranates" (55:68). There will also enjoy "the flesh of fowls, any that they may desire" (Qur'an 56:21). Paradise itself consists of "gardens, with rivers flowing beneath" (3:198; cf. 3:136; 13:35; 15:45; 22:23). In it are "two springs pouring forth water in continuous abundance" (55:66), along with "rivers of milk of which the taste never changes; rivers of wine, a joy to those who drink; and rivers of honey pure and clear" (47:15). That wine is "free from headiness," so that those who drink it will not "suffer intoxication therefrom" (37:47).

"Reclining in the Garden on raised thrones," the blessed "will see there neither the sun's excessive heat nor the moon's excessive cold. And the shades of the Garden will come low over them, and the bunches of fruit, there, will hang low in humility" (76:13-14).

The food and comforts would never run out: "its food is everlasting, and its shade" (13:35).

And above all, of course, there will be "voluptuous women of equal age" (78:31): "those of modest gaze, with lovely eyes" (37:48), "fair women with beautiful, big, and lustrous eyes" (44:54), "like unto rubies and coral" (55:58) to whom the blessed will be "joined" (52:20). These women would be "maidens, chaste, restraining their glances, whom no man or Jinn [spirit being] before them has touched" (55:56). Allah "made them virgins" (56:36), and according to Islamic tradition, virgins they would remain forever. Also "round about them will serve, devoted to them, young male servants handsome as pearls well-guarded" (52:24), "youths of perpetual freshness" (56:17): "if thou seest them, thou wouldst think them scattered pearls" (76:19).

None of this, of course, can be found in the Jewish or Christian Scriptures, but it is in the writings of the Zoroastrians of Persia, who were a considerable presence in the areas around the Persian Empire before the advent of Islam. According to historian W. St. Clair Tisdall, who did pioneering work on these questions in his monograph "The Sources of Islam," which he later expanded into a book, and in his other writings, "the books of the Zoroastrians and Hindus...bear the most extraordinary likeness to what we find in the Koran and Hadith. Thus in Paradise we are told of 'houris having fine black eyes,' and again of 'houris with large black eyes, resembling pearls hidden in their shells.'...The name *houry* too is derived from an Avesta or Pehlavi Source, as well as *jinn* for genii, and *bihisht* (Paradise), signifying in Avestic 'the better land.' We also have very similar tales in the old Hindu writings, of heavenly regions with their boys and girls resembling the houris and *ghilman* of the Koran."[10]

Revelations of convenience?

Aisha once asked Muhammad what the experience of receiving revelations was like, and he responded: "Sometimes it is (revealed) like the ringing of a bell, this form of Inspiration is the hardest of all and then this state passes off after I have grasped what is inspired. Sometimes the Angel comes in the form of a man and talks to me and I grasp whatever he says."[11] On another occasion he explained: "The revelation dawns upon me in two ways— Gabriel brings it and conveys to me as a man conveys to another man and that makes me restless. And it dawns upon me like the sound of a bell till it enters my heart and this does not make me restless."[12] Aisha noted:

"When revelation descended upon Allah's Messenger (may peace be upon him) even during the cold days, his forehead perspired."[13] Also, when inspiration came to him "he felt a burden on that account and the colour of his face underwent a change," and "he lowered his head and so lowered his Companions their heads, and when (this state) was over, he raised his head."[14]

A Muslim once said: "I wish I could see Allah's Apostle at the time he is being inspired Divinely." Obligingly, another asked Muhammad a question. Muhammad "waited for a while, and then the Divine Inspiration descended upon him.... The Prophet's face was red and he kept on breathing heavily for a while and then he was relieved." Then he gave an answer to the questioner.[15]

Some of the other difficulties non-Muslims have had with accepting Muhammad as a prophet come from the circumstances of many of the revelations he received. As we shall see, quite often during his prophetic career he received revelations that answered critics, or solved a disputed question, or gave his particular perspective on a series of events.

On more than a few occasions the circumstances of these revelations seemed to manifest Allah's anxiety to grant his prophet his heart's desires—as in the notorious story of one of Muhammad's wives, Zaynab bint Jahsh. Zaynab had been married to Muhammad's adopted son Zayd bin Haritha—a union that neither of them had wanted, according to Islamic tradition, but upon which Muhammad insisted: it would show the equality of all believers, for Zaynab was from a notable family while Zayd was but a freed slave. Muhammad received divine validation for his insistence: "It is not fitting for a Believer, man or woman, when a matter has been decided by Allah and His Messenger to have any option about their decision: if any one disobeys Allah and His Messenger, he is indeed on a clearly wrong Path" (Qur'an 33:36).

Zaynab bint Jahsh was apparently remarkably beautiful. According to the *Tafsir al-Jalalayn*, an ancient Islamic commentary on the Qur'an, after her marriage to Zayd, "Muhammad's eye fell on her, and love for Zaynab budded in his heart."[16] One day, seeking Zayd, Muhammad went to their house and chanced upon her wearing only a chemise. Zaynab exclaimed, "He is not here, Messenger of God. Come in, you who are as dear to me as my father and mother!" But the Prophet of Islam hastened away in considerable agitation, murmuring something unheard and then adding audibly, "Glory be to God the Almighty! Glory be to God, who causes hearts to turn!"[17]

Zayd, saddled with a marriage he had not wanted, saw his way out. He went to see Muhammad and echoed Zaynab's language: "Messenger of God, I have heard that you came to my house. Why didn't you go in, you who are as dear to me as my father and mother?" Then he got to the point: "Messenger of God, perhaps Zaynab has excited your admiration, and so I will separate myself from her." Muhammad told him: "Keep thy wife to thyself, and fear Allah" (Qur'an 33:37). Zayd returned on many occasions, but Muhammad would only repeat this admonition. Aisha later remarked, "If Allah's Apostle were to conceal anything (of the Qur'an) he would have concealed this Verse."[18] Finally Zayd separated from her anyway, and shortly thereafter, Allah himself intervened. According to the Muslim historian Abu Ja'far Muhammad bin Jarir al-Tabari (839–923), one day Muhammad was talking with Aisha when "a fainting overcame him." Then he smiled and asked, "Who will go to Zaynab to tell her the good news, saying that God has married her to me?"

He then recited the revelation Allah had just given him, scolding him for being concerned about what people might think and thus refusing to marry Zaynab. (Qur'an 33:37). So Muhammad took Zaynab as his wife, protected by a direct revelation from Allah from the appearance of scandal. To this day, Muslims in reciting the Qur'an recite these warnings to the Prophet that he should not turn aside from the gifts of Allah, and not hesitate to marry his former daughter-in-law.

This new wife, and the circumstances of her betrothal to Muhammad, worried Aisha. "I became very uneasy because of what we heard about her beauty and another thing, the greatest and loftiest of matters—what God had done for her by giving her in marriage. I said that she would boast of it over us."[19] And sure enough, Zaynab did, saying to Muhammad's other wives: "You were given in marriage by your families, while I was married (to the Prophet) by Allah from over seven Heavens."[20] Whereupon Aisha responded: "I am the one whose innocence was revealed from heaven" — and thereby hangs another tale of the questionable circumstances of Muhammad's revelations.[21]

Muhammad had recently ordered the veiling of women, so Aisha, when she accompanied him to a battle, was carried in a curtained howdah on the back of a camel — triggering a crisis whose effects are still being felt in the Islamic world. Aisha tells the story:

> (We camped) as we approached near the city of Medina. Then he announced for departure at night. I got up when they announced the departure, and went away from the army camps, and after finishing from the call of nature, I came back to my riding animal. I touched my chest to find that my necklace which was made of *Zifar* beads (i.e. Yemenite beads partly black and partly white) was missing. So I returned to look for my necklace and my search for it detained me. (In the meanwhile) the people who used to carry me on my camel, came and took my *Hawdaj* and put it on the back of my camel on which I used to ride, as they considered that I was in it. In those days women were light in weight for they did not get fat, and flesh did not cover their bodies in abundance as they used to eat only a little food. So, those people did not feel the difference in the heaviness of the *Hawdaj* while lifting it, and they put it near the camel. At that time I was still a young lady. They made the camel rise and all of them left (along with it). I found my necklace after the army had gone.

Since the order for veiling meant that no one could look at her or speak to her, and her weight didn't make any significant difference, the people loading Aisha's howdah onto her camel had no way of telling she wasn't there. And so Muhammad's favorite wife was stranded.

While I was sitting in my resting place, I was overwhelmed by sleep and slept. Safwan bin Al-Muattal As-Sulami Adh-Dhakwani was behind the army. When he reached my place in the morning, he saw the figure of a sleeping person and he recognized me on seeing me as he had seen me before the order of compulsory veiling (was prescribed). So I woke up when he recited *Istirja'* (i.e. *"Inna lillahi wa inna llaihi raji'un"* ["Truly to Allah we belong and truly to him we shall return"]) as soon as he recognized me.[22] I veiled my face with my head cover at once, and by Allah, we did not speak a single word, and I did not hear him saying any word besides his *Istirja'*. He dismounted from his camel and made it kneel down, putting his leg on its front legs and then I got up and rode on it. Then he set out leading the camel that was carrying me till we overtook the army in the extreme heat of midday while they were at a halt (taking a rest).

Aisha had been alone with a man who was not her husband. For some, that was enough to begin circulating ugly rumors about her: "(Because of the event) some people brought destruction upon themselves," Aisha said, "and the one who spread the *Ifk* (i.e. slander) more, was 'Abdullah bin Ubai Ibn Salul"—along with three others (including another man named Mistah bin Uthatha and the sister of Zaynab bint Jahsh), along with some secondary figures. The rumors flew, and even Muhammad was affected by them, drawing back from Aisha, who explains:

After we returned to Medina, I became ill for a month. The people were propagating the forged statements of the slanderers while I was unaware of anything of all that, but I felt that in my present ailment, I was not receiving the usual kindness from Allah's Messenger which I used to receive when I got sick. (But now) Allah's Messenger would only come, greet me and say, 'How is that (lady)?' and leave. That roused my doubts, but I did not discover the evil (i.e. slander) till I recovered from my ailment and I went out with Umm Mistah [that is, Mistah's mother] to Al-Manasi' where we used to answer the call of nature...

Umm Mistah ultimately tells Aisha about the rumors, which of course made an already ailing Aisha feel even worse:

So my ailment was aggravated, and when I reached my home, Allah's Messenger came to me, and after greeting me, said, 'How is that (lady)?' I said, 'Will you allow me to go to my parents?' as I wanted to be sure about the news through them. Allah's Messenger allowed me (and I went to my parents) and asked my mother, 'O mother! What are the people talking about?' She said, 'O my daughter! Don't worry, for scarcely is there a charming woman who is loved by her husband and whose husband has other wives besides herself that they (i.e. women) would find faults with her.' I said, 'Subhan Allah! [Glory be to Allah!] Are the people really talking in this way?' I kept on weeping that night till dawn, I could neither stop weeping nor sleep, then in the morning again, I kept on weeping.

And she had good reason to weep: Muhammad evidently believed the rumors, although Aisha had defenders:

(When the Divine Revelation was delayed), Allah's Messenger called 'Ali bin Abi Talib and Usama bin Zaid to ask and consult them about divorcing me. Usama bin Zaid said what he knew of my innocence, and the respect he had for me. Usama said, "(O Allah's Messenger!) She is your wife, and we do not know anything except good about her."

Rather ungallantly, 'Ali, who later became the great saint and hero of the Shi'ite Muslims, reminds Muhammad that there are "plenty of women" available to the Prophet (Aisha never forgot this, and later disputed Ali's claim that Muhammad had appointed him as his successor: "When did he appoint him by will? Verily when he died he was resting against my chest and he asked for a wash-basin and then collapsed while in that state, and I could not even perceive that he had died, so when did he appoint him by will?").[23] Aisha's account continues:

> 'Ali bin Abi Talib said, "O Allah's Messenger! Allah does not put you in difficulty, and there are plenty of women other than she, yet, ask the maid-servant (Aishah's slave-girl) who will tell you the truth." On that Allah's Messenger called Barira (i.e. the maid-servant) and said, "O Barira! Did you ever see anything which aroused your suspicion?" Barira said to him, "By Him Who has sent you with the Truth, I have never seen anything in her (i.e., Aishah) which I would conceal, except that she is a young girl who sleeps leaving the dough of her family exposed so that the domestic goats come and eat it."

Muhammad was satisfied with this, and turned on Aisha's accusers. Aisha recounts:

> So, on that day, Allah's Messenger got up on the pulpit and complained about 'Abdullah bin Ubai (bin Salul) before his Companions,[24] saying, "O you Muslims! Who will relieve me from that man who has hurt me with his evil statement about my family? By Allah, I know nothing except good about my family and they have blamed a man about whom I know nothing except good and he used never to enter my home except in my company"....All that day I kept on weeping with my tears never ceasing, and I could never sleep.
>
> In the morning my parents were with me and I wept for two nights and a day, neither my tears ceased nor could I sleep till I thought that my liver would burst from weeping. While my

parents were sitting with me and I was weeping, an *Ansari* woman asked me to grant her admittance, and I allowed her to come in. She came in, and sat down and started weeping with me. While we were in this state, Allah's Messenger came, greeted us and sat down. He had never sat with me since that day of the slander. A month had elapsed and no Divine Revelation came to him about my case. Allah's Messenger then recited *Tashahhud* (i.e., *La ilaha illallah wa anna Muhammad-ur-Rasul Allah*—none has the right to be worshipped but Allah and Muhammad is Allah's Messenger) and then said, "'*Amma Ba'du* [Now to the point], O 'Aishah! I have been informed such-and-such about you; if you are innocent, then soon Allah will reveal your innocence, and if you have committed a sin, then repent to Allah and ask Him for forgiveness, for when a person confesses his sins and asks Allah for forgiveness, Allah accepts his repentance."

At that point Aisha began to fight back against her accusers, even quoting the Qur'an in her own defense:

When Allah's Messenger finished his speech, my tears ceased flowing completely and there remained not even a single drop of it. I said to my father, "Reply to Allah's Messenger on my behalf concerning what he has said." My father said, "By Allah, I do not know what to say to Allah's Messenger." Then I said to my mother, "Reply to Allah's Messenger on my behalf concerning what he has said." She said, "By Allah, I do not know what to say to Allah's Messenger." In spite of the fact that I was a young girl and had a little knowledge of the Qur'an, I said, "By Allah, no doubt I know that you heard this (slanderous) speech so that it has got fixed up in your minds and you have taken it as a truth. Now, if I tell you that I am innocent, you will not believe me, and if confess to you falsely that I am guilty, and Allah knows that I am innocent, you will surely believe me." [Qur'an 12:18].... Then I turned to the other side of my bed; hoping that Allah would prove my innocence.

Allah does:

By Allah, Allah's Messenger had not got up and nobody had left the house before the Divine Revelation came to Allah's Messenger. So, there overtook him the same state which used to overtake him, (when he used to be inspired Divinely). The sweat was dropping from his body like pearls, though it was a (cold) wintry day and that was because of the weighty statement which was being revealed to him. When that state of Allah's Messenger was over, he got up smiling, and the first word he said was, "O 'Aishah! Allah has declared your innocence!" (V. 24.11-21).[25]

Here is the full passage of the Qur'an declaring Aisha's innocence, scolding the Muslims for ever believing the accusations, and setting a standard for evidence in crimes of sexual impurity that remains part of Islamic law to this day:

Why did they not produce four witnesses? Since they produce not witnesses, they verily are liars in the sight of Allah. Had it not been for the grace of Allah and His mercy unto you in the world and the Hereafter an awful doom had overtaken you for that whereof ye murmured. When ye welcomed it with your tongues, and uttered with your mouths that whereof ye had no knowledge, ye counted it a trifle. In the sight of Allah it is very great. Wherefore, when ye heard it, said ye not: It is not for us to speak of this. Glory be to Thee (O Allah)! This is awful calumny. (Qur'an 24:11-20)

The consequences

Certainly Muhammad loved Aisha, and was clearly relieved when the revelation of her innocence came to him from Allah. But here, as in the case of Zaynab, it seems as if Allah's solicitude for his Prophet takes the Qur'an, which is supposed to be a universal message applicable to all people in all times and places, into some rather surprisingly localized areas. Even Aisha herself was amazed: "But by Allah, I did not think that Allah, (to confirm my innocence), would reveal Divine Revelation which would be recited, for I consider myself too unimportant to be talked about by Allah through Divine Revelation revealed for recitation, but I hoped that Allah's Messenger might have a dream in which Allah would reveal my innocence."[26] Indeed, many others have marveled at this over the centuries.

Of course, in this case as in Zaynab's, there is a stated justification beyond Muhammad's immediate desires: Muslims are instructed by the tale of Zaynab that a man may marry the divorced wife of his adopted son — however curious it may be that there was any need for legislation on such a matter at any time, much less a serious incident involving the Prophet of Allah and divine revelation. A consequence of this has been the weakening of adoption in Islamic culture, as Zayd was no longer known as "Zayd bin Muhammad," Zayd son of Muhammad, but as Zayd bin Haritha, the name of his birth father. Says the Qur'an: "Allah has not made for any man two hearts in his (one) body: nor has He made your wives whom ye divorce by Zihar your mothers: nor has He made your adopted sons your sons. Such is (only) your (manner of) speech by your mouths. But Allah tells (you) the Truth, and He shows the (right) Way. Call them by (the names of) their fathers: that is juster in the sight of Allah" (33:5).[27]

And the false accusations against Aisha brought about the requirement that four male Muslim witnesses must be produced in order to establish a crime of adultery or related indiscretions. In cases of sexual misbehavior, four male witnesses are required to establish the deed — in accord with the revelation that came to Muhammad to exonerate his youthful wife (Qur'an 24:13).[28] And just as Aisha's own word counted for nothing to establish the falsity of the accusations against her, so to this day Islamic law restricts the validity of a woman's testimony—particular in cases involving sexual immorality. Says the Qur'an: "Call in two male witnesses from among you, but if two men cannot be found, then one man and two women whom you, judge fit to act as witnesses; so that if either of them commit an error, the other will remember" (2:282). And Islamic legal theorists have restricted women's testimony even farther by limiting it to, in the words of one Muslim legal manual, "cases involving property, or transactions dealing with property, such as sales."[29] Otherwise only men can testify.

Consequently, it is even today virtually impossible to prove rape in lands that follow the dictates of the sharia. Unscrupulous men can commit rape with impunity: as long as they deny the charge and there are no witnesses, they get off scot-free, because the victim's account is inadmissible. Even worse, if a woman accuses a man of rape, she may end up incriminating herself. If the required male witnesses can't be found, the victim's charge of rape becomes an admission of adultery. That accounts for the grim fact that as many as 75 percent of the women in prison in Pakistan are, in fact, behind bars for the crime of being a victim of rape.[30] Several high-profile cases in Nigeria recently have also revolved around rape accusations being turned around by Islamic authorities into charges of fornication, resulting in death sentences that were only modified after international pressure.[31]

Moreover, such abuses are extraordinarily resistant to criticism and reform—they are, after all, based on the example of the Prophet, the perfect model for human behavior.

Modern embarrassment

At the same time, however, many modern Muslims and spokesmen for Islam do indeed seem embarrassed by this material—or at least they don't seem to want their readers to know much about it. Yahiya Emerick in *The Life and Work of Muhammad* says of Zaynab bint Jahsh only that the Prophet married her, and that she "had recently divorced Zayd bin

Harithah because of his humble background."[32] He makes no mention of the incident involving Muhammad's confusion at her state of undress, or the subsequent divine revelation recorded in sura 33. He recounts Muhammad's adoption of Zayd and his becoming known as Zayd bin Muhammad, without ever mentioning his subsequent divinely mandated reversion to being Zayd bin Haritha.[33]

Muhammad Husayn Haykal, in his *Life of Muhammad*, sputters with indignation at the "Orientalists" who use the story of Zaynab to besmirch Muhammad:

> Western Orientalists and missionaries pause in order to give full vent to their resentment and imagination. In this chapter of Muhammad's biography, some of them take inordinate pain to paint a sensual portrait of Zaynab. They relate that when Muhammad saw her, she was half-naked, that her fine black hair was covering half her body, and that every curve of her body was full of desire and passion. Others relate that when Muhammad opened the door of the house of Zayd the breeze played with the curtains of the room of Zaynab, thus permitting Muhammad to catch a glimpse of her stretched out on her mattress in a nightgown. They then tell their readers that this view of her stormed the heart of Muhammad who was extremely passionate in his love and desire for women. They relate that Muhammad had hidden his secret desire, though he could hardly bear to conceal it for long!

This and many like pictures have been painted arduously by Orientalists and missionaries and may be read in the work of Muir, Dermenghem, Washington Irving, Lammens, and others. It cannot be denied that these stories are based upon reports in fanciful Muslim biographies and Hadith books. But these books are questionable. And it is extremely regrettable that our authors have used them without scrutiny. It is inexcusable that these scholars had built "Castles in Spain" regarding Muhammad's relations with women, castles which they thought were sufficiently justified by the fact that Muhammad married a plurality of wives, probably nine, or even more according to some versions.

Haykal responds to this first by asserting that even if the story of Zaynab's marriage to Muhammad were true, that would still "constitute no flaw in the prophethood of Muhammad, in his own greatness or that of his message."

Why not? Because "the rules which are law to the people at large do not apply to the great. A fortiori, they have no application on prophets, the messengers of God." And beyond this rather surprising Romantic view, "the fact is that Muhammad was not a man given to passion and desire as the Orientalists and missionaries have pictured him. He did not marry his wives for lust, desire, or love. If some Muslim writers in certain periods of history have allowed themselves to attribute such things to the Prophet and thereby to present with good intent an argument to the enemies of Islam, that is because their conservatism caused them to adopt a materialistic view of things. In such a manner they pictured Muhammad as superlative in everything including the lusts of this world. But the picture they drew was clearly false. The history of Muhammad denies it outright, and the logic of Muhammad's life is utterly inconsistent with it."[34]

Karen Armstrong, by contrast, starts out being somewhat more realistic. She even records Aisha's sharp comment after Muhammad received his divine scolding for hesitating to marry Zaynab: "Truly thy Lord makes haste to do thy bidding." But then she explains that "today Muslims deny that Muhammad married Zaynab out of lust, and, indeed, it seems most unlikely that a woman of thirty-nine, who had been living on the brink of malnutrition all her life and exposed to the merciless sun of Arabia would inspire such a storm of emotion in anybody's breast, let alone that of a cousin who had known her since she was a child."[35]

This, however, contradicts the earliest accounts, in which, as we have seen, Muhammad is indeed overcome by a storm of emotion on seeing Zaynab wearing only her shift, and Zayd tells his adoptive father that he will divorce her if she has "excited your admiration."

Regarding the rumors swirling around Aisha, Armstrong doesn't discuss the implications of the fact that Muhammad would not take her at her word, but apparently needed a divine revelation to exonerate her. She focuses not on the peculiarity of a revelation being necessary, and doesn't mention the evidentiary disadvantage under which Muslim women have consequently suffered. On the contrary, she sees in Aisha's "dignified handling of the situation" evidence of "the confidence that Islam could give to a woman."[36]

Nor does Armstrong mention another statement of Aisha's: "I have not seen any woman suffering as much as the believing women."[37]

And they continue to suffer.

CHAPTER FIVE

"A warner in the face of a terrific punishment"

- Initial opposition to Muhammad from his own tribe
- Evolution of the Qur'an's teaching on warfare against unbelievers
- The Satanic verses: Muhammad's attempt to win over his opponents
- How Islamic apologists try to explain away the Satanic verses incident
- Muhammad's Night Journey to Jerusalem

Difficulties with the Quraysh

AFTER MUHAMMAD DETERMINED, WITH HELP FROM KHADIJA AND Waraqa, that he was a prophet, he began to speak with people privately about the new religion. At first the substance of his preaching was simple monotheism: "It is God's religion which He has chosen for Himself and sent His apostles with it. I call you to God, the One without an associate, to worship Him and to disavow al-Lat and al-'Uzza."[1] His wife Khadija became the first Muslim, followed by Ali bin Abu Talib, then a boy of ten, who would much later loom so large in the Sunni-Shi'ite schism, and a few others. Three years after his initial visitation from the one he came to believe was

Gabriel, which took place around the year 610, Allah commanded him to "proclaim what you have been ordered and turn aside from the polytheists."[2]

Muhammad summoned his kinsmen, the Quraysh, climbing a mountain and calling the names of the various Quraysh clans. He asked them, "Suppose I told you that there is an (enemy) cavalry in the valley intending to attack you, would you believe me?"

They responded, "Yes, for we have not found you telling anything other than the truth."

Muhammad's riposte to this was: "I am a warner to you in face of a terrific punishment." In other words, the dreadful judgment of Allah would be far worse than the enemy cavalry.

This pious warning annoyed Muhammad's uncle, Abu Lahab, who did not believe his nephew's prophetic claims. He called out to Muhammad, "May your hands perish all this day. Is it for this purpose you have gathered us?"[3] Turning to the assembled Quraysh, Abu Lahab declared, "Your host has bewitched you."[4]

Allah himself gave Muhammad his response to Abu Lahab in a new revelation: "May the hands of Abu Lahab perish! May he himself perish! Nothing shall his wealth and gains avail him. He shall be burnt in a flaming fire, and his wife, laden with faggots, shall have a rope of fibre around her neck!" (Qur'an 111:1-5). A hadith informs us that Abu Lahab "indeed perished."[5] The hadith does not record the manner of his death, but one possible cause may be ruled out: at this point the Muslims were not targeting their enemies for violent attacks.

Yahiya Emerick gives this story a very different spin in his apologetic biography of Muhammad. After Muhammad delivered his message, he says, "Abu Lahab, who was standing nearby, angrily cursed Muhammad and told him he should die. Muhammad held his tongue, because the ancient code of respect for elders was ingrained in him. Soon thereafter, a small couplet of verses was revealed to him in which Abu Lahab was told that he would be the one who was doomed."[6]

Muhammad continued to preach, to little effect. His detractors asked him why he performed no miracle, asking him to turn the mountains around Mecca into gold for them, or to clear them away altogether so that their farming would be easier. Allah replied to Muhammad: "If you wish, I will be patient and give them more time, or if you wish, I will do what they are asking, but if they then disbelieve, they will be destroyed as the nations before them were destroyed."[7] Muhammad asked that they be granted more time, and replied to his foes that his miracle was the Qur'an.

At one point one of the Quraysh asked him to send Gabriel or some other angel to tell them to believe in him: "O Muhammad, if an angel had been sent with thee to speak to men about thee and to be seen with thee!"[8] But Allah replied in a revelation that in order to send an angel, he would have had to make him appear as a man, and that would have left the Quraysh back where they started. (Qur'an 6:9). He consoled Muhammad, telling him that his was the common lot of the prophets before him: "Mocked were (many) messengers before thee; but their scoffers were hemmed in by the thing that they mocked" (Qur'an 6:10). Though the Muslims were only a tiny band at this point, violence connected with the new religion began early. Ibn Ishaq tells the story:

> When the apostle's companions prayed they went to the glens so that their people could not see them praying, and while Sa'd bin Abu Waqqas was with a number of the Prophet's companions in one of the glens of Mecca, a band of polytheists came upon them while they were praying and rudely interrupted them. They blamed them for what they were doing until they came to blows, and it was on that occasion that Sa'd smote a polytheist with the jawbone of a camel and wounded him. This was the first blood to be shed in Islam.[9]

Much more would come in due course. But Muhammad didn't begin his prophetic career as a warrior, although he had participated in two local wars between his Quraysh tribe and a neighboring clan.[10] He confined his activities to preaching, although his preaching threatened the pagan Meccans with annihilation.

How many were the populations We utterly destroyed because
of their iniquities, setting up in their places other peoples? Yet,
when they felt Our Punishment (coming), behold, they (tried
to) flee from it. Flee not, but return to the good things of this
life which were given you, and to your homes in order that ye
may be called to account. They said: "Ah! woe to us! We were
indeed wrong-doers!"

And that cry of theirs ceased not, till We made them as a field
that is mown, as ashes silent and quenched. (Qur'an 21:11-15)

The Quraysh were completely surprised by the killing committed by Sa'd b.
Abu Waqqas, and as Muhammad began to attack them and their gods with
increasing vehemence, they began to see Islam and its prophet as a threat.
In due course they began to strike back. According to Ibn Ishaq, they
"stirred up against him foolish men who called him a liar, insulted him, and
accused him of being a poet, a sorcerer, a diviner, and of being possessed.
However, the apostle continued to proclaim what God had ordered him to
proclaim, concealing nothing, and exciting their dislike by contemning
their religion, forsaking their idols, and leaving them to their unbelief."[11]

Things got so bad between the Muslims and the Quraysh that Muhammad told his small band of followers: "If you were to go to Abyssinia (it
would be better for you), for the king will not tolerate injustice and it is a
friendly country, until such time as Allah shall relieve you from your distress."[12] A number of the Muslims took his advice, but Muhammad himself stayed in Mecca and kept trying to bring the Quraysh to Islam.

The evolution of the command to wage war

On one occasion Muhammad's anger and frustration over his failure to
convert the Quraysh boiled over. He approached a group of Quraysh at the
Ka'bah, kissed the black stone, and walked around the shrine three times.
On his third pass he stopped and declared: "Will you listen to me, O
Quraysh? By him who holds my life in His hand, I bring you slaughter."[13]
This was one prophecy of Muhammad that would indisputably prove true.

Muhammad's messages began to change in character. Early in his career a group of twelve converts to Islam from the Khazraj tribe of the city of the Medina gathered with Muhammad in the city of Al-'Aqaba, made what is known as the first covenant of 'Aqaba: a pledge of fealty to the Prophet of Islam. One of them explained: "We gave allegiance to the apostle that we would associate nothing with God, not steal, not commit fornication, not kill our offspring, not slander our neighbor, not disobey him in what was right; if we fulfilled this paradise would be ours; and if we committed any of those sins we should be punished in this world and this would serve as expiation; if the sin was concealed until the Day of Resurrection, then it would be for God to decide whether to punish or to forgive."[14]

There was nothing in this pledge about warring for Islam. But a year later, around the year 622, that was to change. Originally, explained Ibn Ishaq, "the apostle had not been given permission to fight or allowed to shed blood....He had simply been ordered to call men to God and to endure insult and forgive the ignorant. The Quraysh had persecuted his followers, seducing some from their religion, and exiling others from their country. They had to choose whether to give up their religion, be maltreated at home, or to flee the country, some to Abyssinia, others to Medina."

But now the time for forgiveness was over:

> When Quraysh became insolent towards God and rejected His
> gracious purpose, accused His prophet of lying, and ill treated
> and exiled those who served Him and proclaimed His unity,
> believed in His prophet, and held fast to His religion, He gave
> permission to His apostle to fight and to protect himself against
> those who wronged them and treated them badly.[15]

Then Ibn Ishaq explains the progression of Qur'anic revelation about warfare. First, he explains, Allah allowed Muslims to wage defensive warfare:

> Assuredly God will help those who help Him. God is Almighty.
> Those who if we make them strong in the land will establish
> prayer, pay the poor-tax, enjoin kindness, and forbid iniquity.

To God belongs the end of matters.[16] The meaning is: "I have allowed them to fight only because they have been unjustly treated while their sole offence against men has been that they worship God. When they are in the ascendant they will establish prayer, pay the poor-tax, enjoin kindness, and forbid iniquity, i.e. the Prophet and his companions all of them."[17]

"When they are in the ascendant," in other words, they will establish an Islamic state, in which Muslims will pray regularly, pay the poor-tax (*zakat*), and institute Islamic laws ("forbid iniquity"). But that was not Allah's last word on the circumstances in which Muslims should fight:

Then God sent down to him: "Fight them so that there be no more seduction," i.e., until no believer is seduced from his religion. "And the religion is God's," i.e., until God alone is worshipped.[18]

The Qur'an verse Ibn Ishaq quotes here (2:193) commands much more than defensive warfare: Muslims must fight until "the religion is God's"—that is, until Allah alone is worshipped. Later Islamic law, based on statements of Muhammad, would offer non-Muslims three options: conversion to Islam, subjugation as inferiors under Islamic law, or warfare.

The Satanic verses

But Muhammad's efforts to bring his tribesmen into his new religion continued to flounder—and this led to the notorious incident of the Satanic verses, immortalized in the equally notorious novel by Salman Rushdie. In 1989, Iran's Ayatollah Khomeini issued a fatwa, ordering Muslims to kill Rushdie—a death sentence that has been perpetually reaffirmed by Iranian leaders, though no assassin has yet carried it out.

According to Islamic tradition, Satan, not Allah, once actually spoke through Muhammad's mouth. The verses that the devil gave to the Prophet of Islam have been known thereafter as "the Satanic verses."

Muhammad was frustrated over his inability to convert his own people, the Quraysh, to Islam. According to Ibn Ishaq, in a section of his Sira preserved by Tabari, "the apostle was anxious for the welfare of his people, wishing to attract them as far as he could." In fact, "he longed for a way to attract them." However, ultimately it was the leaders of the Quraysh who came to him with an offer. They would give him wives and money, and even make him their king—if he would in turn accept their condition. "This is what we will give you, Muhammad, so desist from reviling our gods and do not speak evilly of them. If you will not do so, we offer you one means which will be to your advantage and to ours."

"What is it?" asked the Prophet of Islam.

"You will worship our gods, al-Lat and al-'Uzza, for a year, and we shall worship your god for a year."

Muhammad responded: "Let me see what revelation comes to me from my Lord."[19] And initially, the answers the Prophet of Islam received were sharply negative: Allah told him to tell the disbelievers that Muslims would not worship what they worshipped. (Qur'an 109:1-6)

But the Quraysh persisted: "Muhammad, come and let us worship that which you worship and you worship that which we worship, and we shall make you a partner in all of our undertakings." But Allah still told Muhammad to stand firm. (Qur'an 39:64-66)

But behind this adamantine posture, Muhammad longed for a way out of the impasse: "When the apostle saw that his people turned their backs on him and he was pained by their estrangement from what he brought them from God he longed that there should come to him from God a message that would reconcile his people to him."[20]

He said: "I wish Allah had not revealed to me anything distasteful to them."[21] And finally he hit on a solution. He received a revelation saying that it was legitimate for Muslims to pray to al-Lat, al-'Uzza, and Manat, the three goddesses favored by the pagan Quraysh, as intercessors before Allah.[22] But his pain and frustration at being rejected by his own people had gotten the better of him: this new message directly contradicted the substance of his preaching up to that point. He had scorned al-Lat, al-'Uzza, and Manat as false gods from the beginning of his proclamation of his prophethood, or even before that if the account of his youthful encounter with the Syrian monk Bahira is to be believed. Was this uncompromising monotheism now to be discarded for the sake of reconciliation with his people?

Reconciliation did seem to be at hand. The Quraysh were elated, and prostrated themselves with Muhammad and the Muslims after Muhammad finished reciting the new revelation. Ibn Ishaq recounts: "Then the people dispersed and Quraysh went out, delighted at what had been said about their gods, saying, 'Muhammad has spoken of our gods in splendid fashion. He alleged in what he read that they are the exalted Gharaniq whose intercession is approved.'"[23]

Word traveled quickly among the Muslims: "the Quraysh have accepted Islam."[24] Since peace seemed to be at hand, some of the Muslims who had earlier fled to Abyssinia for their safety returned. But one principal player in the drama was not at all pleased: the angel Gabriel, the one whose appearance to Muhammad had given birth to Islam. He came to Muhammad and said: "What have you done, Muhammad? You have read to these people something I did not bring you from God and you have said what He did not say to you."

Muhammad began to realize just how severely he had compromised his entire enterprise. "I have fabricated things against God and have imputed to Him words which He has not spoken."[25] He "was bitterly grieved and was greatly in fear" of Allah for having allowed his message to be adulterated by Satan. And Allah gave Muhammad a stern warning (Qur'an 17:73-75) but was ultimately merciful to his prophet:

> So God sent down (a revelation), for He was merciful to him,
> comforting him and making light of the affair and telling him
> that every prophet and apostle before him desired as he desired
> and wanted what he wanted and Satan interjected something
> into his desires as he had on his tongue. So God annulled what
> Satan had suggested and God established His verses i.e., you
> are just like the prophets and apostles.[26]

This reassurance is enshrined in the Qur'an: "Never did We send a messenger or a prophet before thee, but, when he framed a desire, Satan threw some (vanity) into his desire: but Allah will cancel anything (vain) that Satan throws in, and Allah will confirm (and establish) His Signs: for Allah is full of Knowledge and Wisdom" (22:52). Indeed, it was all a test of the unbelievers: "That He may make the suggestions thrown in by Satan, but a trial for those in whose hearts is a disease and who are hardened of heart: verily the wrong-doers are in a schism far (from the Truth)" (22:53).

Allah, says Ibn Ishaq, thereby "relieved his prophet's grief, and made him feel safe from his fears." He also sent down a new revelation to replace Satan's words about al-Lat, al-'Uzza, and Manat:

> Have ye thought upon Al-Lat and Al-'Uzza and Manat, the
> third, the other? Are yours the males and His the females? That
> indeed were an unfair division! They are but names which ye
> have named, ye and your fathers, for which Allah hath revealed
> no warrant. They follow but a guess and that which (they)
> themselves desire. And now the guidance from their Lord hath
> come unto them. (Qur'an 53:19-23)

In other words, does Allah have only daughters while even the unbelievers have sons ("are yours the males and His the females")? To a seventh-century Arab, that would be preposterous. And what's more, al-Lat, al-'Uzza and Manat are just figments of the pagan imagination, "names which ye have named, ye and your fathers, for which Allah hath revealed no warrant."

Muhammad returned to his original uncompromising monotheism. Unsurprisingly, his about-face only enflamed tensions with the Quraysh all the more. Ibn Ishaq recalls that the polytheists began to use this episode against him:

> When the annulment of what Satan had put upon the
> Prophet's tongue came from God, Quraysh said: "Muhammad
> has repented of what he said about the position of your gods
> with Allah, altered it and brought something else." Now those

two words which Satan had put upon the apostle's tongue were
in the mouth of every polytheist and they became more vio-
lently hostile to the Muslims and the apostle's followers.[27]

The Satanic verses incident has naturally caused Muslims acute embarrassment for centuries. Indeed, it casts a shadow over the veracity of
Muhammad's entire claim to be a prophet. After all, if Satan could put
words into Muhammad's mouth once, and make him think they were revelations from Allah, who is to say that Satan did not use Muhammad as his
mouthpiece on other occasions? Thus Islamic scholars, apologists, and historians have attacked the Satanic verses with particular ferocity. Muhammad Husayn Haykal argues in his *Life of Muhammad* that the incident
never happened at all, and indeed could not have happened, for after all,
Muhammad is a prophet:

> This story arrested the attention of the western Orientalists who
> took it as true and repeated it ad nauseam. . . . It is a story whose
> incoherence is evident upon the least scrutiny. It contradicts
> the infallibility of every prophet in conveying the message of
> his Lord.

He marvels that even some Muslim scholars take it to be true. But is quick
to add: "Ibn Ishaq, for his part, did not hesitate at all to declare it a fabri-
cation by the zindiqs [Non-Muslims concealing their unbelief, falsely pre-
tending that they are members of the ummah; mostly Zoroastrians and
Manicheans. -Tr.]."[28]

Yahiya Emerick doesn't mention the Satanic verses incident at all, and
explains that the Muslims who had emigrated to Abyssinia began to return
when "word came from Mecca through travelling merchants that the conversion of a high-ranking noble had improved the Muslims' situation."[29]

Karen Armstrong denies the authenticity of the story: "We have to be
clear here that many Muslims believe this story to be apocryphal. They
point out that there is no clear reference to it in the Qur'an, that it is not

mentioned by Ibn Ishaq in the earliest and most reliable account of Muhammad's life..."[30]

However, it is not certain that Ibn Ishaq does not mention the incident. Tabari attributes his version to Ibn Ishaq, and would have had no reason for saying this if it were not so.[31] Ibn Sa'd also notes the incident.[32]

It is hard to see how and why such a story would have been fabricated and accepted as authentic by such pious Muslims as Ibn Ishaq, Ibn Sa'd, and Tabari, as well as by the later Qur'anic commentator Zamakhshari (1074–1143), who is unlikely to have recounted it if he did not trust the sources. Here, as in many other areas, the witness of the early Islamic sources is compelling. While events may be explained in other ways, those who would wish away the Satanic verses cannot get around the fact that these elements of Muhammad's life were not the inventions of his enemies, but were passed along by men who believed he was indeed the Prophet of Allah.

In the hadith collection of Bukhari we are told that on one occasion, after reciting sura 53 of the Qur'an, Muhammad prostrated himself, and all the pagans and unbelievers also prostrated themselves.[33] Sura 53 contains the reference to the goddesses al-Lat, al-'Uzza, and Manat. There is no other incident in Muhammad's prophetic career recounted by anyone in which unbelievers (*al-Mushrikun*) prostrate themselves along with the Muslims after the recitation of a passage of the Qur'an. Non-Muslims to this day are not generally welcome to join in prayer with Muslims. Why were the unbelievers then present for the recitation of this sura?

The Night Journey

It was around this time that Muhammad went on his famous Night Journey (*Miraj*, or Ascension), which Islamic tradition identifies as a miraculous trip from Mecca to Jerusalem. In Jerusalem, according to these traditions, Muhammad ascended into heaven from the Temple Mount and met the other prophets. The only thing the Qur'an has to say about it is this: "Glory to (Allah) Who did take His servant for a Journey by night from the Sacred Mosque to the farthest Mosque, whose precincts We did bless, in order that We might show him some of Our Signs: for He is the One Who heareth and seeth (all things)" (17:1). There is no Qur'anic identification of the "farthest Mosque" with any mosque in Jerusalem, but the Hadith is very clear on the identification of its location with Jerusalem.

The vision was as dramatic as his initial encounter with Gabriel. Muhammad described the vision to one of the Muslims as beginning "while I was lying in Al-Hatim or Al-Hijr," that is, an area in Mecca opposite the Ka'bah, identified by Islamic tradition as the burial place of Hagar and Ishmael, when "Gabriel came and stirred me with his foot. I sat up but saw nothing and lay down again. He came a second time and stirred me with his foot. I sat up but saw nothing and lay down again. He came to me the third time and stirred me with his foot."[34] And "suddenly someone came to me and cut my body open from here to here"—and he gestured from his throat to his pubic area. The one who had come to him, Muhammad continued, "then took out my heart. Then a golden tray full of Belief was brought to me and my heart was washed and was filled (with Belief) and then returned to its original place. Then a white animal which was smaller than a mule and bigger than a donkey was brought to me."[35] This was the Buraq, which Muhammad further described as "an animal white and long, larger than a donkey but smaller than a mule, who would place his hoof a distance equal to the range of vision."[36] It was, he said, "half mule, half donkey, with wings on its sides with which it propelled its feet."

"When I came up to mount him," Muhammad reports, "he shied. Gabriel placed his hand on its mane and said, 'Are you not ashamed, a Buraq, to behave in this way? By God, none more honorable before God than Muhammad has ever ridden you before.' The animal was so ashamed that he broke out into a sweat and stood still so that I could mount him."[37]

They went to the Temple Mount, and from there to heaven itself: "I was carried on it, and Gabriel set out with me till we reached the nearest heaven. When he asked for the gate to be opened, it was asked, 'Who is it?' Gabriel answered, 'Gabriel.' It was asked, 'Who is accompanying you?' Gabriel replied, 'Muhammad.' It was asked, 'Has Muhammad been called?' Gabriel replied in the affirmative. Then it was said, 'He is wel-comed. What an excellent visit his is!'"

Muhammad enters the first heaven, where he encounters Adam. Gabriel prods Muhammad: "This is your father, Adam; pay him your greet-ings." The Prophet of Islam duly greets the first man, who responds, "You are welcome, O pious son and pious Prophet." Gabriel then carries Muhammad to the second heaven, where the scene at the gate is reen-acted, and once inside, John the Baptist and Jesus greet him: "You are wel-come, O pious brother and pious Prophet." In the third heaven, Joseph greets him in the same words, and Muhammad and Gabriel go on, greeted by other prophets at other levels of heaven.

Moses is in the sixth heaven, occasioning another dig at the Jews. "When I left him," Muhammad says, "he wept. Someone asked him, 'What makes you weep?' Moses said, 'I weep because after me there has been sent (Muhammad as a Prophet) a young man, whose followers will enter Paradise in greater numbers than my followers.'"

In the seventh heaven, Muhammad meets Abraham, has further visions, and receives the command that the Muslims pray fifty times daily. When Muhammad started on his journey back, he passed by Moses, who asked him, "What have you been ordered to do?"

Muhammad replied, "I have been ordered to offer fifty prayers a day."

Moses offered him some advice: "Your followers cannot bear fifty prayers a day, and by Allah, I have tested people before you, and I have tried my level best with Bani Israel (in vain). Go back to your Lord and ask for reduction to lessen your followers' burden." So Muhammad returned to Allah and got the number of daily prayers reduced to forty, but Moses still thought that was too many. The Prophet of Islam kept going between Allah and Moses until the number of daily prayers for the Muslims was only five. At this point Moses still doubted that Muhammad's followers were up to this challenge, saying again: "Your followers cannot bear five prayers a day, and no doubt, I have got an experience of the people before you, and I have tried my level best with Bani Israel, so go back to your Lord and ask for reduction to lessen your followers' burden."

But this time Muhammad would not go back. "I have requested so much of my Lord that I feel ashamed, but I am satisfied now and surrender to Allah's Order." And as he left, he says, "I heard a voice saying, 'I have passed My Order and have lessened the burden of My Worshipers.'"[38]

The Prophet of Islam also described the other prophets for his followers: "On the night of my *Al-Isra* (Journey by Night) (to the heavens), I saw (the prophet) Musa (Moses) who was a thin person with lank hair, looking like one of the men of the tribe of Shanu'a; and I saw Isa (Jesus) who was of average height with red face as if he had just come out of a bathroom. And I resemble Prophet Ibrahim (Abraham) more than any of his offspring does. Then I was given two cups, one containing milk and the other wine. Gabriel said, 'Drink whichever you like.' I took the milk and drank it. Gabriel said, 'You have accepted what is natural, (True Religion i.e., Islam) and if you had taken the wine, your followers would have gone astray.'"[39]

When they heard the stories of his Night Journey, the Quraysh again scoffed at the Prophet of Islam: "By God, this is a plain absurdity! A caravan takes a month to go to Syria and a month to return and can Muhammad do the return journey in one night?" Challenged by some who had been to Jerusalem, Muhammad claimed one further miracle in connection with the Night Journey: "When the people of Quraish did not believe me, I stood up in *Al-Hijr* and Allah displayed Jerusalem in front of me, and I began describing it to them while I was looking at it."[40] Asked how many doors were in the "farthest Mosque," Muhammad later recalled: "I had not counted them so I began to look at it and counted them one by one and gave them information concerning them. I also gave information about their caravan which was on the way and its signs. They found them as I had related."[41]

Evidently, however, his descriptions of Jerusalem were not altogether convincing: even some of the Muslims abandoned their faith and challenged Muhammad's most faithful follower, Abu Bakr, to do the same. Abu Bakr was contemptuous: "If he says so then it is true. And what is so surprising in that? He tells me that communications from God from heaven to earth come to him in an hour of a day or night and I believe him, and that is more extraordinary than that at which you boggle!"[42]

Allah consoled Muhammad: "Behold! We told thee that thy Lord doth encompass mankind round about: We granted the vision which We showed thee, but as a trial for men, as also the Cursed Tree (mentioned) in the Qur'an: We put terror (and warning) into them, but it only increases their inordinate transgression!" (Qur'an 17:60) Later Muhammad seems to have retreated from the claim that this was a bodily journey. Aisha explained: "The apostle's body remained where it was but God removed his spirit by night."[43]

The Night Journey has become firmly embedded in the Islamic consciousness, such that it today serves as the foundation of the Islamic claim to Jerusalem as one of the holy cities of Islam. But at the time that Muhammad first spoke about it, it only further enflamed his already poor relationship with the Quraysh.

CHAPTER SIX

Muhammad becomes a warlord

- Islam's real beginning: when Muhammad becomes a military leader
- The covenant between the Muslims and the Jews, and how their relations soured
- The Nakhla raid and the beginnings of Islamic violence
- The definitive break with the Jews
- Muhammad commands stoning for adultery

The Hijra

IN 622, AFTER YEARS OF INCREASING TENSIONS WITH THE QURAYSH,
Muhammad and his followers finally fled Mecca for a nearby town, Yathrib
(now known as Medina, which is a shortening of *Medinat al-Nabi*, or City
of the Prophet), at the invitation of some of the Muslim converts in that
city. This was thirteen years after the beginning of his prophetic career.[1]
The flight or emigration (*Hijra*, or often in English *Hegira*) of Muhammad
and the Muslims from Mecca to Medina was a major turning point for the
community. No longer would they be a tiny, persecuted band. Muhammad

was now much more than just an apocalyptic preacher: he was a political and military leader. It is noteworthy that the year of the Hijra, not the year of Muhammad's birth or of his first revelation—both milestones that non-Muslims might expect to receive this honor—is the first year of the Muslim calendar. The beginning of Islam as a political and social entity is the beginning of the calendar—for Muslims an event almost as significant as the Exodus for Jews.

Once settled in Medina, the character of Muhammad's revelations began to change. The brief and arresting poetic apocalyptic of the early Meccan suras of the Qur'an (which are now found mostly at the back of the book, since the Qur'an is arranged not chronologically but from the longest chapter to the shortest) began to give way to long, discursive, prosaic material, much of which involved making laws for the new community.

Many of these laws were formulated in dialogue and debate with the Jews of Medina. Muhammad's arrival in the city brought him into close proximity with the three Jewish tribes there, the Banu Qaynuqa, Banu Nadir, and Banu Qurayzah. From nearly the beginning of his prophetic career Muhammad was strongly influenced by Judaism—situating himself within the roster of Jewish prophets, forbidding pork for his followers, and adapting for the Muslims the practice of several daily prayers and other aspects of Jewish ritual. Now he began to try to gain their acceptance of his prophetic status. For the first year and a half after the Muslims' arrival in Medina he even had them face Jerusalem for their prayers.[2]

The covenant between the Muslims and the Jews

During that period Muhammad concluded a pact with the Jewish tribes of Medina—the "world's first constitution" according to Muslims. Ibn Ishaq describes this as a "friendly agreement" between the Jews and the Muslims. It also contains instructions for the two groups of Muslims, the emigrants (*muhajiroun*), the Muslims who came from Mecca, and the helpers (*ansari*), the Muslims who converted in Medina. This document affirms the sharp distinction between believers and unbelievers that would be a hallmark of Islamic history, while granting various rights to the Jews in a manner that foreshadowed Muslim treatment of the dhimmis—the People of the Book in Islamic lands. (Some features of this agreement were superseded by revelations Muhammad received later in his career, which made things more difficult for non-Muslims—with effects that are still being felt.)

The document begins by declaring that all Muslims, whether they are Meccan or Medinan, are a single united community—another principle that Muslims have affirmed throughout history, although it would not always be uniformly upheld once non-Arabs began to join the *umma*. Here the unity of all believers, and the sharp distinction between believers and unbelievers, is clearly delineated:

> A believer shall not take as an ally the freedman of another Muslim against him. The God-fearing believers shall be against the rebellious or him who seeks to spread injustice, or sin or enmity, or corruption between believers; the hand of every man shall be against him even if he be a son of one of them. A believer shall not slay a believer for the sake of an unbeliever, nor shall he aid an unbeliever against a believer. God's protection is one, the least of them may give protection to a stranger on their behalf. Believers are friends one to the other to the exclusion of outsiders.... The peace of the believers is indivisible. No separate peace shall be made when believers are fighting in the way of God. Conditions must be fair and equitable to all. In every foray a rider must take another behind him. The believers must avenge the blood of one another shed in the way of God. The God-fearing believers enjoy the best and most upright guidance. No polytheist shall take the property or person of Quraysh under his protection nor shall he intervene against a believer. Whosoever is convicted of killing a believer without good reason shall be subject to retaliation

unless the next of kin is satisfied (with blood-money), and the believers shall be against him as one man, and they are bound to take action against him.

The document also details the rights and responsibilities of outsiders, outlining in relatively generous terms the rights of the Banu Auf (Auf tribe) and other Jewish tribes, mandating mutual defense and declaring off-limits any cooperation with the Quraysh:

> To the Jew who follows us belong help and equality. He shall not be wronged nor shall his enemies be aided.... The Jews shall contribute to the cost of war so long as they are fighting alongside the believers. The Jews of the B. 'Auf are one community with the believers (the Jews have their religion and the Muslims have theirs), their freedmen and their persons except those who behave unjustly and sinfully, for they hurt but themselves and their families. The same applies to the Jews of the B. al-Najjar, B. al-Harith, B. Sa'ida, B. Jusham, B. al-Aus, B. Tha'laba, and the Jafna, a clan of the Tha'laba and the B. al-Shutayba.

"The Jews of the B. 'Auf are one community with the believers" is a remarkable statement, and one which Islamic apologists of today never tire of quoting. It would, however, soon be superseded in the life of the Muslims by statements of a vastly different kind. Furthermore, the mutual defense provision had one exception. The Jews agreed to fight alongside the Muslims "except in the case of a holy war."[3]

The conversion of Abdullah and tensions with the rabbis

Despite the concord suggested by this agreement (if it actually existed—neither Muhammad nor the Jewish leaders mention it in their subsequent interaction), Muhammad's relationship with the Jewish leaders of Medina was steadily worsening. They could not accept the idea that a prophet in the line of Abraham and Moses could have arisen from the Gentiles, and began, as Ibn Ishaq puts it, to "annoy the apostle with questions."[4]

But one of the rabbis of Medina, al-Husayn, who was also known as Abdullah bin Salam (some say Muhammad renamed him Abdullah after his conversion), was not hostile to the Muslims. Echoing the stories of Bahira the monk and others who recognized Muhammad by descriptions supposedly found in the Jewish and Christian Scriptures, Abdullah was deeply impressed: "When I heard about the apostle I knew by his description, name, and the time at which he appeared that he was the one we were waiting for, and I rejoiced greatly there at, though I kept silent about it until the apostle came to Medina."

When Abdullah heard that Muhammad was moving to Medina, he shouted, "Allahu akbar"—Allah is greater—and hurried to see him.[5] Admitted to Muhammad's presence, he asked him "about three things which nobody knows unless he be a Prophet. What is the first portent of the Hour? What is the first meal of the people of Paradise? And what makes a baby look like its father or mother?"

The Prophet coolly told him, "Just now Jibril (Gabriel) has informed me about that."

Abdullah was surprised. "Gabriel?"

"Yes," said Muhammad.

"He, among the angels is the enemy of the Jews," noted Abdullah, whereupon Muhammad recited a verse of the Qur'an: "Say: Whoever is an enemy to Gabriel—for he brings down the (revelation) to thy heart by Allah's will, a confirmation of what went before, and guidance and glad tidings for those who believe—Whoever is an enemy to Allah and His angels and messengers, to Gabriel and Michael, lo! Allah is an enemy to those who reject Faith" (Qur'an 2:97).

Then he proceeded to answer Abdullah's three questions:

> As for the first portent of the Hour, it will be a fire that will collect the people from the east to west. And as for the first meal

of the people of Paradise, it will be the caudite (i.e. extra) lobe
of the fish liver. And if a man's discharge preceded that of the
woman, then the child resembles the father, and if the
woman's discharge preceded that of the man, then the child
resembles the mother.

Hearing these answers, Abdullah immediately converted to Islam and exco-
riated his own people, exclaiming: "I testify that *La ilaha illallah* (none has
the right to be worshipped but Allah) and that you are the Messenger of
Allah, O Allah's Messenger; the Jews are liars, and if they should come to
know that I have embraced Islam, they would accuse me of being a liar."[6]

Abdullah recounted that he "became a Muslim, and when I returned
to my house I ordered my family to do the same."[7] He asked for Muhammad's help in laying a trap for the Jews: "The Jews are a nation of liars and
I wish you would take me into one of your houses and hide me from them,
then ask them about me so that they may tell you the position I hold
among them before they know that I have become a Muslim. For if they
know it beforehand they will utter slanderous lies against me." Muhammad
agreed, summoned the Jewish leaders with Abdullah present but hidden,
and asked them what they thought of Abdullah. They replied: "He is our
chief, and the son of our chief; our rabbi, and our learned man."

Muhammad asked them, "What would you think if 'Abdullah bin
Salam embraced Islam?"

The Jewish leaders answered, "May Allah protect him from this!"

The trap was sprung. Abdullah appeared and cried: "I testify that *La ilaha
illallah* (none has the right to be worshipped but Allah) and that Muhammad is the Messenger of Allah.[8] O Jews, fear God and accept what He has
sent you. For by God you know that he is the apostle of God. You will find
him described in your Torah and even named. I testify that he is the apostle
of God, I believe in him, I hold him to be true, and I acknowledge him."[9]

But the Jews now said: "Abdullah is the worst of us, and the son of the
worst of us."

Abdullah exclaimed, "O Allah's Messenger! This is what I was afraid of!"[10] He later recounted: "I reminded the apostle that I had said that they would do this, for they were a treacherous, lying, and evil people."[11]

Such tales would only reinforce for Muslims throughout history the idea that the Jewish (as well as Christian) Scriptures really did bear witness to Muhammad in clear terms. Another Muslim tradition holds that Muhammad went to a Jewish seminary, where he challenged the rabbis: "Bring forward the most learned among you before me." When that man came forward, he and Muhammad spoke in private. Finally Muhammad asked him, "Do you know that I am the Apostle of Allah?"

The rabbi answered, "By Allah! Yes, and the people know what I know. Verily your attributes and qualities are clearly mentioned in the Torah, but they are jealous of you."[12] It was only the sinful obstinacy of the Jews and Christians that prevented them from acknowledging this—indeed, that sin was so great that ultimately it led them to alter their Scriptures in order to remove all references to Muhammad. The idea of Jews and Christians as sinful renegades from the truth of Islam would become a cornerstone of Islamic thought regarding non-Muslims.

Muhammad composed for the Muslims a brief prayer, known as the *Fatiha* (Opening), that became the cornerstone of Muslim prayer (it is recited seventeen times a day by the Muslim who performs the five daily prayers) and the first sura of the Qur'an:

In the name of Allah, the Beneficent, the Merciful.
Praise be to Allah, Lord of the Worlds,
The Beneficent, the Merciful.
Master of the Day of Judgment,
Thee (alone) we worship; Thee (alone) we ask for help.
Show us the straight path,
The path of those whom Thou hast favoured;
Not the (path) of those who earn Thine anger nor of those who go astray. (Qur'an 1:1-7)

Even this, which has a status among Muslims analogous to the centrality of the Lord's Prayer for Christians, has a polemical edge. Traditionally Muslim divines have identified those who have earned Allah's anger with the Jews and those who have gone astray with the Christians. The Qur'anic commentator Ibn Kathir (Isma'il bin 'Amr bin Kathir al Dimashqi) (1301–1372) represents a broad mainstream in Islamic tradition. The Muslim scholar Ahmad von Denffer calls his Qur'an commentary (*tafsir*) one of the "better-known" and "more valuable books of *tafsir*," and notes that it is "of greatest importance to Muslims."[13] In it, Ibn Kathir explains that "these two paths are the paths of the Christians and Jews, a fact that the believer should be aware of so that he avoids them. The path of the believers is the knowledge of truth and abiding by it. In comparison, Jews abandoned practicing the religion, while the Christians lost the true knowledge. This is why 'anger' descended upon the Jews, while being described as 'led astray' is more appropriate of the Christians."[14]

The Hypocrites

At this point, according to Ibn Ishaq, some of the Hypocrites (*munafiqin*) of Medina began to make common cause with the Jews who opposed Muhammad. The Hypocrites were members of the tribes of Medina who had become Muslim; they converted out of fear and convenience and began, according to the early Muslim sources, to act as a fifth column within the Muslim community. The Qur'an is full of furious invective against them and their plots against Muhammad. Muhammad also received revelations attacking the Hypocrites for their dishonesty, warning them of the dreadful punishment that awaited them, and redolent with frustration and anger at their duplicity. (Qur'an 2:8-15)

An entire sura of the Qur'an is devoted to the insincerity and deceptiveness of the Hypocrites, in which Allah vows that he will not forgive them:

> That is because they believed, then they rejected Faith: So a
> seal was set on their hearts: therefore they understand not.

When thou lookest at them, their exteriors please thee; and when they speak, thou listenest to their words. They are as (worthless as hollow) pieces of timber propped up, (unable to stand on their own). (Qur'an 63:1-8)

At one point Muhammad spotted a group of these Hypocrites talking together in the mosque and ordered they be expelled. This was accomplished, says Ibn Ishaq, "with some violence."

> 'Umara b. Hazm went for Zayd b. 'Amr who had a long beard and seized him by it and dragged him violently out of the mosque. Then clenching his fists he punched him in the chest and knocked him down, Zayd crying the meanwhile, "You have torn my skin off!" "God get rid of you, you hypocrite," he answered, "God has a worse punishment than that in store for you, so don't come near the apostle's mosque again!"[15]

The Nakhla raid

With his new, stronger base of support in Medina, Muhammad felt more confident in confronting the Quraysh. The Muslims began raiding Quraysh caravans, with Muhammad himself leading many of these raids. Muhammad's first raid was at a site known as Al-Abwa or Waddan, where the Prophet of Islam hoped to meet and overpower a Quraysh caravan. They did not find the Quraysh there, but during the expedition Muhammad issued a fateful edict when one of the Muslims asked him a question:

> The Prophet passed by me at a place called Al-Abwa' or Waddan, and was asked whether it was permissible to attack *Al-Mushrikun* [unbelieving] warriors at night with the probability of exposing their women and children to danger. The Prophet replied, "They (i.e. women and children) are from them (i.e. *Al-Mushrikun*)."[16]

From then on, innocent non-Muslim women and children could legiti-
mately suffer the fate of male unbelievers.

These raids were not solely designed to exact revenge from the people who had rejected the Prophet who had arisen among them. They
served a key economic purpose, keeping the Muslim movement solvent.
They also became the occasion for the formation of some key elements
of Islamic theology—as in one notorious incident when a band of Muslims raided a Quraysh caravan at Nakhla, a settlement not far from
Mecca. Muhammad sent one of his most trusted lieutenants, Abdullah
bin Jahsh, along with eight of the emigrants—long-standing Muslims
who had left Mecca for Medina with Muhammad—on a journey. He
gave Abdullah a letter with the order that he not open it until he had traveled for two days.

Abdullah complied, reading the letter after two days of journeying.
"When you have read this letter of mine proceed until you reach Nakhla
between Mecca and Al-Ta'if. Lie in wait there for Quraysh and find out for
us what they are doing." Abdullah seemed to suspect that this mission
would be perilous; he told the others: "The apostle has commanded me to
go to Nakhla to lie in wait there for Quraysh so as to bring us news of them.
He has forbidden me to put pressure on any of you, so if anyone wishes for
martyrdom let him go forward, and he who does not, let him go back; as
for me I am going on as the Prophet has ordered." All went with him.
Abdullah used the word "martyrdom" just as modern-day jihad terrorists
do: referring to one who (in the words of a revelation that came to Muhammad much later) "slays and is slain" for Allah (Qur'an 9:111), rather than
in the Christian sense of suffering unto death at the hands of the unjust for
the sake of the faith.

Abdullah and his band came upon a caravan of Quraysh carrying
leather and raisins. They considered the matter: "If you leave them alone
tonight they will get into the sacred area and will be safe from you; and if
you kill them, you will kill them in the sacred month"—for it was the last
day of the sacred month of Rajab, when fighting was forbidden. They
decided, according to Ibn Ishaq, to "kill as many as they could of them and

take what they had." On the way home to Medina Abdullah set aside a fifth of the booty for Muhammad. When they returned to the Muslim camp, Muhammad refused to share in the loot or to have anything to do with them, saying only: "I did not order you to fight in the sacred month." He was put in a politically uncomfortable position as well, for the Quraysh began to say: "Muhammad and his companions have violated the sacred month, shed blood therein, taken booty, and captured men."[17]

But then another helpful revelation came from Allah, explaining that the Quraysh's opposition to Muhammad was more offensive in his eyes than the Muslims' violation of the sacred month: the raid was therefore justified. "They question thee, O Muhammad, with regard to warfare in the sacred month. Say: warfare therein is a great transgression, but to turn men from the way of Allah, and to disbelieve in Him and in the Inviolable Place of Worship, and to expel His people thence, is a greater transgression with Allah; for persecution is worse than killing" (Qur'an 2:214). Whatever sin the Nakhla raiders had committed in violating the sacred month was nothing compared to the Quraysh's sins. Ibn Ishaq explained this verse: "they have kept you back from the way of God with their unbelief in Him, and from the sacred mosque, and have driven you from it when you were with its people. This is a more serious matter with God than the killing of those whom you have slain."[18] Once he received this revelation, Muhammad took Abdullah's booty and prisoners. Abdullah was considerably relieved, and asked, "Can we hope that it will count as a raid for which we shall be given the reward of combatants?" Here again Allah answered in a revelation: "Lo! those who believe, and those who emigrate (to escape the persecution) and strive in the way of Allah, these have hope of Allah's mercy. Allah is Forgiving, Merciful" (Qur'an 2:218). The redemption of Abdullah and his band of emigrants was complete.

This was a momentous incident, for it would set a pattern: good became identified with anything that redounded to the benefit of Muslims, and evil with anything that harmed them, without reference to any larger moral standard. Moral absolutes were swept aside in favor of the overarching principle of expediency.

The break with the Jews and the
change of qibla (direction for prayer)

Muhammad continued to appeal to the Jews to accept his prophetic status.
He wrote a letter to the Jews of Khaybar, an oasis around a hundred miles
north of Medina, explaining who he was and why they should accept his
claims. The letter began by quoting the Qur'an and asserting that the Jews
would find the same material in their own Scriptures. (Qur'an 48:29) Then
Muhammad challenged them directly to search their books for signs of his
coming:

> I adjure you by God, and by what He has sent down to you, by
> the manna and quails He gave as food to your tribes before you,
> and by His drying up the sea for your fathers when He deliv-
> ered them from Pharaoh and his works, that you tell me: Do
> you find in what He has sent down to you that you should
> believe in Muhammad?[19]

In this Muhammad quoted part of what is today the most famous verse in
all the Qur'an, 2:256, which also contains the maxim, "There is no com-
pulsion in religion." The subsequent fortunes of the Jews of Arabia, however, indicate that this verse was not considered even in Muhammad's day
to be an open-ended invitation to religious pluralism and a call to Muslims
to coexist peacefully as equals with non-Muslims.

Some hints of this would come in the immediate aftermath of his letter
to the Jews of Khaybar. Some of the Jews answered Muhammad's challenge the only way they could. One explained that Muhammad "has not
brought us anything we recognize and he is not the one we spoke of to
you"—that is, he is not the Messiah of whom the Jews had spoken to the
Arabs before Muhammad began his prophetic career. Muhammad in
response received a revelation: "And when there cometh unto them a scripture from Allah, confirming that in their possession—though before that
they were asking for a signal triumph over those who disbelieved—and
when there cometh unto them that which they know (to be the truth) they

disbelieve therein. The curse of Allah is on disbelievers" (Qur'an 2:89). Another Jewish leader noted that "No covenant was ever made with us about Muhammad." Allah again responded through his Prophet: "Is it ever so that when they make a covenant a party of them set it aside? The truth is, most of them believe not" (Qur'an 2:100).

Around the time of the Nakhla raid Muhammad began to give up on the idea that the Jews would ever accept him as a prophet. Before this, at time of the Night Journey, he was already obliquely laying claim to a stronger connection to Abraham than they had: "I resemble Prophet Ibrahim (Abraham) more than any of his offspring does."[20]

At this point he received a revelation from Allah instructing the Muslims to face Mecca instead of Jerusalem for prayers and declaring that the prayers in the direction of Jerusalem were only a test for the believers.

Then Allah revealed the new qibla, telling Muhammad that it would bring him joy: "We see the turning of thy face (for guidance) to the heavens: now shall We turn thee to a Qibla that shall please thee. Turn then thy face in the direction of the sacred mosque [in Mecca]: Wherever ye are, turn your faces in that direction." The revelation even asserted that the Jews and Christians ("the People of the Book") knew that the Muslims' new direction for prayer was the correct one: "The People of the Book know well that that is the truth from their Lord. Nor is Allah unmindful of what they do" (Qur'an 2:143-144). Dissenters were warned: "So from whencesoever thou startest forth, turn thy face in the direction of the sacred Mosque...." (Qur'an 2:150).

News traveled quickly among the Muslims. "While some people were at Quba (offering) morning prayer, a man came to them and said, 'Last night Qur'anic Verses have been revealed whereby the Prophet has been ordered to face the Ka'bah [at Mecca], so you, too, should face it.' So they, keeping their postures, turned towards the Ka'bah. Formerly the people were facing Sham (Jerusalem)."[21]

Some traditions report that some of the rabbis came to Muhammad at this point and told him that they would declare him a prophet and accept Islam if he turned his people's prayers back to Jerusalem.[22] The Prophet of

Islam refused, receiving another revelation: "The fools among the people will say: 'What hath turned them from the Qibla to which they were used?' Say: To Allah belong both east and West: He guideth whom He will to a Way that is straight" (2:142).

Departing from his earlier tendency to appeal to the Jews as the authorities on what Allah had revealed, Muhammad began to criticize them for concealing parts of that revelation. On one occasion, the Prophet of Islam challenged them over the appropriate punishment for a couple that had been accused of adultery: "What do you find in the Torah," Muhammad asked them, "about the legal punishment of Ar-Rajm (stoning)?"

The Jews answered, "We announce their crime and lash them."

At this point, however, Abdullah bin Salam, the former rabbi and convert to Islam, rushed to Muhammad's aid. "You are telling a lie," Abdullah said. "Torah contains the order of Rajm." One of the Jews then began to read from the Torah, but he skipped the verse mandating stoning for adultery, covering it with his hand.[23] "Lift your hand!" Abdullah cried, and, the verse duly read, Muhammad exclaimed, "Woe to you Jews! What has induced you to abandon the judgment of God which you hold in your hands?" And he asserted: "I am the first to revive the order of God and His Book and to practice it."[24]

Muhammad ordered the couple to be stoned to death; another Muslim remembered, "I saw the man leaning over the woman to shelter her from the stones."[25]

Not only does this episode reveal the sharp distinction between Jewish and Islamic concepts of compassion, but the contrast between Muhammad's teaching and that of Jesus ("let he who is without sin cast the first stone") could not be more marked—and that difference has shaped Muslim and Christian history, culture, and ideas of mercy and justice.

CHAPTER SEVEN

"War is deceit"

The Battle of Badr

AS THE MUSLIMS' RELATIONS WITH THE JEWS STEADILY deteriorated, they reached their final breaking point with the Quraysh. The Muslim raids on Quraysh caravans precipitated the Muslims' first major battle. Muhammad heard that a large Quraysh caravan, laden with money and goods, was coming from Syria. "This is the caravan of the Quraysh possessing wealth," he told his followers. "It is likely that Allah may give it to you as booty."[1] Ibn Ishaq reports that "the people answered his summons, some eagerly, others reluctantly because they had not thought that the apostle would go to war."

Muhammad received a revelation from Allah berating those Muslims who were reluctant to wage war for the Prophet of Islam: "Those who believe say, 'Why is not a sura sent down (for us)?' But when a sura of basic or categorical meaning is revealed, and fighting is mentioned therein, thou wilt see those in whose hearts is a disease looking at thee with a look of one in swoon at the approach of death" (Qur'an 47:20).

Allah told Muhammad's followers to fight fiercely and behead their enemies: "Therefore, when ye meet the Unbelievers (in fight), smite at their necks. At length, when ye have thoroughly subdued them, bind a bond firmly (on them): thereafter (is the time for) either generosity or ransom, until the war lays down its burdens." He reminded them that this was his will, and a test he was giving them: "Thus (are ye commanded): but if it had been Allah's Will, He could certainly have exacted retribution from them (Himself); but (He lets you fight) in order to test you, some with others. But those who are slain in the Way of Allah, He will never let their deeds be lost" (Qur'an 47:4).

Muhammad set out toward Mecca to lead the raid. He knew that the Quraysh would be defending their caravan with an army this time, but he was confident: "Forward in good heart," he told his men, "for God has promised me one of the two parties"—that is, either the caravan or the army. "And by God, it is as though I now see the enemy lying prostrate."[2] When he saw the Quraysh marching toward the Muslims, he prayed: "O God, here come the Quraysh in their vanity and pride, contending with Thee and calling Thy apostle a liar. O God, grant the help which Thou didst promise me. Destroy them this morning!"[3] One of the Quraysh leaders, Abu Jahl (which means "Father of Ignorance," a name given him by Muslim chroniclers; his real name was 'Amr ibn Hisham), also felt as if a defining moment was at hand. Oiling a coat of mail before the battle, he declared: "No, by God, we will not turn back until God decide between us and Muhammad."[4]

And this time the Quraysh were much more prepared to face the Muslims than they had been at Nakhla. They came out to meet Muhammad's three hundred men with a force nearly a thousand strong.[5] Muhammad seems not to have expected these numbers and cried out to Allah in anxiety: "O God, if this band perish today Thou wilt be worshipped no more." But after a short rest Muhammad felt better, telling his key follower Abu Bakr, who was to succeed him as the leader of the Muslims: "Be of good cheer, O Abu Bakr. God's help is come to you. Here is Gabriel holding the rein of a horse and leading it. The dust is upon his front teeth."[6]

Muhammad strode among his troops and issued a momentous promise—one that has given heart to Muslim warriors throughout the ages: "By God in whose hand is the soul of Muhammad, no man will be slain this day fighting against them with steadfast courage advancing not retreating but God will cause him to enter Paradise." One of the assembled Muslim warriors, 'Umayr bin al-Humam, exclaimed: "Fine, Fine! Is there nothing between me and my entering Paradise save to be killed by these men?" He flung away some dates that he had been eating, rushed into the thick of the battle, and fought until he was killed. In a similar vein, another Muslim warrior, 'Auf bin Harith, asked Muhammad, "O apostle of God, what makes the Lord laugh with joy at His servant?" Muhammad answered: "When he plunges into the midst of the enemy without mail." 'Auf threw off his coat of mail and plunged into the thick of the battle, fighting tenaciously until he was killed.[7]

The Prophet of Islam picked up a few pebbles and threw them in the direction of the Quraysh, saying, "Foul be those faces!" Then he ordered the Muslims to charge.[8] Despite their superior numbers, the Quraysh were routed. Some Muslim traditions say that Muhammad himself participated in the fighting; others that it was more likely that he exhorted his followers from the sidelines. In any event, it was an occasion for him to avenge years of frustration, resentment, and hatred toward his people who had rejected him. One of his followers later recalled a curse Muhammad had pronounced on the leaders of the Quraysh: "The Prophet said, 'O Allah! Destroy the chiefs of Quraish, O Allah! Destroy Abu Jahl bin Hisham, 'Utba bin Rabi'a, Shaiba bin Rabi'a, 'Uqba bin Abi Mu'ait, 'Umaiya bin Khalaf (or Ubai bin Kalaf).'"[9]

All these men were captured or killed during the battle of Badr. One Quraysh leader named in this curse, 'Uqba, pleaded for his life: "But who will look after my children, O Muhammad?"

In the confrontation, 'Uqba had thrown camel dung, blood, and intestines on the Prophet of Islam, to the great merriment of the Quraysh chieftans, while Muhammad prostrated himself in prayer.[10] Muhammad had pronounced a curse on them, and now it was being fulfilled. Who would care for 'Uqba's children? "Hell," Muhammad declared, and ordered 'Uqba killed.[11]

Abu Jahl of the Quraysh was beheaded. The Muslim who severed his head proudly carried the trophy to Muhammad: "I cut off his head and brought it to the apostle saying, 'This is the head of the enemy of God, Abu Jahl.'"

Muhammad was delighted. "By God than Whom there is no other, is it?" he exclaimed, and gave thanks to Allah for the death of his enemy.[12]

According to another account, two young Muslims murdered Abu Jahl as he was "walking amongst the people." One of the murderers explains why: "I have been informed that he abuses Allah's Messenger. By Him in Whose Hands my soul is, if I should see him, then my body will not leave his body till either of us meet his fate." After they have done the deed, they go to see the Prophet of Islam, who asks, "Which of you has killed him?"

Both youths answered, "I have killed him."

Muhammad thought of a way to resolve the dispute, asking them: "Have you cleaned your swords?" They answered that they had not, so Muhammad inspected their weapons and announced: "No doubt, you both have killed him and the spoils of the deceased will be given to Mu'adh bin 'Amr bin Al-Jamuh,'" who was one of the murderers.[13]

The bodies of all those named in the curse were thrown into a pit. As an eyewitness recalled: "Later on I saw all of them killed during the battle of Badr and their bodies were thrown into a well except the body of Umaiya or Ubai, because he was a fat man, and when he was pulled, the parts of his body got separated before he was thrown into the well."[14] Then Muhammad taunted them as "people of the pit" and posed a theological question: "Have you found what God promised you is true? I have found that what my Lord promised me is true." When asked why he was speaking to dead bodies, he replied: "You cannot hear what I say better than they, but they cannot answer me."[15]

Allah fights for the Muslims

The victory at Badr was the turning point for the Muslims. It became the stuff of legend, a cornerstone of the new religion. Muhammad even received a revelation announcing that armies of angels joined with the Muslims to smite the Quraysh—and that similar help would come in the future to Muslims who remained faithful to Allah: "Allah had helped you at Badr, when ye were a contemptible little force; then fear Allah; thus may ye show your gratitude. Remember thou saidst to the Faithful: 'Is it not enough for you that Allah should help you with three thousand angels specially sent down? Yea, if ye remain firm, and act aright, even if the enemy should rush here on you in hot haste, your Lord would help you with five thousand angels making a terrific onslaught" (Qur'an 3:123-125). Allah told Muhammad: "Remember ye implored the assistance of your Lord, and He answered you: 'I will assist you with a thousand of the angels, ranks on ranks.'... Remember thy Lord inspired the angels (with the message): 'I am with you: give firmness to the Believers: I will instill terror into the hearts of the Unbelievers: smite ye above their necks and smite all their fin-ger-tips off them.' This because they contended against Allah and His Mes-senger: If any contend against Allah and His Messenger, Allah is strict in punishment" (Qur'an 8:9, 12-13). The latter verse, with its exhortation to the angels to behead the enemies of Allah and Muhammad, became one of the chief justifications for the Islamic practice—then and now—of beheading hostages and war captives.

Ibn Ishaq says that Muhammad received another revelation consigning to hell some ex-Muslims who had fought alongside the Quraysh: "When angels take the souls of those who die in sin against their souls, they say: 'In what (plight) were ye?' They reply: 'Weak and oppressed were we in the earth.' Then say: 'Was not the earth of Allah spacious enough for you to move yourselves away (from evil)?' Such men will find their abode in Hell. What an evil refuge!" (Qur'an 4:99).

Yet another revelation from Allah emphasized that it was piety, not military might, that brought victory at Badr: "There has already been for you a sign in the two armies that met in combat: one was fighting in the cause of Allah, the other resisting Allah; these saw with their own eyes twice their number. But Allah doth support with His aid whom He pleaseth. In this is a warning for such as have eyes to see" (Qur'an 3:13). Allah warned the Quraysh not to attempt another attack, telling them they would again be defeated no matter how much more numerous they were than the Muslims. (8:19)

Still another Qur'anic passage asserts that the Muslims were merely passive instruments at Badr. Even the pebbles Muhammad threw toward the Quraysh were not thrown by him, but by Allah: "It is not ye who slew them; it was Allah. When thou threwest (a handful of dust), it was not thy act, but Allah's: in order that He might test the Believers by a gracious trial from Himself: for Allah is He Who heareth and knoweth (all things)" (8:17). And Allah would grant such victories to pious Muslims even though they faced odds even more prohibitive than those they had overcome at Badr: "O Prophet! Rouse the Believers to the fight. If there are twenty amongst you, patient and persevering, they will vanquish two hundred: if a hundred, they will vanquish a thousand of the unbelievers: for these are a people without understanding" (Qur'an 8:65).

These became recurring themes of jihad literature throughout the centuries, up to the present day: piety will bring military victory, Allah will send angels to fight with the believing Muslims, and they will conquer even against overwhelming odds. The victory at Badr continues to resound through history. At the beheading of American hostage Nicholas Berg in May 2004, for example, Iraqi jihad leader Abu Musab al-Zarqawi invoked the great battle: "Is it not time for you [Muslims] to take the path of jihad and carry the sword of the Prophet of prophets?... The Prophet, the most merciful, ordered [his army] to strike the necks of some prisoners in [the battle of] Badr and to kill them.....And he set a good example for us."[16]

The problem of booty

Allah rewarded those to whom he had granted victory. There was great booty for the victors—so much, in fact, that it became a bone of contention. So divisive did this threaten to become that Allah himself spoke about it in a chapter of the Qur'an devoted entirely to reflections on the battle of Badr: the eighth chapter, entitled Al-Anfal, "the Spoils of War" or "Booty." Allah warns the Muslims not to consider booty won at Badr to belong to anyone but Muhammad: "They ask thee concerning things taken as spoils of war. Say: '(Such) spoils are at the disposal of Allah and the Messenger: so fear Allah, and keep straight the relations between yourselves. Obey Allah and His Messenger, if ye do believe" (8:1). Ultimately, Muhammad distributed the booty among the Muslims equally, keeping a fifth for himself. (8:41). This was in accord with a special privilege that Allah had granted to Muhammad. Muhammad explained: "I have been given five (things) which were not given to any amongst the Prophets before me." These included the fact that "Allah made me victorious by awe (by His frightening my enemies)" and "the booty has been made *Halal* (lawful) to me (and was not made so to anyone else)."[17]

Muhammad exercised this privilege at Badr when two of his most important companions, Abu Bakr and Umar, disagreed over what they should do with the prisoners:

> The Muslims that day (i. e. the day of the Battle of Badr) killed seventy persons and captured seventy. The Messenger of Allah (may peace be upon him) said to Abu Bakr and 'Umar (Allah be pleased with them): What is your opinion about these captives? Abu Bakr said: They are our kith and kin. I think you should release them after getting from them a ransom. This

will be a source of strength to us against the infidels. It is quite possible that Allah may guide them to Islam.

The ransom, of course, would increase the booty for the Muslims. But Umar disagreed:

> Then the Messenger of Allah (may peace be upon him) said: What is your opinion, Ibn Khattab [that is, Umar]? He said: Messenger of Allah. I do not hold the same opinion as Abu Bakr. I am of the opinion that you should hand them over to us so that we may cut off their heads. Hand over 'Aqil to 'Ali that he may cut off his head, and hand over such and such relative to me that I may cut off his head. They are leaders of the disbelievers and veterans among them.

Muhammad sided with Abu Bakr, but the next day Umar was appalled to come upon Muhammad and Abu Bakr weeping. "Messenger of Allah," he cried, "why are you and your Companion shedding tears?"

Muhammad answered: "I weep for what has happened to your companions for taking ransom (from the prisoners). I was shown the torture to which they were subjected. It was brought to me as close as this tree." And he pointed to a nearby tree. The Prophet of Islam was referring to the tortures of hellfire, for Allah sided with Umar, revealing to Muhammad that "it is not for any prophet to have captives until he hath made slaughter in the land." He scolded Muhammad for desiring booty instead of doing as Allah wished by making slaughter: "Ye desire the lure of this world and Allah desireth (for you) the Hereafter, and Allah is Mighty, Wise." However, the Companions would be spared the tortures that would otherwise have awaited them because of Allah's previous grant to Muhammad of permission to take booty: "Had it not been for an ordinance of Allah which had gone before, an awful doom had come upon you on account of what ye took. Now enjoy what ye have won, as lawful and good, and keep your duty to Allah. Lo! Allah is Forgiving, Merciful" (8:67-69).[18] Since then,

innumerable Muslims have taken to heart the concept that killing the enemies of Allah helps to, according to Ibn Isaq, "manifest the religion which
He wishes to manifest."[19]

The Muslims had grown from a tiny, despised community into a force
with which the pagan Arabs had to reckon. They began to strike terror in
the hearts of their enemies: "Against them make ready your strength to the
utmost of your power, including steeds of war, to strike terror into (the
hearts of) the enemies, of Allah and your enemies, and others besides,
whom ye may not know, but whom Allah doth know. Whatever ye shall
spend in the cause of Allah, shall be repaid unto you, and ye shall not be
treated unjustly" (Qur'an 8:60).

The battle of Badr was the first practical example of what came to be
known as the Islamic doctrine of jihad.

The Qaynuqa Jews

Flushed with victory, Muhammad stepped up his raiding operations. During one of them, against the pagan Ghatafan tribe, he was surprised by an
enemy warrior while resting. The warrior asked him: "Who will defend you
from me today?"

The Prophet of Islam replied coolly, "Allah"—whereupon the warrior
dropped his sword. Muhammad seized it quickly and asked, "Who will
defend you from me?"

"None," said the warrior, and he recited the Shahada, the Islamic pro-
fession of faith ("there is no god but Allah and Muhammad is his
prophet"), and became a Muslim.[20]

Around this time Muhammad's attitude hardened toward the Jewish
tribes of the region. His prophetic calls to them began to emphasize earthly
chastisement more than punishment in the next world—earthly chastisement at the hands of the Muslims. Allah gave him a revelation allowing
him to break treaties he had made with groups that he feared would betray
him: "If thou fearest treachery from any group, throw back (their covenant)
to them, (so as to be) on equal terms: for Allah loveth not the treacherous"

(Qur'an 8:58). After he received this revelation, Muhammad said, "I fear the Banu Qaynuqa"—a Jewish tribe with whom he had a truce.[21] He resolved to move against them.

Striding into the center of the marketplace of the Qaynuqa, the Prophet of Islam announced to the crowds: "O Jews, beware lest God bring upon you the vengeance that He brought upon Quraysh and become Muslims. You know that I am a prophet who has been sent—you will find that in your scriptures and God's covenant with you." He buttressed this threat with a revelation from Allah: "Say to those who reject Faith: 'Soon will ye be vanquished and gathered together to Hell, an evil bed indeed (to lie on)! There has already been for you a Sign in the two armies that met (in combat): one was fighting in the cause of Allah, the other resisting Allah; these saw with their own eyes twice their number. But Allah doth support with His aid whom He pleaseth. In this is a warning for such as have eyes to see" (Qur'an 3:10). The two armies that met, of course, were the Muslims and the Quraysh at Badr.

The Qaynuqa Jews replied with disdain, infuriating the Prophet of Islam still more by denigrating him for his hope that the Jews would accept him as a prophet: "O Muhammad, you seem to think that we are your people. Do not deceive yourself because you encountered a people with no knowledge of war and got the better of them; for by God if we fight you, you will find that we are real men!"[22]

Muhammad's forces laid siege to the Qaynuqa until they offered him unconditional surrender. But the Qaynuqa had made alliances among the Muslims, and now some of them came forward to plead their case before the Prophet of Islam. Muhammad wanted to have all the men of the tribe put to death.[23] However, a Muslim—one of the Hypocrites—named Abdullah bin Ubayy told Muhammad: "O Muhammad, deal kindly with my clients." Muhammad ignored him, so Abdullah repeated the request, whereupon the Prophet of Islam turned his face away from Abdullah. Abdullah bin Ubayy then impetuously caught Muhammad by the collar of his robe, whereupon, according to Ibn Ishaq, "the apostle was so angry that his face became almost black." Muhammad said to Abdullah, "Confound you, let me go."

But Abdullah replied, "No, by God, I will not let you go until you deal kindly with my clients. Four hundred men without mail and three hundred mailed protected me from all mine enemies; would you cut them down in one morning? By God, I am a man who fears that circumstances may change." Muhammad then granted him his request, agreeing to spare the Qaynuqa as long as they turned over their property as booty to the Muslims and left Medina, which they did forthwith.

Still, Muhammad was unhappy with the alliance Abdullah had made with the Jewish tribe. It was at this point that he received a key revelation about the relationships that should prevail between Muslims and non-Muslims: "O ye who believe! Take not the Jews and the Christians for your friends and protectors: They are but friends and protectors to each other. And he amongst you that turns to them (for friendship) is of them. Verily Allah guideth not a people unjust" (Qur'an 5:51). And Allah scolded in harsh terms those who, like Abdullah bin Ubayy, feared a loss of business prospects because of the misfortune of the Qaynuqa. (5:52).[24]

Anger toward Jews and Christians

Clearly Abdullah bin Ubayy's pleading for the lives of this Jewish tribe did not sit well with Muhammad, and he grew angrier toward the Jews. A revelation pronounced them under Allah's curse for changing the content of his earlier revelations, and declared that most of them could not be trusted: "But because of their breach of their covenant, We cursed them, and made their hearts grow hard; they change the words from their (right) places and forget a good part of the message that was sent them, nor wilt thou cease to find them—barring a few—ever bent on (new) deceits." Still, Allah counseled mercy: "But forgive them, and overlook (their misdeeds): for Allah loveth those who are kind" (Qur'an 5:13). Forgive them, but give up any hope of their conversion to Islam: "Have ye any hope that they will be true to you when a party of them used to listen to the word of Allah, then used to change it, after they had understood it, knowingly?" (Qur'an 2:75).

A delegation of Christians came from Najran to discuss theology with Muhammad, and the Prophet of Islam was no less impatient with them. He was particularly incensed by their avowal of Jesus as the Son of God, for—as he often repeated—"It befitteth not (the Majesty of) Allah that He should take unto Himself a son" (Qur'an 19:35). The Prophet of Islam took it upon himself again to correct the errors of Christian theology: "They indeed have disbelieved who say: Lo! Allah is the Messiah, son of Mary. Say: Who then can do aught against Allah, if He had willed to destroy the Messiah son of Mary, and his mother and everyone on earth? Allah's is the Sovereignty of the heavens and the earth and all that is between them. He createth what He will. And Allah is able to do all things" (5:17). Jesus was not divine, and was not crucified—and the Prophet of Islam rebuked the Jews for boasting that they had indeed crucified him: "And because of their saying: We slew the Messiah, Jesus son of Mary, Allah's messenger—they slew him not nor crucified him, but it appeared so unto them. And lo! Those who disagree concerning it are in doubt thereof; they have no knowledge thereof save pursuit of a conjecture; they slew him not for certain" (Qur'an 4:157).

Demonstrating only a dim grasp of the Christian doctrine of the Trinity, Muhammad announced in another revelation that Jesus himself would deny this doctrine when questioned by Allah: "And when Allah saith: 'O Jesus, son of Mary! Didst thou say unto mankind: "Take me and my mother for two gods beside Allah"?' He saith: 'Be glorified! It was not mine to utter that to which I had no right. If I used to say it, then Thou knewest it. Thou knowest what is in my mind, and I know not what is in Thy Mind. Lo! Thou, only Thou, art the Knower of Things Hidden'" (Qur'an 5:116).

How then did the Christians get these ideas? Because they strayed from what Jesus had actually taught: "And with those who say: 'Lo! We are Christians,' We made a covenant, but they forgot a part of that whereof they were admonished. Therefore We have stirred up enmity and hatred among them till the Day of Resurrection, when Allah will inform them of their handiwork" (5:14).

Muhammad called both Jews and Christians to Islam, presenting it as the correction of the Judaism and Christianity of his day, and the restoration of the original messages of Moses and Jesus: "O People of the Scripture! Now hath Our messenger come unto you, expounding unto you much of that which ye used to hide in the Scripture, and forgiving much. Now hath come unto you light from Allah and plain Scripture...." (5:15-16).

Assassination and deceit

After the Battle of Badr and the attack against the Qaynuqa Jews, the Prophet of Islam directed his anger at the Jewish poet Ka'b bin Al-Ashraf, who, according to Ibn Ishaq, "composed amatory verses of an insulting nature about the Muslim women."[25] Incensed, Muhammad asked his followers: "Who is willing to kill Ka'b bin Al-Ashraf who has hurt Allah and His Apostle?"[26]

He found a volunteer in a young Muslim named Muhammad bin Maslama: "Messenger of Allah, do you wish that I should kill him?"

The Prophet of Islam answered in the affirmative, and Muhammad bin Maslama made a request: "Then allow me to say a (false) thing (i.e. to deceive Ka'b)."

The Prophet of Islam again took the path of expediency over moral absolutes: "You may say it."

Then Muhammad bin Maslama went to Ka'b and began to complain about his master. "That man [i.e. Muhammad] demands *Sadaqa* [that is, *zakat*, alms] from us, and he has troubled us, and I have come to borrow something from you."

Ka'b was not surprised, exclaiming, "By Allah, you will get tired of him!"[27]

Muhammad bin Maslama played his role to the hilt. "The coming of this man [that is, the Prophet] is a great trial to us. It has provoked the hostility of the Arabs, and they are all in league against us. The roads have become impassable so that our families are in want and privation, and we and our families are in great distress."[28] Muhammad bin Maslama then offered Ka'b a deal, trying to enlist the poet's help in aiding him to break from Islam and its Prophet: "Now as we have followed him, we do not want to leave him unless and until we see how his end is going to be. Now we want you to lend us a camel load or two of food." It would not be the last time in history that a Muslim professed to be disenchanted with Muhammad and his religion, and interested in striking a deal with non-Muslims. And it would not be the first time that those non-Muslims would be deceived, even at the cost of their lives.

Ka'b agreed to Muhammad bin Maslama's plan, but with a caveat: "Yes, (I will lend you), but you should mortgage something to me.... Mortgage your women to me."

Muhammad bin Maslama was incredulous: "How can we mortgage our women to you and you are the most handsome of the Arabs?" Finally they struck a deal on other terms, and Muhammad bin Maslama promised to return that night. He did, along with his foster brother Abu Na'ila and some others. Having gained Ka'b's trust, Muhammad bin Maslama and the men with him were admitted into Ka'b's presence. To get close enough to Ka'b to be able to kill him, Muhammad bin Maslama professed to admire Ka'b's perfume: "I have never smelt a better scent than this.... Will you allow me to smell your head?" Ka'b agreed; Muhammad bin Maslama's companions smelled it also. Muhammad bin Maslama thereupon caught Ka'b in a strong grip, and commanded his companions: "Get at him!" They killed Ka'b, and then hurried to inform the Prophet, carrying Ka'b's head with them.[29] When Muhammad heard the news, he cried out, "Allahu akbar!" and praised Allah for the death of his enemy.[30]

The outraged Jews said to Muhammad, "Our chief has been killed treacherously." Muhammad, according to Ibn Sa'd, "reminded them of his misdeeds and how he had been instigating them and exciting them to fight with them (Muslims) and how he had been harming them."[31] The murder, in other words, came after intense provocation—a line of defense that jihadists to this day use to justify their actions.

After the murder of K'ab, Muhammad issued a blanket command: "Kill any Jew that falls into your power."[32] This was not a military order: the first victim was a Jewish merchant, Ibn Sunayna, who had "social and business relations" with the Muslims. The murderer, Muhayissa, was rebuked for the deed by his brother Huwayissa, who was not yet a Muslim. Muhayissa was unrepentant. He told his brother: "Had the one who ordered me to kill him ordered me to kill you I would have cut your head off."

Huwayissa was impressed: "By God, a religion which can bring you to this is marvelous!" He became a Muslim.[33] The world still sees such marvels even today: Mohammed Robert Heft, a Canadian convert to Islam who was personally acquainted with several of the seventeen jihad terror plotters arrested in June 2006, explained that he personally had gone through a bout of extremism, during which time he would have killed his parents if they had interfered with his commitment to Islam.[34] Muhayissa and Huwayissa would have understood.

On another occasion Muhammad allowed one of his followers to use deception again in order to kill another of his enemies, Sufyan ibn Khalid al-Hudhali, whom the Prophet of Islam likened to the devil himself: "When you see him," he told the assassin, "you will be frightened and bewildered and you will recall Satan." When the mission was accomplished and Sufyan was dead, Muhammad praised the killer and gave him a staff, saying, "Walk with it to Paradise."[35]

The Quraysh strike back

After their humiliation at Badr, the Quraysh were anxious for revenge. They assembled three thousand troops against one thousand Muslims at a mountain near Mecca named Uhud. Muhammad wore two coats of mail and, brandishing a sword, led the Muslims into battle. Muhammad was confident: when one of the Muslims asked him, "O apostle, should we not ask help from our allies, the Jews?" the Prophet of Islam replied: "We have no need of them."[36] Or perhaps he was thinking of how bitter his relationship with the Jews had become.

This time, the Quraysh were far more determined, and the Muslims were routed. Muhammad himself fought along with his men, wounding a

Quraysh warrior named Ubayy bin Khalaf in the back of the neck. Years before, Ubayy had taunted the new prophet in Mecca: "Muhammad, I have got a horse called 'Aud which I feed every day on many measures of corn. I shall kill you when I am riding it."

Muhammad replied, "No, I shall kill you, if God wills." Ubayy remembered this when he returned to the Quraysh encampment, wounded very slightly in the neck and exclaiming, "By God! Muhammad has killed me." When the Quraysh responded, "By God! You have lost heart. You are not hurt," Ubayy insisted: "He said to me in Mecca that he would kill me, and, by God, if he had spat on me he would have killed me." He died as he was being transported back to Mecca, killed by the warrior prophet just as he had predicted.[37]

Aisha later recounted that the Muslims were initially winning at Uhud, but then their lines collapsed in confusion due to a supernatural intervention: "Satan, Allah's Curse be upon him, cried loudly, 'O Allah's Worshippers, beware of what is behind!' On that, the front files of the (Muslim) forces turned their backs and started fighting with the back files."[38]

In the confusion, the Prophet of Islam himself had his face bloodied and a tooth knocked out; rumors even flew around the battlefield that he had been killed. Muhammad washed the blood off his face and vowed revenge: "The wrath of God is fierce against him who bloodied the face of His prophet."[39] He lamented again the Quraysh's rejection of the man Allah had chosen from among them to be a prophet: "How can a nation who injured their Prophet's face be successful?"[40] But in this Allah admonished him: "It is no concern at all of thee (Muhammad) whether He relent toward them or punish them; for they are evil-doers" (Qur'an 3:128). When Abu Sufyan, the Quraysh leader, taunted the Muslims, Muhammad reaffirmed that the Quraysh were indeed all evildoers. He told his lieutenant Umar to respond: "God is most high and most glorious. We are not equal. Our dead are in paradise; your dead in hell."[41]

Muhammad vowed revenge again when he found the body of his uncle Hamza. Hamza had been killed at Uhud and his body horribly mutilated by a woman named Hind bint 'Utba, who cut off Hamza's nose and ears and ate a part of his liver. She did this in revenge for the Muslims' killing of her father, brother, uncle, and eldest son at Badr. Muhammad did not hesitate to extend the cycle of revenge: "If God gives me victory over Quraysh in the future," he exclaimed, "I will mutilate 30 of their men." Touched by his grief and anger, his followers made a similar vow: "By God, if God gives us victory over them in the future we will mutilate them as no Arab has ever mutilated anyone."[42]

Similar incidents still fill the newspapers today. After jihadist strikes in Iraq or Israel, jihad warriors treat any counter-measures by American or Israeli forces as unprovoked attacks, deserving swift and fierce revenge. Ever since Muslims began fighting in imitation of their warrior prophet, this has been their standard of behavior. It is not "turn the other cheek," it is visiting enormities against one's enemies.

Hamza's killer, Wahshi, learned that Muhammad would not exact his revenge and kill him if he became a Muslim. Wahshi promptly recited the Shahada and went to see the Prophet of Islam. Muhammad asked him to tell the story of how he had killed his uncle, and then said, "Woe to you, hide your face from me and never let me see you again."[43] Wahshi did as he was told, and outlived the Prophet. Also outliving the Prophet was this distinction between believers and unbelievers, such that Muslims would ever after hesitate to kill other Muslims (excepting, of course, those whom they considered heretics or apostates), but would hold the lives of non-Muslims cheap.

Assuaging doubts after Uhud

One might have expected the defeat at Uhud to shake the Muslims' faith, since after Badr Muhammad had frequently insisted that Allah himself had been fighting for the Muslims. But Muhammad was ready with more revelations. This time the theme was that the Muslims were defeated because they had disobeyed Allah and focused on booty rather than victory. (Qur'an 3:152). Another revelation exhorted the Muslims to fight valiantly, assuring them that their lives were in no danger until the day Allah had decreed that they must die: "Nor can a soul die except by Allah's leave, the term being fixed as by writing. If any do desire a reward in this life, We shall give it to him; and if any do desire a reward in the Hereafter, We shall give it to him. And swiftly shall We reward those that (serve us with) gratitude" (Qur'an 3:145).

Allah reminded them of his help for the Muslims in the past, and made future help dependent on their obedience: "Allah had helped you at Badr, when ye were a contemptible little force; then fear Allah; thus may ye show your gratitude. Remember thou saidst to the Faithful: 'Is it not enough for you that Allah should help you with three thousand angels (specially) sent down?' Yea, if ye remain firm, and act aright, even if the enemy should rush here on you in hot haste, your Lord would help you with five thousand angels making a terrific onslaught" (Qur'an 3:123-127).

Again a pattern was set: when things go wrong for the Muslims, Muslim leaders inevitably insist it is because they are not Islamic enough. In 1948, Sayyid Qutb, the great theorist of the Muslim Brotherhood, the first modern Islamic terrorist group, declared about the Islamic world that "we only have to look in order to see that our social situation is as bad as it can be." Yet "we continually cast aside all our own spiritual heritage, all our intellectual endowment, and all the solutions which might well be revealed by a glance at these things; we cast aside our own fundamental principles and doctrines, and we bring in those of democracy, or socialism, or communism."[44] In other words, the only path to success is Islam, and all failures stem from the abandonment of Islam. After Uhud, Allah promised the Muslims that victory would soon be theirs again, if they depended solely on him and rejected all accord with the non-Muslims. (Qur'an 3:149-151).

The stark theological connection between victory and obedience on the one hand and defeat and disobedience on the other was reinforced after the Muslims' victory at a later battle, the Battle of the Trench in 627. Muhammad again received a revelation that attributed the victory to Allah's supernatural intervention: "O ye who believe! Remember Allah's favor unto you when there came against you hosts, and We sent against them a great wind and hosts ye could not see" (Qur'an 33:9).

The deportation of the Banu Nadir

Not long after the Battle of Uhud, some members of a Jewish tribe, the Banu Nadir, conspired to kill Muhammad by dropping a large stone on his head as he passed one of their houses. Some Muslims learned of the plot, and warned Muhammad. Rather than appealing to the Nadir leaders to turn over the guilty men, Muhammad sent word to the Nadir: "Leave my country and do not live with me. You have intended treachery." His messenger was Muhammad bin Maslama (the killer of Ka'b bin Al-Ashraf), a member of the Aws tribe of Medina with whom the Nadir had formerly had a covenant. But when the men of the Nadir protested and invoked that covenant, Muhammad bin Maslama replied: "Hearts have changed, and Islam has wiped out the old covenants."[45]

Abdullah bin Ubayy and some of the other Hypocrites urged the Banu Nadir not to go, and promised to come to their aid if attacked. Relying on this, the Nadir told Muhammad: "We will not leave our settlements; so do as you see fit." With the displacement of responsibility onto the enemy that would become characteristic of jihad warriors throughout the ages, Muhammad told the Muslims, "The Jews have declared war."[46] Allah gave him a revelation, assuring him that the Hypocrites would prove just as false to the Jews as they had to Muhammad. He promised the Prophet of Islam victory over the Nadir. Had he not delivered victory over those who "lately preceded them," the Qaynuqa Jews? Allah would strike "terror" into the Jews' hearts: "Of a truth ye are stronger (than they) because of the terror in their hearts, (sent) by Allah" (Qur'an 59:11-17).

The Prophet of Islam ordered his Muslims to march out against the tribe and lay siege to them. During the siege, he ordered that the date palms of the Banu Nadir be burnt.[47] The Nadir, surprised, asked him: "Muhammad, you have prohibited wanton destruction and blamed those guilty of it. Why then are you cutting down and burning our palm-trees?"[48] Allah justified Muhammad's action in a new revelation: "Whatsoever palm-trees ye cut down or left standing on their roots, it was by Allah's leave, in order that He might confound the evil-livers" (Qur'an 59:5). Islamic apologists frequently cite Muhammad's prohibition against wanton destruction—but don't mention Muhammad's own violation of this decree, and Allah's endorsement of the violation.

The siege of the Banu Nadir lasted two weeks, before they agreed to go into exile. Muhammad allowed the Jews to carry what they could on their camels, but demanded that they turn over all weapons.[49] Some of the Nadir destroyed their own houses.[50] What the Jews couldn't carry with them became Muhammad's personal property, which he distributed as booty among the *muhajiroun*, the Muslims who had emigrated with him from Mecca to Medina.[51] He also kept some of it for his own expenses and for preparing for future jihad wars, as Umar later recounted: "The properties abandoned by Banu Nadir were the ones which Allah bestowed upon His Apostle.... These properties were particularly meant for the Holy Prophet (may peace be upon him). He would meet the annual expenditure of his family from the income thereof, and would spend what remained for purchasing horses and weapons as preparation for Jihad."[52] Muhammad was well known as a man of simple tastes: he did not indulge in lavish displays, live in sumptuous quarters, or adorn himself in pomp and splendor. He spent as much as he could on jihad.

In a revelation, Allah told Muhammad that it was divine terror that had defeated the Banu Nadir, and that they were all bound for hell: "But the (wrath of) Allah came to them from quarters from which they little expected (it), and cast terror into their hearts, so that they destroyed their dwellings by their own hands and the hands of the Believers.... And had it not been that Allah had decreed banishment for them, He would certainly have punished them in this world. And in the hereafter they shall (certainly) have the punishment of the fire" (Qur'an 59:2-3).

The remaining Jews of Medina were next to receive the wrath of Muhammad.

CHAPTER EIGHT

Casting terror into their hearts

- The Battle of the Trench and Muhammad's imperial ambitions
- Muhammad and the massacre of the Jewish Qurayzah tribe
- The abuse of the women of the Mustaliq tribe
- The Treaty of Hudaybiyya: an arrangement of convenience
- The siege of Khaybar and the poisoning of Muhammad

The Battle of the Trench

AFTER THE EXPULSION OF THE QAYNUQA AND NADIR JEWS FROM Medina, some of those who remained approached the Quraysh, offering an alliance against Muhammad and the Muslims. The Quraysh readily accepted and asked them: "You, O Jews, are the first scripture people and know the nature of our dispute with Muhammad. Is our religion the best or is his?"[1] The Jews replied, as might be expected under the circumstances, that of course the pagan Quraysh religion was better. When Muhammad heard of this, Allah gave him a revelation: "Hast thou not seen those unto whom a portion of the Scripture hath been given, how they believe in idols and false deities, and how they say of those (idolaters) who disbelieve: 'These are more rightly guided than those who believe'? Those are they whom Allah hath cursed, and he whom Allah hath cursed, thou (O Muhammad) wilt find for him no helper" (Qur'an 4:51-52).

Muhammad, forewarned of this new alliance, had a trench dug around Medina. This huge effort required a great deal of manpower: many of the Muslims pressed into this service, however, would slip away. Only a few would ask Muhammad permission to leave, and some of those offered only some trifling excuse. Muhammad accordingly received another revelation, warning them that true Muslims do not take lightly the commands of the Prophet of Islam:

> They only are the true believers who believe in Allah and His messenger and, when they are with him on some common errand, go not away until they have asked leave of him.... Deem not the summons of the Messenger among yourselves like the summons of one of you to another: Allah doth know those of you who slip away under shelter of some excuse: then let those beware who withstand the Messenger's order, lest some trial befall them, or a grievous penalty be inflicted on them. (Qur'an 24:62-63)

Such incidents reinforced the divinely commanded and exalted status of Muhammad among the Muslims. When the riots over the Danish Muhammad cartoons rocked the world in late 2005 and early 2006, many non-Muslims were puzzled by the fury of the Muslim reaction. At least some of that fury must be ascribed to the fact that in the Qur'an again and again Allah is quite solicitous of his prophet, and ready to command what will please him. To the mind of someone who accepts the Qur'an as an authentic revelation, this places Muhammad in a particularly important position.

During the digging of the trench Muhammad had visions of conquering the areas bordering on Arabia. This story has a legendary cast, but whether it originated with Muhammad or with the Muslim community, it indicates the imperialistic designs the early Muslims had on the territories surrounding Arabia. One of the earliest Muslims, Salman the Persian, was working on the trench when he began having trouble with a particularly large rock. "The apostle," explained Salman, "who was near at hand, saw me hacking and saw how difficult the place was. He dropped down into the trench and took the pick from my hand and gave such a blow that lightning showed beneath the pick."[2] The flash of lightning "shot out, illuminating everything between the two tracts of black stones—that is, Medina's two tracts of black stones—like a lamp inside a dark room." Muhammad shouted with the Islamic cry of victory, "Allahu akbar," and all the Muslims responded with the same shout.[3] This happened again and then a third time, in exactly the same way. Finally Salman asked Muhammad: "O you, dearer than father or mother, what is the meaning of this light beneath your pick as you strike?"

The Prophet of Islam responded: "Did you really see that, Salman? The first means that God has opened up to me the Yaman; the second Syria and the west; and the third the east."[4] Or, according to another version of the same story, Muhammad declared: "I struck my first blow, and what you saw flashed out, so that the palaces of al-Hirah [in what is today southern Iraq] and al-Madai'in of Kisra [the winter capital of the Sassanian empire] lit up for me as if they were dogs' teeth, and Gabriel informed me that my nation would be victorious over them." The second blow illuminated in the same way "the palaces of the pale men in the lands of the Byzantines," and the third, "the palaces of San'a"—that is, Yemen.[5] Gabriel promised Muhammad victory over each, repeating three times: "Rejoice; victory shall come to them!" To this Muhammad replied, "Praise be to God! The promise of One who is true and faithful! He has promised us victory after tribulation."

Decades later, when the countries named in this legend were indeed conquered by the warriors of jihad, an old Muslim used to say: "Conquer where you will, by God, you have not conquered and to the resurrection day you will not conquer a city whose keys God had not given beforehand to Muhammad."[6] But all that conquest was far in the future. In the present was only the siege of the Medina.

As the Quraysh, along with another tribe, the Ghatafan (known collectively in Islamic tradition as "the Confederates"), laid siege to Medina, the
trench prevented the invaders from entering the city, but the Muslims were
unable to force them to end the siege. Then to make matters even worse,
a tribe of Jews in Medina, the Banu Qurayzah, broke their covenant with
the Prophet of Islam (perhaps after reflecting upon the fate of the Banu
Qaynuqa and Banu Nadir) and began collaborating with the Quraysh.[7]

Muhammad sent spies among the Qurayzah to find out if what he was
hearing was true, and if they had really broken their agreement with him.
The worst news confirmed, he stood strong amid the fears of his people,
saying only: "God is greatest! Rejoice, people of the Muslims!"[8]

As the three-week siege dragged on, the situation of the Muslims grew
more perilous. Conditions grew so bad that one Muslim remarked bitterly
about Muhammad's territorial ambitions and his designs on the two great
powers that bordered Arabia, the Persian empire of Chosroes and the Eastern Roman (Byzantine) empire of Caesar: "Muhammad used to promise
us that we should eat the treasures of Chosroes and Caesar and today not
one of us can feel safe in going to the privy!"[9] The Hypocrites pointed to
the irony of Muhammad's visions in light of the present difficult position
of the Muslims. Muhammad in response delivered this revelation from
Allah: "And behold! The Hypocrites and those in whose hearts is a disease
(even) say: 'Allah and His Messenger promised us nothing but delusion!'"
(Qur'an 33:12).

Muhammad accused the Hypocrites of demoralizing the Muslims and
treasonous plotting with the enemies of Islam, and received a revelation to
back him up (Qur'an 33:13-14). Allah also told Muhammad to tell the people that desertion would be useless: "Say: 'Running away will not profit you
if ye are running away from death or slaughter; and even if (ye do escape),
no more than a brief (respite) will ye be allowed to enjoy!'" (Qur'an 33:16).

Muhammad, meanwhile, sent out feelers for peace negotiations, offering the Quraysh a third of the date harvest of Medina if they would withdraw, but then one of the Muslims, Sa'd ibn Mu'adh, reminded him of the
exalted status of the Muslims, saying it was disgraceful to contemplate put-

ting the Muslim Medinans in a worse position before the pagan Quraysh than they had been in when they too were pagans: "Now that God has conferred Islam on us, guided us to it, and strengthened us with your presence, shall we give them our wealth? We have no need for this! By God, we will offer them only the sword, until God judge between us and them."

Muhammad replied, "As you wish," and did not pursue the idea of paying tribute any further.[10]

As the siege continued, one warrior of the Quraysh, Amr, challenged the Muslims to send out one man for hand-to-hand combat and taunted them about Muhammad's promises of Paradise: "Where is your garden of which you say that those you lose in battle will enter it? Can't you send a man to fight me?" As might be expected since Muhammad was himself from Mecca, the home of the Quraysh, Amr had relatives among the Muslims. His nephew was Ali, Muhammad's cousin and son-in-law and later the revered figure of Shi'a Islam. To his uncle Ali said: "I invite you to God and His apostle and to Islam."

Amr rebuffed the overture and refused to dismount. But he added, "O son of my brother, I do not want to kill you."

Ali was less sentimental. He replied to his uncle: "But I want to kill you," and he did.[11] Islamic loyalty was deeper than blood.

The Qurayzah agreed to attack the Muslims from one side while the Quraysh besieged them from the other. But then events took a turn for the Muslims. A new convert to Islam, Nu'aym bin Mas'ud, came to the Prophet with a proposition: since his own people, the Ghatafan, did not know that he had become a Muslim, Muhammad could perhaps make use of him to gain an advantage over his enemies. Muhammad immediately recognized the potential of the situation, saying: "You are only one man among us, so go and awake distrust among the enemy to draw them off us if you can, for war is deceit."[12] Nu'aym went to the Qurayzah Jews and reminded them that they had much more at stake than the Quraysh and Ghatafan; after all, their wives and property were close at hand, while those of the Quraysh were back in Mecca. The Qurayzah should demand some assurance that the Quraysh would indeed fight to defend them: they should ask for hostages from among the Quraysh leaders, who would be released once Muhammad and the Muslims were defeated. The Qurayzah accepted his suggestion, whereupon Nu'aym hurried to the leaders of the Quraysh and Ghatafan and told them that the Jews were having second thoughts about their alliance, and wanted to reconcile with Muhammad. They had gone to the Prophet of Islam, said Nu'aym, offering him the heads of some of the Quraysh and Ghatafan, and Muhammad accepted. "So," Nu'aym concluded, "if the Jews send to you to demand hostages, don't send them a single man."[13]

Soon afterward, Abu Sufyan, a Quraysh chief, sent word to the Qurayzah that the attack must begin immediately. But the Qurayzah protested that it was the Sabbath and also, "we will not fight Muhammad along with you until you give us hostages whom we can hold as security until we make an end of Muhammad; for we fear that if the battle goes against you and you suffer heavily you will withdraw at once to your country and leave us while the man is in our country, and we cannot face him alone." Of course, this reply only confirmed for the Quraysh the suspicions that Nu'aym had fanned, and they indignantly refused to send any hostages. A strong wind blew up around this time also, making it impossible for the Quraysh to keep their tents up or fires going.

Abu Sufyan had had enough. He said to his men: "O Quraysh, we are not in a permanent camp; the horses and camels are dying; the B. Qurayza have broken their word to us and we have heard disquieting reports of them. You can see the violence of the wind which leaves us neither cooking-pots, nor fire, nor tents to count on. Be off, for I am going!"[14] The Quraysh began to abandon their positions around Medina, and soon the Ghatafan followed. Nu'aym's deception had broken the siege and saved Islam.

Dealing with the Banu Qurayzah

After the successful resolution of the Battle of the Trench, the Angel Gabriel made sure that Muhammad settled accounts with the Qurayzah Jews. According to Aisha, "When Allah's Messenger returned on the day (of the battle) of *Al-Khandaq* (i.e., Trench), he put down his arms and took a bath. Then Jibril (Gabriel) whose head was covered with dust, came to him saying, 'You have put down your arms! By Allah, I have not put down my arms yet.' Allah's Messenger said, 'Where (to go now)?' Jibril said, 'This way,' pointing towards the tribe of Bani Quraiza. So Allah's Messenger went out towards them."[15]

As his armies approached the fortifications of the Qurayzah, Muhammad addressed them in terms that have become familiar usage for Islamic jihadists when speaking of Jews today—language that also made its way into the Qur'an: "You brothers of monkeys, has God disgraced you and brought His vengeance upon you?" The Qur'an in three places (2:62-65; 5:59-60; and 7:166) says that Allah transformed the Sabbath-breaking Jews into pigs and monkeys.

The Qurayzah Jews tried to soften his wrath, saying: "O Abu'l-Qasim [Muhammad], you are not a barbarous person." But the Prophet of Islam was in no mood to be appeased. He told the Muslims who were with him that a warrior who passed by on a white mule was actually Gabriel, "who has been sent to Banu Qurayza to shake their castles and strike terror to their hearts." The Muslims laid siege to the Qurayzah strongholds for twenty-five days, until, according to Ibn Ishaq, "they were sore pressed" and, as Muhammad had warned, "God cast terror into their hearts."[16]

Also casting terror in their hearts may have been the choices offered them by their own chief Ka'b ibn Asad, who had made and broken the treaty with Muhammad. The first was to accept Muhammad and Islam, "for by God it has become plain to you that he is a prophet who has been sent and that it is he that you find mentioned in your scripture; and then your lives, your property, your women and children will be saved."[17] The second choice was to kill their wives and children, "leaving no encumbrances behind us," and go fight Muhammad. The third choice was to ambush the Prophet on the Sabbath. The Qurayzah rejected all three, but chose to surrender to the Muslims.

After some deliberations Muhammad decided to put the fate of the tribe into the hands of the Muslim warrior Sa'd bin Mu'adh. Sa'd was a member of the Aws tribe that had previously had an alliance with the Jews of Medina, so perhaps Muhammad thought that the Qurayzah would accept his judgment as impartial, or at least that it would appear to be to any of the followers of the Prophet of Islam who might otherwise question his own ruling because of the close ties many of the Muslims had with the Jews of Medina. When Sa'd rode up on his donkey, Muhammad told him, "These people are ready to accept your judgment."

Sa'd replied: "I give the judgment that their warriors should be killed and their children and women should be taken as captives."

The Prophet of Islam was pleased. "O Sa'd! You have judged amongst them with (or similar to) the judgment of the King (Allah)."[18] He confirmed Sa'd's judgment as that of Allah himself: "You have decided in confirmation to the judgment of Allah above the seven heavens."[19] (Later, when Sa'd died, Ibn Ishaq records several early Muslim traditions asserting that the very throne of Allah shook.[20])

Sa'd's sentence was duly carried out, with Muhammad himself actively participating. According to Ibn Ishaq, "The apostle went out to the market of Medina (which is still its market today) and dug trenches in it. Then he sent for [the men of the Qurayzah] and struck off their heads in those trenches as they were brought out to him in batches." One of the Prophet's fiercest enemies among the Qurayzah, Huyayy, proclaimed: "God's command is right. A book and a decree, and massacre have been written against the Sons of Israel." Then Muhammad struck off his head.

In light of Sa'd's judgment to kill the men and enslave the women and children, one of the captives, Attiyah al-Qurazi, explained how the Muslims determined who was a man and who wasn't: "I was among the captives of Banu Qurayzah. They (the Companions) examined us, and those who had begun to grow hair (pubes) were killed, and those who had not were not killed. I was among those who had not grown hair."[21]

Ibn Ishaq puts the number of those massacred at "600 or 700 in all, though some put the figure as high as 800 or 900."[22] Ibn Sa'd says "they were between six hundred and seven hundred in number."[23] As the Qurayzah were being led to Muhammad in groups, someone asked Ka'b bin Asad what was happening. "Will you never understand?" replied the distraught leader of the Qurayzah. "Don't you see that the summoner never stops and those who are taken away do not return? By Allah it is death!"[24]

This mass killing is amply attested in various ahadith. One summarizes Muhammad's dealings with the three Jewish tribes of Medina: "Bani An-Nadir and Bani Quraiza fought (against the Prophet violating their peace treaty), so the Prophet exiled Bani An-Nadir and allowed Bani Quraiza to remain at their places (in Medina) taking nothing from them till they fought against the Prophet again. He then killed their men and distributed their women, children and property among the Muslims, but some of them came to the Prophet and he granted them safety, and they embraced Islam. He exiled all the Jews from Medina. They were the Jews of Bani Qainuqa', the tribe of 'Abdullah bin Salam and the Jews of Bani Haritha and all the other Jews of Medina."[25]

Allah also sent down a revelation referring obliquely to the massacre: "And those of the People of the Book who aided them—Allah did take them down from their strongholds and cast terror into their hearts. (So that) some ye slew, and some ye made prisoners" (Qur'an 33:26). And Muhammad again delivered revelations ascribing victory to Allah alone (Qur'an 33:9-11).

Meanwhile, Muhammad's cool head and trust in Allah when things looked bleakest for the Muslims stood him in good stead. Allah gave him a revelation, telling the Muslims to imitate him: "Ye have indeed in the Messenger of Allah a beautiful pattern (of conduct) for any one whose hope is in Allah and the Final Day, and who engages much in the praise of Allah" (Qur'an 33:21). Befitting his lofty status, Muhammad also received a revelation in which Allah admonishes the Muslims not to be so familiar with their prophet or his wives:

> O ye who believe! Enter not the dwellings of the Prophet for a
> meal without waiting for the proper time, unless permission be
> granted you. But if ye are invited, enter, and, when your meal

is ended, then disperse. Linger not for conversation. Lo! That
would cause annoyance to the Prophet, and he would be shy
of (asking) you (to go); but Allah is not shy of the truth. And
when ye ask of them (the wives of the Prophet) anything, ask it
of them from behind a curtain. That is purer for your hearts
and for their hearts. And it is not for you to cause annoyance to
the messenger of Allah, nor that ye should ever marry his wives
after him. Lo! That in Allah's sight would be an enormity.
(Qur'an 33:53)

Finding excuses for a massacre

The massacre of the Banu Qurayzah has been understandably a source of
embarrassment to Muslims. Various Muslim apologists have attempted to
deny the incident altogether or to minimize the number of casualties. One
Islamic scholar, W. N. Arafat, published a lengthy article in 1976 arguing
that the massacre never happened, chiefly for the anachronistic reason that
it would have violated Islamic law.[26] This is rather an odd argument given
the fact that Muhammad readily set aside his principles on other occasions,
as in the incident when his raiders killed Quraysh during the sacred
month, and when he conceived his powerful attraction to Zaynab bint
Jahsh. Others point to the treachery of the Banu Qurayzah as justifying
Sa'd's sentence and Muhammad's approval of it. Yahiya Emerick, in his
biography of Muhammad, says of Sa'd's judgment that "Muhammad did
not intervene because he had already given up his right to alter the judgment." He does not repeat Muhammad's words affirming Sa'd's judgment
as that of Allah.[27]

Karen Armstrong argues that "it is not correct to judge the incident by
twentieth-century standards" and that "in the early seventh century, an
Arab chief would not be expected to show any mercy to traitors like
Qurayzah."[28] That is true, but Armstrong misses the larger issue; as in all
the incidents of Muhammad's life, he is still held up by Muslims around
the world as "an excellent model of conduct" (Qur'an 33:21). In July 2006,

as Israeli forces prepared to move into Gaza in the wake of the kidnapping of an Israeli soldier by Hamas, a writer on a British Muslim Internet forum declared: "I'm so fed up with these dirty, filthy Israeli dogs. May Allah curse them and destroy them all, and may they face the same fate as Banu Qurayzah!"[29] No one accused him of illicitly importing seventh-century models into the present day.

The women of the Banu Mustaliq

Muhammad was now the undisputed master of Medina, and the Prophet of Islam enjoyed an immediate economic advantage. A hadith records that "people used to give some of their date-palms to the Prophet (as a gift), till he conquered Bani Quraiza and Bani An-Nadir, whereupon he started returning their favours."[30] But challengers to his consolidation of power over all Arabia still remained. He received word that the Banu al-Mustaliq, an Arab tribe related to the Quraysh, were gathering against the Muslims, so he led the Muslims out to attack them. And Allah, according to Ibn Ishaq, "put the B. al-Mustaliq to flight and killed some of them and gave the apostle their wives, children and property as booty."[31]

There were, according to one of the Muslim warriors, Abu Sa'id al-Khadri, "some excellent Arab women" among the captives of the Banu Mustaliq. "We desired them, for we were suffering from the absence of our wives, (but at the same time) we also desired ransom for them." The Qur'an permitted them to have sexual intercourse with slave girls captured in battle—"those captives whom your right hands possess" (4:24)—but if they intended to keep the women as slaves, they couldn't collect ransom money for them. "So," Abu Sa'id explained, "we decided to have sexual intercourse with them but by observing 'azl'—that is, *coitus interruptus*. Muhammad, however, told them this was not necessary: "It does not matter if you do not do it, for every soul that is to be born up to the Day of Resurrection will be born."[32] Conceptions and births were up to Allah alone.

From a twenty-first-century perspective this is one of the most problematic aspects of Muhammad's status as "an excellent model of conduct": the treatment of women as war prizes, with no consideration of their will. Even a contemporary Islamic legal manual stipulates that when a woman is taken captive, her "previous marriage is immediately annulled."[33] If a jihad warrior takes her captive, she has no say in the matter. The number of women victimized by this across the Islamic centuries cannot be calculated; and even today, women are all too often treated as commodities all across the Islamic world. Of course, this phenomenon has manifested itself to varying degrees in all cultures and societies, but in the Islamic world it is particularly hard to eradicate because of the prophetic sanction it has received.

Muhammad participated in the seizure of female captives. And he gained a wife from among the Banu Mustaliq, but in a way that suggests that at least sometimes, under special circumstances, a captive woman might have some say in her fate. Among the captives from among the Mustaliq was a strikingly beautiful woman named Juwayriya, whom the Prophet of Islam assigned by lot to one of his cousins, Thabit bin Qays bin al-Shammas. Juwayriya thought this was beneath her station, as she was the daughter of the chief of the Mustaliq. So she went to Muhammad to appeal: "You can see the state to which I have been brought. I have fallen to the lot of Thabit or his cousin and have given him a deed for my ransom and have come to ask your help in the matter."

Muhammad replied, "Would you like something better than that? I will discharge your debt and marry you." His marriage to Juwayriya made the Mustaliq relatives of the Prophet; on the day he married her, therefore, a hundred families enslaved by the Muslims were released from bondage.[34] Muhammad changed the woman's name; it had originally been Barra, which means Pious. Said the Prophet of Islam: "I did not like that it should be said: He had come out from Barra (Pious)."[35]

Abdullah bin Ubayy and praying for one's enemies

Shortly after this battle, Abdullah bin Ubayy, the Hypocrite who had annoyed the Prophet of Islam with his scheming and pleading for the Jewish tribes of the Qaynuqa and Nadir, began to challenge Muhammad more openly. He called upon the Medinans to rise up against the Muslims who had come from Mecca and expel them from the city. "Nothing so fits us and the vagabonds of the Quraysh," he exclaimed, "as the ancient saying, 'Feed a dog and it will devour you.' By Allah when we return to Medina the stronger will drive out the weaker."[36] But when several of the Muslims reported this to Muhammad, Abdullah bin Ubayy denied having said it, and the Prophet of Islam accepted his denial. Umar, however, doubted Abdullah bin Ubayy, and went to Muhammad with an offer: "Permit me so that I should strike the neck of this hypocrite."

Muhammad refused: "Leave him, the people may not say that Muhammad kills his companions."[37] Then Abdullah's son came to Muhammad offering to kill his father for him. The young man hoped thereby to save himself from the dilemma of having to avenge his father's killing by killing the man Muhammad sent to end his father's life:

> I have heard that you want to kill 'Abdullah b. Ubayy for what you have heard about him. If you must do it, then order me to do it and I will bring you his head, for al-Khazraj know that they have no man more dutiful to his father than I, and I am afraid that if you order someone else to kill him my soul will not permit me to see his slayer walking among men and I shall kill him, thus killing a believer for an unbeliever, and so I should go to hell.[38]

Again, Islamic loyalty was thicker than blood. But Muhammad declined, saying, "Nay, but let us deal kindly with him and make much of his companionship while he is with us."[39]

Muhammad's kindness did not move Abdullah bin Ubayy, who continued to be at odds with the Prophet of Islam until his death. Muhammad never gave up on him, however, and even prayed over his grave when he died. Umar, who was with him, was aghast: "Allah's Messenger, are you going to conduct prayer for this man, whereas Allah has forbidden you to offer prayer for him?"

Muhammad answered by interpreting a verse from the Qur'an: "Whether thou ask for their forgiveness, or not, (their sin is unforgivable): if thou ask seventy times for their forgiveness, Allah will not forgive them: because they have rejected Allah and His Messenger: and Allah guideth not those who are perversely rebellious" (9:80). He told Umar that Allah had given him a choice by saying: "Whether thou ask for their forgiveness, or not..." and said that while he knew that seventy prayers would be fruitless, he had hope for those beyond seventy.

But Allah put an end to this magnanimity with a new revelation: "And never (O Muhammad) pray for one of them who dieth, nor stand by his grave. Lo! They disbelieved in Allah and His messenger, and they died while they were evil-doers" (Qur'an 9:84).[40]

After that, Muhammad stopped praying at the gravesites of those who opposed him.[41] It is noteworthy that when Yahiya Emerick relates the story of Muhammad's difficulties with Abdullah bin Ubayy, he concludes: "He soon fell ill, and on his deathbed, Muhammad came to visit him and asked God to forgive him, telling his stunned companions that he hoped God would."[42] Emerick says nothing about the divine rebuke that Muhammad received for this display of mercy after praying at Abdullah's gravesite.

The Treaty of Hudaybiyya

Yet another key Islamic principle was formulated by the Treaty of Hudaybiyya and the events surrounding it. In 628, Muhammad had a vision in which he performed the pilgrimage to Mecca—a pagan custom that he very much wanted to make part of Islam, but had thus far been prevented by the Quraysh control of Mecca. But at this time he directed Muslims to prepare to make the pilgrimage to Mecca, and advanced upon the city with fifteen hundred men. The Quraysh met him outside the city, and the two sides concluded a ten-year truce (*hudna*), the treaty of Hudaybiyya.

Some leading Muslims were unhappy with the prospect of a truce. After all, they had broken the Quraysh siege of Medina and were now more powerful than ever. Were they going to bargain away their military might for the sake of being able to make the pilgrimage? A furious Umar went to Abu Bakr and said, "Is he not God's apostle, and are we not Muslims, and are they not polytheists? Then why should we agree to what is demeaning to our religion?" The two of them went to Muhammad, who attempted to reassure them: "I am God's slave and His apostle. I will not go against His commandment and He will not make me the loser."[43]

But it certainly did not seem as if the treaty was being concluded to the Muslims' advantage. When the time came for the agreement to be written, Muhammad called for Ali and told him to write, "In the name of Allah, the Compassionate, the Merciful." But the Quraysh negotiator, Suhayl bin 'Amr, stopped him: "I do not recognize this; but write 'In thy name, O Allah." Muhammad told Ali to write what Suhayl had directed.

But Suhayl was not finished. When Muhammad directed Ali to continue by writing, "This is what Muhammad, the apostle of God, has agreed with Suhayl bin 'Amr," he protested again. "If I witnessed that you were God's apostle," Suhayl told Muhammad, "I would not have fought you. Write your own name and the name of your father." Again the Prophet of Islam, to the increasing dismay of his followers, told Ali to write the document as Suhayl wished.

The treaty finally agreed to read this way:

> This is what Muhammad b. 'Abdullah has agreed with Suhayl b. 'Amr: they have agreed to lay aside war for ten years during which men can be safe and refrain from hostilities on condition that if anyone comes to Muhammad without the permission of his guardian he will return him to them; and if anyone of those with Muhammad comes to Quraysh they will not return him to him. We will not show enmity one to another and there shall be no secret reservation or bad faith. He who wishes to enter into a bond and agreement with Muhammad may do so and he who wishes to enter into a bond and agreement with Quraysh may do so.

The Quraysh added: "You must retire from us this year and not enter Mecca against our will, and next year we will make way for you and you can enter it with your companions, and stay there three nights. You may carry a rider's weapons, the swords in their sheaths. You can bring in nothing more."[44]

Muhammad had shocked his men by agreeing to provisions that seemed highly disadvantageous to the Muslims: those fleeing the Quraysh and seeking refuge with the Muslims would be returned to the Quraysh, while those fleeing the Muslims and seeking refuge with the Quraysh would not be returned to the Muslims.

The treaty concluded, Muhammad insisted that the Muslims had been victorious despite all appearances to the contrary. He produced a new revelation from Allah: "Verily We have granted thee a manifest victory" (Qur'an 48:1). Muhammad also revealed that "Allah promiseth you much booty that ye will capture, and hath given you this in advance, and hath withheld men's hands from you, that it may be a token for the believers, and that He may guide you on a right path" (Qur'an 48:18-20).

If any of his followers were still skeptical, their fears would soon be assuaged. A woman of the Quraysh, Umm Kulthum, joined the Muslims in Medina; her two brothers came to Muhammad, asking that they be returned "in accordance with the agreement between him and the Quraysh at Hudaybiya."[45] But Muhammad refused: Allah forbade it. He gave Muhammad a new revelation: "O ye who believe! When there come to you believing women refugees, examine and test them: Allah knows best as to their faith: if ye ascertain that they are believers, then send them not back to the unbelievers" (Qur'an 60:10).

In refusing to send Umm Kulthum back to the Quraysh, Muhammad broke the treaty. Although Muslim apologists have claimed throughout history that the Quraysh broke it first, this incident came before all those by the Quraysh that Muslims point to as treaty violations. Emerick asserts that Muhammad based his case on a bit of legal hair-splitting: the treaty stipulated that the Muslims would return to the Quraysh any *man* who came to them, not any *woman*.[46] Even if that is true, Muhammad soon—as Emerick acknowledges—began to accept men from the Quraysh as well, thus definitively breaking the treaty.[47] The breaking of the treaty in this way, would reinforce the principle that nothing was good except what was advantageous to Islam, and nothing evil except what hindered Islam. Once the treaty was formally discarded, Islamic jurists enunciated the principle that truces in general could only be concluded on a temporary basis of up to ten years, and that they could only be entered into for the purpose of allowing weakened Muslim forces to gather strength to fight again more effectively.

Subsequent events would illustrate the dark implications of this episode.

The raid at Khaybar

Allah had promised the Muslims disgruntled by the Treaty of Hudaybiyya "much booty" (Qur'an 48:19). Perhaps to fulfill this promise, Muhammad led them against the Khaybar oasis, which was inhabited by Jews—many of them exiles from Medina. One of the Muslims later remembered: "When the apostle raided a people he waited until the morning. If he heard a call to prayer he held back; if he did not hear it he attacked. We came to Khaybar by night, and the apostle passed the night there; and when morning came he did not hear the call to prayer, so he rode and we rode with him. . . . We met the workers of Khaybar coming out in the morning with their spades and baskets. When they saw the apostle and the army they cried, 'Muhammad with his force,' and turned tail and fled. The apostle said, 'Allah Akbar! Khaybar is destroyed. When we arrive in a people's square it is a bad morning for those who have been warned.'"[48]

The Muslim advance was inexorable. "The apostle," according to Ibn Ishaq, "seized the property piece by piece and conquered the forts one by one as he came to them."[49] Ibn Sa'd reports that the battle was fierce: the "polytheists . . . killed a large number of [Muhammad's] Companions and he also put to death a very large number of them. . . . He killed ninety-three men of the Jews. . . ."[50] Muhammad and his men offered the *fajr* prayer, the

Islamic dawn prayer, before it was light, and then entered Khaybar itself. The Muslims immediately set out to locate the inhabitants' wealth. Kinana bin al-Rabi, a Jewish leader of Khaybar who was supposed to have been entrusted with the treasure of the Banu Nadir, was brought before Muhammad. Kinana denied knowing where this treasure was, but Muhammad pressed him: "Do you know that if we find you have it I shall kill you?" Kinana said yes.

Some of the treasure was found. To find the rest, Muhammad gave orders concerning Kinana: "Torture him until you extract what he has." One of the Muslims built a fire on Kinana's chest, but Kinana would not give up his secret. When he was at the point of death, Muhammad bin Maslama, killer of the poet Ka'b bin Al-Ashraf, beheaded him.[51]

Muhammad agreed to let the people of Khaybar go into exile, allowing them, as he had the Banu Nadir, to keep as much of their property as they could carry.[52] However, he commanded them to leave behind all their gold and silver.[53] He had intended to expel all of them, but some, who were farmers, begged him to allow them to let them stay if they gave him half their yield annually.[54] Muhammad agreed: "I will allow you to continue here, so long as we would desire."[55] He warned them: "If we wish to expel you we will expel you."[56] They no longer had any rights that did not depend upon the good will and sufferance of Muhammad and the Muslims. And indeed, when the Muslims discovered some treasure that some of the Khaybar Jews had hidden, he ordered the women of the tribe enslaved and seized the perpetrators' land.[57] A hadith notes that "the Prophet had their warriors killed, their offspring and woman taken as captives."[58]

Later, during the caliphate of Umar (634-644), the Jews who remained at Khaybar were banished to Syria, and the rest of their land seized.[59]

The poisoning of Muhammad

One of the Jewish women of Khaybar, Zaynab bint al-Harith, was brought in to prepare dinner for Muhammad. She prepared a roast lamb—and poisoned it. Muhammad took a bite and spit it out, exclaiming, "This bone tells me that it is poisoned." A dinner companion, Bishr bin al-Bara, had already eaten some and died soon thereafter. Zaynab bint al-Harith readily confessed, explaining to Muhammad: "You know what you have done to my people. I said to myself, If he is a king I shall ease myself of him and if he is a prophet he will be informed (of what I have done)." Because she had thus obliquely confessed his prophethood, Muhammad spared her life.[60] According to another tradition, however, he did have her put to death.[61]

The poison had a definite effect on him; afterward one of the Muslims observed, "I continued to see the effect of the poison on the palate of the mouth of Allah's Messenger."[62] On his deathbed three years after the poisoning, Muhammad told Bishr's sister, "This is the time in which I feel a deadly pain from what I ate with your brother at Khaybar."[63] And likewise he cried out to Aisha: "O 'Aisha! I still feel the pain caused by the food I ate at Khaibar, and at this time, I feel as if my aorta is being cut from that poison."[64]

Another tradition represents the poisoning not as the work of an individual woman, but as a plot of the Jews, who are again portrayed as inveterate liars and schemers. According to this version, after the conquest of Khaybar, the Jews gave Muhammad the gift of a roasted sheep which had been poisoned. Muhammad, sensing the plot, commanded: "Let all the Jews who have been here, be assembled before me." When this was done, Muhammad said: "I am going to ask you a question. Will you tell the truth?" After their affirmative reply, he asked them: "Who is your father?" On hearing their answer (which is not recorded by the tradition), the Prophet of Islam declared, "You have told a lie," and gave them the correct answer.

The Jews acknowledged that Muhammad was right. He then asked them: "Will you now tell me the truth, if I ask you about something?" Again receiving an affirmative reply, he asked, "Who are the people of the hellfire?"

According to the hadith, they answered: "We shall remain in the (Hell) Fire for a short period, and after that you will replace us."

Muhammad would have none of this: "You may be cursed and humiliated in it! By Allah, we shall never replace you in it." And again: "Will you now tell me the truth if I ask you a question?" Receiving yet another assurance that they would, Muhammad asked: "Have you poisoned this sheep?"

They admitted that they had indeed poisoned it. Asked why, they answered as did Zaynab bint al-Harith: "We wanted to know if you were a liar in which case we would get rid of you, and if you are a prophet then the poison would not harm you."[65]

The spoils of Khaybar

With Khaybar conquered, it was time to divide up the spoils. Aisha remembered that as the Muslims entered the Khaybar oasis, they exclaimed, "Now we will eat our fill of dates!"[66]

One of the Muslim warriors, Dihya bin Khalifa, came to Muhammad and said: "O Allah's Prophet! Give me a slave girl from the captives." The Prophet of Islam was agreeable, telling Dihya: "Go and take any slave girl." Dihya chose a woman named Safiyya bint Huyayy.[67] Safiyya was the daughter of Huyayy bin Akhtab, who had induced the Banu Qurayzah Jews to repudiate their alliance with Muhammad. Muhammad had killed Huyayy along with the rest of the men of the Qurayzah. Safiyya's husband was Kinana ibn Rabi, who had just been tortured and killed by the warriors of jihad. Once captured herself, she had won the admiration of the warriors of Islam, who told their prophet: "We have not seen the like of her among the captives of war."[68] One man added: "O Allah's Messenger! You gave Safiya bint Huyai to Dihya and she is the chief-mistress of (the ladies) of the tribes of Quraiza and An-Nadir, she befits none but you."[69]

Muhammad accordingly called for Dihya and Safiyya. When the Prophet of Islam saw Safiyya, he told Dihya: "Take any slave girl other than her from the captives." Muhammad then immediately freed her and married her himself—since she agreed to convert to Islam, she was able to be elevated beyond the position of a slave. That night Safiyya was dressed as a bride and a wedding feast was hastily arranged. On the way out of Khaybar that night, Muhammad halted his caravan as soon as they were outside the oasis, pitched a tent, and consummated the marriage.[70] Safiyya's feelings on going from wife of a Jewish chieftain, to widow, to captive, to wife of the Prophet of Islam in the course of a single day are not recorded.

Khaybar has become a watchword for present-day jihadists. The chant is popular among Palestinians and their allies: "Khaybar, Khaybar, O Jews, the army of Muhammad will return."[71] That can mean nothing less than the destruction of the State of Israel, as surely as the Jewish stronghold of Khaybar was destroyed.

CHAPTER NINE

Victorious through terror

- Muhammad becomes the master of Mecca
- Muhammad orders the killing of apostates from Islam
- Muhammad becomes the master of Arabia
- Muhammad calls the rulers of neighboring states to Islam
- The Tabuk expedition and warfare against Christians and Jews
- The cardinal importance of the non-Muslim poll tax
- Muhammad's final illness and death
- After Muhammad: the Islamic schism

The conquest of Mecca

THE STAGE WAS NOW SET FOR THE CONQUEST OF MECCA AND Muhammad's triumphant return to his home city, where he had first begun to proclaim the message of Allah. He ordered his men to prepare for a foray to Mecca, and prayed: "O God, take eyes and ears from Quraysh so that we may take them by surprise in their land."[1] The surprise was almost given away by a Muslim who sent a letter to the Quraysh informing them of Muhammad's plans; however, the Muslims intercepted the letter. The traitor, Hatib bin Abu Balta'a, explained that he was a believing Muslim but he had relatives among the Quraysh, including a son. Muhammad forgave him because Hatib was a veteran of the Battle of Badr. Then he received another revelation from Allah, telling Hatib that as a Muslim, his feelings of filial piety toward the Quraysh were misplaced:

> Your ties of kindred and your children will avail you naught upon the Day of Resurrection. He will part you. Allah is Seer of what ye do. There is a goodly pattern for you in Abraham and those with him, when they told their folk: Lo! We are guiltless of you and all that ye worship beside Allah. We have done with you. And there hath arisen between us and you hostility and hate for ever until ye believe in Allah only. (Qur'an 60:1–4)

Muhammad then marched on Mecca with an army of, according to some reports, ten thousand Muslims.[2] When the Meccans saw the size of their force, which Muhammad exaggerated by ordering his men to build many extra fires during the night as his men were assembled outside the city, they knew that all was lost. Many of the most notable Quraysh warriors now deserted and, converting to Islam, joined Muhammad's forces. As they advanced, they were met by Abu Sufyan himself, who had opposed Muhammad bitterly as a leader of the Quraysh; but now Abu Sufyan wanted to become a Muslim. Allowed into Muhammad's presence, Abu Sufyan recited a poem including these lines:

> I was like one going astray in the darkness of the night,
> But now I am led on the right track.
> I could not guide myself, and he who with God overcame me
> Was he whom I had driven away with all my might.

According to Ibn Ishaq, when he got to the lines "he who with God overcame me was he whom I had driven away with all my might," Muhammad "punched him in the chest and explained, 'You did indeed!'"[3] But when

Muhammad said, "Woe to you, Abu Sufyan, isn't it time that you recognize that I am God's apostle?," Abu Sufyan replied, "As to that I still have some doubt."[4] At that, one of Muhammad's lieutenants, Abbas, responded to Abu Sufyan: "Submit and testify that there is no God but Allah and that Muhammad is the apostle of God before you lose your head." Abu Sufyan complied.[5]

Apostates to be killed

When Muhammad "forced his entry" into Mecca, according to Ibn Sa'd, "the people embraced Islam willingly or unwillingly."[6] The Prophet of Islam ordered the Muslims to fight only those individuals or groups who resisted their advance into the city—except for a list of people who were to be killed, even if they had sought sanctuary in the Ka'bah itself. One of those was Abdullah bin Sa'd, a former Muslim who at one time had been employed by Muhammad to write down the Qur'anic revelations; but he had subsequently apostatized and returned to the Quraysh. He was found and brought to Muhammad along with his brother, and pleaded with the Prophet of Islam for clemency: "Accept the allegiance of Abdullah, Apostle of Allah!" Abdullah repeated this twice, but Muhammad remained impassive. After Abdullah repeated it a third time, Muhammad accepted.

As soon as Abdullah had left, Muhammad turned to the Muslims who were in the room and asked: "Was not there a wise man among you who would stand up to him when he saw that I had withheld my hand from accepting his allegiance, and kill him?"

The companions, aghast, responded: "We did not know what you had in your heart, Apostle of Allah! Why did you not give us a signal with your eye?"

"It is not advisable," said the Prophet of Islam, "for a Prophet to play deceptive tricks with the eyes."[7]

Apostasy from Islam had always been for Muhammad a supreme evil. When he was master of Medina, some livestock herders came to the city and accepted Islam. But they disliked Medina's climate, so Muhammad gave them some camels and a shepherd; once away from Medina, the herders killed the shepherd, released the camels, and renounced Islam. Muhammad had them pursued. When they were caught, he ordered that their hands and feet be amputated (in accord with Qur'an 5:33, which directs that those who cause "corruption in the land" be punished by the amputation of their hands and feet on opposite sides) and their eyes put out with heated iron bars, and that they be left in the desert to die. Their pleas for water, he ordered, must be refused.[8]

The traditions are clear that one of the main reasons that the punishment was so severe was because these men had been Muslims but had "turned renegade." Muhammad legislated for his community that no Muslim could be put to death except for murder, unlawful sexual intercourse, and apostasy.[9] He said flatly: "Whoever changed his Islamic religion, then kill him."[10]

It stains credulity, in light of all this, that Islamic apologists in the West assert that, in the words of one Ibrahim B. Syed, President of the Islamic Research Foundation International of Louisville, Kentucky, "there is no historical record, which indicates that Muhammad (pbuh) or any of his companions ever sentenced anyone to death for apostasy."[11] This kind of assertion may be comforting to non-Muslims who would prefer to believe that the notorious capital charges levied in early 2006 against the Afghan convert from Islam to Christianity, Abdul Rahman, were some sort of anomaly. Unfortunately, this claim simply does not accord with the facts of Muhammad's life. That such assertions pass unchallenged only underscores the need for Westerners to become informed about the actual words and deeds of Muhammad—which make the actions of Islamic states much more intelligible than do the words of Islamic apologists in the West.

There were several others in Mecca who were on the list of those to be killed immediately: Abdullah bin Khatal, another apostate from Islam; al-Huwayrith bin Nuqaydh, who had insulted Muhammad, and some others.[12]

Muhammad at the Ka'bah

Once the city was entirely pacified, the Prophet of Islam rode a camel to the Ka'bah. He found it full of idols—360 in all—and quoted his Qur'an: "Truth hath come and falsehood hath vanished away. Lo! Falsehood is ever bound to vanish" (17:81). He ordered that all the idols be burned except for an icon of Jesus and Mary.[13] Then he stood at the door of the shrine and announced:

> Every claim of privilege or blood or property are abolished by me except the custody of the temple and the watering of the pilgrims. The unintentionally slain in a quasi-intentional way by club or whip, for him the bloodwit is most severe: a hundred camels, forty of them to be pregnant. O Quraysh, God has taken from you the haughtiness of paganism and its veneration of ancestors. Man springs from Adam and Adam sprang from dust.

The Quraysh leaders were assembled and listened avidly, waiting for the Prophet of Islam to tell them their fate. Finally he turned to them and asked, "O Quraysh, what do you think that I am about to do with you?"

They answered that they were sure he was about to do good to them: "You are a noble brother, son of a noble brother."

And it was so. "Go your way," said the Prophet of Islam, "for you are the freed ones." He spared their lives though, according to early Islamic tradition, "God had given him power over their lives and they were his spoil."[14]

The people of Mecca now gathered to pay homage to Muhammad. It was the crowning moment of his prophetic career; eight years before he had been exiled from his home city, and now it lay at his feet. One of his chief companions, Umar, made all the men promise to obey Allah and Muhammad, as the Prophet looked on. When the men had finished with this, the women began to approach—including Hind bint 'Utba, the woman who had mutilated the body of Muhammad's uncle Hamza at the Battle of Uhud. Hind, fearful of how Muhammad might punish her, came before him disguised and veiled. Muhammad gave her a series of Islamic moral instructions: do not associate others with Allah, do not steal, do not commit adultery, and more. By her answers, he came to realize it was Hind, whereupon she asked his forgiveness. When he said to her, "And you shall not kill your children," Hind told Muhammad: "I brought them up when they were little and you killed them on the day of Badr when they were grown up, so you are the one to know about them!" This made Umar laugh heartily.

The homage of the women accepted, Ali presented Muhammad with the key to the Ka'bah, but Muhammad returned it to the caretaker of the shrine when it was a center of pagan pilgrimages, saying: "Here is your key; today is a day of good faith."[15]

The day after the conquest of Mecca, one of the Muslims killed a pagan. Muhammad thereupon delivered this address, emphasizing the sanctity of Mecca, forbidding killings within its confines:

> God made Mecca holy the day He created heaven and earth, and it is the holy of holies until the resurrection day. It is not lawful for anyone who believes in God and the last day to shed blood therein, nor to cut down trees therein. . . . If anyone should say, The apostle killed men in Mecca, say God permitted His apostle to do so but He does not permit you. . . . If anyone is killed after my sojourn here his people have a choice: they can have his killer's life or the blood-money.[16]

The Battle of Hunayn and mastery of Arabia

Muhammad was the master of Mecca, but there was one additional great obstacle between him and mastery of all Arabia. Malik ibn 'Awf, a member of the Thaqif tribe of the city of Ta'if, south of Mecca, began to assemble a force to fight the Muslims. The people of Ta'if had rejected Muhammad and treated him shabbily when he presented his prophetic claim to them ten years earlier. They were historic rivals of the Quraysh, and viewed the conversion of the latter to Islam with disdain. Malik assembled a force and marched out to face the Muslims; Muhammad met him with an army 12,000 strong, saying, "We shall not be worsted today for want of numbers."[17]

The two forces met at a wadi—a dry riverbed—called Hunayn, near Mecca. Malik and his men had arrived first and taken up positions that gave them an immense tactical advantage. The Muslims, despite their superior numbers, were routed. As they broke ranks and fled, Muhammad called out: "Where are you going, men? Come to me. I am God's apostle. I am Muhammad the son of 'Abdullah."[18] Some of the Muslims did take heart, and gradually the tide began to turn—although with tremendous loss of life on both sides.

The Muslims eventually prevailed, wiping out the last major force that stood between the Prophet of Islam and mastery of Arabia. After the battle Muhammad received another revelation explaining that the Muslims had won because of supernatural help: "Then Allah sent His peace of reassurance down upon His messenger and upon the believers, and sent down hosts ye could not see, and punished those who disbelieved." (9:26)

With Malik defeated, the Muslims later conquered Ta'if with little resistance. On his way into the city, Muhammad stopped under a tree, and, finding the property to his liking, sent word to the owner: "Either come out or we will destroy your wall."[19] But the owner refused to appear before Muhammad, so the Muslims indeed destroyed his property.[20] Endeavoring, however, to win the tribesmen of Ta'if to Islam, Muhammad was lenient toward them. In his distribution of the booty, he also favored some of the recent converts among the Quraysh, hoping to cement their allegiance to Islam. His favoritism, however, led to grumbling. One Muslim approached him boldly: "Muhammad, I've seen what you have done today....I don't think you have been just."

The Prophet of Islam was incredulous. "If justice is not to be found with me then where will you find it?"[21]

Indeed, Muslims ever after have found justice in Muhammad, and only in him. His words and deeds exemplify their highest pattern of conduct, forming the only absolute standard within Islam: anything sanctioned by the example of the Prophet, with the sole exception of incidents such as that of the Satanic verses, in which he was repentant, is good.

Invitations to Islam

The Prophet of Islam now faced little opposition, becoming the ruler of all Arabia. He began to set his sights on even larger quarry, eyeing the adjacent Byzantine and Persian territories. Earlier he had written a series of letters to the rulers of the great nations surrounding Arabia, calling them to his new faith. To Heraclius, the Eastern Roman Emperor in Constantinople, he wrote:

> Now then, I invite you to Islam (i.e. surrender to Allah), embrace Islam and you will be safe; embrace Islam and Allah will bestow on you a double reward. But if you reject this invitation of Islam, you shall be responsible for misguiding the peasants (i.e. your nation).[22]

Then the letter quoted the Qur'an: "Say: 'O People of the Scripture! Come to an agreement between us and you: that we shall worship none but Allah, and that we shall ascribe no partner unto Him, and that none of us shall take others for lords beside Allah.'" (3:64)

Heraclius did not accept Islam, and soon the Byzantines would know well that the warriors of jihad indeed granted no safety to those who made such a choice. Perhaps Heraclius had some inkling of this; according to a hadith, after the letter was read he turned to the interpreter and remarked: "If what you say is true, then he (the Prophet) will take over the place underneath my two feet."[23] According to some traditions transmitted by Ibn

Sa'd and others Heraclius did want to accept Islam, but at this his nobles "ran away like wild asses, snorting and with their crosses raised." To keep peace with them, Heraclius abandoned this idea.[24]

Muhammad did not get a satisfactory answer either from Chosroes, ruler of the Persians. After reading the letter of the Prophet of Islam, Chosroes contemptuously tore it to pieces. When news of this reached Muhammad, he called upon Allah to tear the Persian emperor and his followers to pieces.[25] "When Khosrau [Chosroes] perishes, there will be no (more) Khosrau after him, and when Caesar perishes, there will be no more Caesar after him. By Him in Whose hands Muhammad's life is, you will spend the treasures of both of them in Allah's Cause."[26]

The Prophet of Islam codified this expansionist imperative as one of the duties of his new community. He received a revelation from Allah that commanded Muslims to fight against Jews and Christians until they accepted Islamic hegemony, symbolized by payment of a poll tax (*jizya*), and submitted to discriminatory regulations that would ensure that they would be constantly reminded of their subordinate position (Qur'an 9:29). He told his followers to offer these unbelievers conversion to Islam, as he had offered to the rulers, and if they refused, to offer them the opportunity to pay tribute as vassals of the Islamic state, and if they refused that also, to go to war.[27]

The Jews and Christians who agreed to pay the jizya were known as *dhimmis*, which means "protected" or "guilty" people—the Arabic word means both. They were "protected" because, as People of the Book, they had received genuine revelations ("the Book") from Allah and thus differed in status from out-and-out pagans and idolaters like Hindus and Buddhists. (Historically, the latter two groups were treated even worse by Islamic conquerors, though as a practical matter their Muslim masters ultimately awarded them dhimmi status.) They were "guilty" because they had not only rejected Muhammad as a prophet, but distorted the legitimate revelations they received from Allah.

Because of that guilt, Islamic law dictates that Jews and Christians may live in Islamic states, but not as equals of Muslims. One Muslim jurist explained that the caliph must "make jihad against those who resist Islam

after having been called to it until they submit or accept to live as a protected dhimmi-community—so that Allah's rights, may He be exalted 'be
made uppermost above all [other] religion' (Qur'an 9:33)."[28] While Jews,
Christians, and other non-Muslims are allowed to practice their religions,
they must do so under severely restrictive conditions that remind them of
their second-class status at every turn.

Muhammad also extended the *dhimma* to Zoroastrians, a Persian religious sect. When a newly converted chieftain wrote to the Prophet of Islam
asking him what to do about the Zoroastrians and Jews in his domains,
Muhammad responded: "He who continues to remain a Magian or a Jew,
shall pay the jizyah." And he wrote to the Zoroastrians in terms that helped
lay the foundations for the Muslim notion that the non-Muslim is unclean:
besides stipulating that they must pay the jizya, he told them that Muslims
would not eat meat that they had slaughtered.[29]

The Tabuk raid

After commanding his followers to make war against Christians, Muhammad resolved to set an example for his followers. In 631, he ordered the
Muslims to begin preparations for a raid on Tabuk, then part of the Byzantine Empire. But many Muslims were reluctant. One came to the Prophet
of Islam and asked to be excused: "Will you allow me to stay behind and
not tempt me, for everyone knows that I am strongly addicted to women
and I am afraid that if I see the Byzantine women I shall not be able to control myself."[30]

Muhammad granted him permission, but then received a revelation
from Allah, counting people who made such requests among the Hypocrites: "Surely it is into temptation that they (thus) have fallen. Lo! Hell
verily is all around the disbelievers" (Qur'an 9:48-9). Others begged off
because of the scorching heat in Arabia at that time of year, making an
expedition particularly trying—and inducing another revelation: "And they
said: Go not forth in the heat! Say: The fire of hell is more intense of heat,
if they but understood." (9:81).

The journey was indeed arduous, and when Muhammad and his large Muslim force arrived at the Byzantine holdings in northwestern Arabia, they found that the Byzantine troops had withdrawn rather than engage them. But the trip was not for naught: Muhammad accepted the submission of several of the area leaders, who agreed to pay the jizya and submit to the "protection of the Muslims." One of them, Ukaydir bin 'Abdu'l-Malik, was the Christian ruler of Duma. Jihad warriors led by the fierce Khalid bin al-Walid captured him while was hunting cattle; Ukaydir's brother was killed in the melee.

The Muslims seized the robe of gold brocade that Ukaydir was wearing and presented it to Muhammad, who sneered: "By Him in whose hand is my life the napkins of Sa'd b. Mu'adh" — the Muslim warrior who had ordered the mass execution of the Qurayzah Jews — "are better than this."[31] Ukaydir agreed to pay the jizya, and Muhammad opted not to have him put to death. Shortly thereafter the Prophet of Islam returned to Medina, where he maintained his headquarters even after the conquest of Mecca.

Revelations Muhammad received referring to the Tabuk raid were among the harshest toward Jews and Christians than any that he had ever received before. They asserted that Jews called Ezra a son of God, just as Christians called Christ the Son of God, and declared that both groups had thereby incurred Allah's curse. (Qur'an 9:30). Allah singled out the Christians for particular criticism:

> They take their priests and their anchorites to be their lords in derogation of Allah, and (they take as their Lord) Christ the son of Mary; yet they were commanded to worship but one Allah.... There are indeed many among the priests and anchorites, who in Falsehood devour the substance of men and hinder (them) from the way of Allah. And there are those who bury gold and silver and spend it not in the way of Allah: announce unto them a most grievous penalty. On the Day when heat will be produced out of that (wealth) in the fire of

Hell, and with it will be branded their foreheads, their flanks,
and their backs, their flanks, and their backs: "This is the (treasure) which ye buried for yourselves: taste ye, then, the (treasures) ye buried!" (Qur'an 9:31-2, 33-5).

Muhammad's wrath could also extend to Muslims who ignored Allah's
messenger. On the way back from Tabuk, he received news about a
mosque that a group of Muslims had built in opposition to his authority.
Allah gave him a revelation making clear the malign intent of the builders:
"They will indeed swear that their intention is nothing but good; but Allah
doth declare that they are certainly liars" (Qur'an 9:107). Muhammad
ordered his followers to burn the mosque to the ground.[32]

The Prophet of Islam received more revelations scolding those who had
declined to go along on the expedition to Tabuk. Allah reminded the Muslims that their first duty was to him and his prophet, and that those who
refused to wage jihad would face terrible punishment:

> Do ye prefer the life of this world to the Hereafter? But little is
> the comfort of this life, as compared with the Hereafter. Unless
> ye go forth, He will punish you with a grievous penalty, and put
> others in your place. . . . (Qur'an 9:38-39)

Not that Muhammad needed their help:

> . . . Allah did indeed help him, when the Unbelievers drove
> him out: he had no more than one companion; they two were
> in the cave, and he said to his companion, "Have no fear, for
> Allah is with us": then Allah sent down His peace upon him,
> and strengthened him with forces which ye saw not, and hum-
> bled to the depths the word of the Unbelievers (Qur'an 9:40)

Though Muhammad may not have needed the help, jihad for the sake of
Allah (jihad fi sabil Allah, which denotes in Islamic theology armed strug-

gle to establish the hegemony of the Islamic social order) is the best deed
a Muslim can perform. (Qur'an 9:41) The Prophet of Islam emphasized
this on many occasions. Once a man asked him, "Guide me to such a deed
as equals *Jihad* (in reward)."

Muhammad answered: "I do not find such a deed."[33]

For the Muslims who had not accompanied him to Tabuk, Muhammad had more harsh words from Allah. He delivered revelations accusing
them of preferring the easy life to a hard journey of jihad:

> If there had been immediate gain (in sight), and the journey
> easy, they would (all) without doubt have followed thee, but
> the distance was long, (and weighed) on them. They would
> indeed swear by Allah, "If we only could, we should certainly
> have come out with you": They would destroy their own souls;
> for Allah doth know that they are certainly lying. (Qur'an
> 9:42)

Allah even rebuked his prophet for excusing Muslims from the Tabuk expedition. (Qur'an 9:43) He told Muhammad that true Muslims did not hesitate to wage jihad, even to the point of risking their property and their very
lives. The ones who refused to do this weren't believers. (Qur'an 9:44-45)

Singled out for especial criticism were the Bedouin Arabs: "The wandering Arabs are more hard in disbelief and hypocrisy, and more likely to
be ignorant of the limits which Allah hath revealed unto His messenger.
And Allah is Knower, Wise" (Qur'an 9:97). Allah accused some of the
Bedouins of plotting against Muhammad, and warned that their plots
would backfire. (9:98).

Muhammad recited a revelation telling him to be firm against such
hypocrites—and against all the Hypocrites, though their plots against him
had failed: "O Prophet! Strive hard against the unbelievers and the Hypocrites, and be firm against them. Their abode is Hell, an evil refuge indeed.
They swear by Allah that they said nothing (evil), but indeed they uttered
blasphemy, and they did it after accepting Islam…" (Qur'an 9:73-4).

This "striving hard" was, in the context of Muhammad's circumstances, unmistakably a military command—particularly in light of the fact that Allah was guaranteeing Paradise to those who would "fight in the way of Allah and shall slay and be slain" (Qur'an 9:111). On another occasion Muhammad said: "I have been commanded to fight against people, till they testify to the fact that there is no god but Allah, and believe in me (that) I am the messenger (from the Lord) and in all that I have brought. And when they do it, their blood and riches are guaranteed protection on my behalf except where it is justified by law, and their affairs rest with Allah."[34] The obverse is also true: if they do not become Muslims, their blood and riches are not guaranteed any protection from the Muslims.

Collecting the jizya

Muhammad was now the undisputed master of Arabia. The Arabian rulers and tribes that had not yet submitted to his authority now began to journey to Medina to accept his religion and pay him homage. To the lands of those who did not come, Muhammad sent jihad warriors. He sent the fearsome fighter Khalid bin al-Walid to the al-Harith tribe, instructing him to call them to accept Islam three days before he attacked them, and to call off the battle if they converted. Khalid duly told the tribe leaders: "If you accept Islam you will be safe"—whereupon the tribe converted. Khalid notified the Prophet of Islam and sent a deputation from the tribe to Medina to see Muhammad, who told them: "If Khalid had not written to me that you had accepted Islam and had not fought I would throw your heads beneath your feet."[35]

From Himyar in south Arabia came a letter informing Muhammad that the kings of the region had accepted Islam and waged war in Allah's name against the area's remaining pagans. Muhammad was pleased, informing them that "your messenger reached me on my return from the land of the Byzantines and he met us in Medina and conveyed your message and your news and informed us of your Islam and of your killing the polytheists. God has guided you with His guidance."

He detailed their obligations as Muslims and directed that Jews and Christians in their domains should be invited to convert to Islam, but if they refused, they were "not to be turned" from their religions. Rather, the Jew or Christian in these newly Muslim lands "must pay the poll tax—for every adult, male or female, free or slave, one full dinar"—and he gave instructions for how that amount was to be calculated—"or its equivalent in clothes." He reminded the kings that the lives of the Jews and Christians depended on their payment of this tax: "He who pays that to God's apostle has the guarantee of God and His apostle, and he who withholds it is the enemy of God and His apostle."[36]

Ultimately the Prophet of Islam determined that Jews and Christians would no longer be allowed in Arabia at all. "I will expel the Jews and Christians from the Arabian Peninsula," he told his companions, "and will not leave any but Muslims."[37] He gave just such an order on his deathbed. Today the Kingdom of Saudi Arabia labors zealously that the Prophet's wishes in this regard are scrupulously honored.

The jizya tax was so important because, besides raiding, which produced inconsistent results, it was the Muslims' chief source of income. This is clear in a letter Muhammad sent to a Jewish tribe, the Banu Janbah. First he assures them that "under the guarantee of Allah and the guarantee of His Apostle there will be no cruelty or oppression on you. Verily, the Apostle of Allah will defend you." However: " Verily, it is binding on you to pay one-fourth of the yield of your date-palms, and one-fourth of your game from the rivers, and one-fourth of what your women spin."[38] Likewise, to a Christian ruler Muhammad wrote:

> I will not fight against you unless I write to you in advance. So, join the fold of Islam or pay the *jizyah*. Obey Allah and His Apostle and the messengers of His Apostle, honour them and dress them in nice clothes.... Provide Zayd with good clothes. If my messengers will be pleased with you, I shall also be pleased with you.... Pay three *wasaq* of barley to Harmalah...[39]

The onerous tax burdens that Jews and Christians in Muslims domains incurred for the privilege of being allowed to live in relative peace would become the key source of income for the great Islamic empires that carried Muhammad's jihad into Africa, Europe, and Asia.[40]

The last pilgrimage: the rights of women and the expulsion of the pagans

After returning from Tabuk, Muhammad made one last pilgrimage to Mecca, during which he instructed the Muslims how they were to perform the hajj, the great pilgrimage that all Muslims must make to Mecca at least once during their lifetimes. He addressed the pilgrims, making various stipulations, including the declaration that "God has decreed that there is to be no usury." With the usual exceptions made for the non-devout, Muslims have more or less scrupulously followed this prohibition throughout history; in our own day it has led to the establishment of interest-free loans and other arrangements to accommodate Muslims in the West.

Muhammad also established the Islamic lunar calendar as consisting of twelve months, without an additional month to make up the difference between the lunar and solar calendars; thus the Islamic months do not occur at fixed times, but move through the year. Then he turned to the relationship between husbands and wives:

> You have rights over your wives and they have rights over you. You have the right that they should not defile your bed and that they should not behave with open unseemliness. If they do, God allows you to put them in separate rooms and to beat them but not with severity. If they refrain from these things they have the right to their food and clothing with kindness. Lay injunctions on women kindly, for they are prisoners with you having no control of their persons. You have taken them only as a trust from God, and you have the enjoyment of their persons by the words of God. . . . [41]

This was in accord with revelations Muhammad had received from Allah concerning women, which included the beating of disobedient wives:

> So good women are the obedient, guarding in secret that which Allah hath guarded. As for those from whom ye fear rebellion, admonish them and banish them to beds apart, and scourge them. Then if they obey you, seek not a way against them. (Qur'an 4:34)

Muhammad also gave the unbelievers four months to leave Arabia, offering a revelation from Allah and calling them one more time to Islam. (Qur'an 9:1-3).

These unbelievers were pagan Arabs, not Jews and Christians—hence here there is no mention of the jizya option he had already offered to the latter. For Jews and Christians the choices were conversion, subjugation, or war; for the pagans the choices were only conversion or war. He noted that only those unbelievers who converted to Islam would be able to maintain the alliances they had established with the Muslims. The Muslims were to kill the others after the four-month guarantee of safety had ended:

> ... if they repent, and establish regular prayers and practice regular charity, then open the way for them: for Allah is Oft-forgiving, Most Merciful. (Qur'an 9:4-6)

To "repent, and establish regular prayers and practise regular charity" meant to adopt Islam: in Arabic the words used here are *salat* for prayers and *zakat* for charity: two of what have come to be known as the pillars of Islam. Only conversion to Islam would save the lives of the unbelievers, and only the hope that they would accept Islam would gain them mercy from the Muslims, for the sins of the unbelievers were egregious. (Qur'an 9:6-11)

Thus when the Islamic jihad armies swept into Hindu India, they were much more brutal than they were in Europe—for Europe's Christians had the option of living as dhimmis, while the pagan Indians did not (though for practical reasons they were later accorded dhimmi status). Historian Sita Ram Goel observes that the Muslim invaders of India paid no respect to codes of warfare that had prevailed there for centuries:

> Islamic imperialism came with a different code—the Sunnah [tradition] of the Prophet. It required its warriors to fall upon the helpless civil population after a decisive victory had been won on the battlefield. It required them to sack and burn down villages and towns after the defenders had died fighting or had fled. The cows, the Brahmins, and the Bhikshus invited their special attention in mass murders of non-combatants. The temples and monasteries were their special targets in an orgy of pillage and arson. Those whom they did not kill, they captured and sold as slaves. The magnitude of the booty looted even from the bodies of the dead, was a measure of the success of the military mission. And they did all this as *mujahids* (holy warriors) and *ghazis* (*kafir* [unbeliever]-killers) in the service of Allah and his Last Prophet.[42]

The murder of the poets

Muhammad at this point was determined to wipe out every remnant of opposition to his rule. He set his sights now on two poets, Abu 'Afak and 'Asma bint Marwan, who had mocked him and his prophetic pretensions in their verses.

Abu 'Afak was reputed to be over one hundred years old, and had dared to criticize in verse Muhammad's killing of another of his opponents. Muhammad asked his men, "Who will deal with this rascal for me?" He found a ready volunteer in a young Muslim named Salim bin 'Umayr, who dispatched the old poet as he lay sleeping.[43]

'Asma bint Marwan, a poetess, was incensed when she heard of the murder of Abu 'Afak. She wrote verses denigrating the men of Medina for obeying "a stranger who is none of yours," and asked, "Is there no man of pride who would attack him by surprise and cut off the hopes of those who expect aught from him?"[44]

When Muhammad heard of this, he looked for a volunteer to kill her: "Who will rid me of Marwan's daughter?" A Muslim named 'Umayr bin 'Adiy al-Khatmi took the job, and killed her along with her unborn child that very night. But after he had done the deed, 'Umayr began to worry that perhaps he had committed a grave sin. Muhammad reassured him: "You have helped God and His apostle, O 'Umayr!" But would he incur punishment?

"Two goats," replied the Prophet of Islam, "won't butt their heads about her."

The men of 'Asma bint Marwan's tribe, the Banu Khatma, "saw the power of Islam" in her killing—so says Ibn Ishaq. They duly acknowledged Muhammad as the Prophet of Allah.[45]

Muhammad's final illness

Muhammad was in the midst of consolidating his power and planning further expansion of his burgeoning empire—he had just ordered jihad warriors into the Byzantine holdings of Syria and Palestine—when he fell ill. According to Islamic tradition, he foresaw his end approaching. A few months before his final illness began he received one last, brief Qur'anic revelation, and he believed it was telling him to ask for Allah's mercy in preparation for his own death: "When comes the help of Allah, and victory, and thou dost see the people enter Allah's religion in crowds, celebrate the praises of thy Lord, and pray for His Forgiveness: for He is Oft-Returning (in Grace and Mercy)" (110:1-3).[46] Aisha said later that he told her: "Gabriel used to recite the Qur'an to me once a year and for this year it was twice and so I perceived that my death had drawn near."[47]

The final illness of the Prophet of Islam began one day when Aisha complained of a headache. Muhammad said he wished he would outlive her, but knew that was not to be. Referring to her headache, he said: "I wish that had happened while I was still living, for then I would ask Allah's forgiveness for you and invoke Allah for you."

Aisha responded to this with tart playfulness: "By Allah, I think you want me to die; and if this should happen, you would spend the last part of the day sleeping with one of your wives!"

But Muhammad was in no mood to be playful. He told Aisha that it was he whose headache was more severe, and intimating that his illness could be terminal.[48] As his illness progressed, he grew anxious over the fact that he had to move, spending each night in the house of a different wife, as had been his practice ever since he began practicing polygamy. He would cry out anxiously, "Where will I be tomorrow? Where will I be tomorrow?" Finally his other wives allowed him to stay in the home of his favorite wife, Aisha.[49]

As we have seen, he experienced pain that reminded him of his poisoning at Khaybar several years earlier: "O 'Aisha! I still feel the pain caused by the food I ate at Khaibar, and at this time, I feel as if my aorta is being cut from that poison."[50]

As he lay ill, he recited over and over the two suras of the Qur'an that are now placed at the book's end, which are known collectively as Al-Mu'awwidhatan (the two suras of taking refuge in Allah from evil):

> Say: I seek refuge with the Lord of the Dawn
> From the mischief of created things;
> From the mischief of Darkness as it overspreads;
> From the mischief of those who practise secret arts;
> And from the mischief of the envious one as he practises envy.
>   (113:1-5)
> Say: I seek refuge with the Lord and Cherisher of Mankind,
> The King (or Ruler) of Mankind,
> The god (or judge) of mankind,
> From the mischief of the Whisperer (of Evil), who withdraws
>   (after his whisper),
> (The same) who whispers into the hearts of mankind,
> Among Jinns and among men. (114:1-6)[51]

He asked the believers who had gathered around his bedside to give him something to write on, "so that I may write to you something after which you will never go astray." But instead the Muslims fell to bickering about how ill Muhammad really was, until finally he ordered them out of the room. But before they left, he gave them two orders: "Turn *Al-Mushrikun* [polytheists, pagans, idolaters, and disbelievers in the Oneness of Allah and in His Messenger Muhammad] out of the 'Arabian Peninsula; respect and give gifts to the foreign delegations as you have seen me dealing with them."[52] (The material in brackets here was added by the Saudi translator of the hadith of Bukhari; the word Al-Mushrikun is generally translated as "unbelievers.")

The unbelievers were much on his mind even as he lay ill. Some Islamic traditions even claim that the Jews "bewitched" Muhammad.[53] When some of his wives began discussing a beautiful church they had seen in Abyssinia, festooned with gorgeous icons, Muhammad sat up and said: "Those are the people who, whenever a pious man dies amongst them, make a place of worship at his grave and then they make those pictures in it. Those are the worst creatures in the sight of Allah."[54] He added: "Allah cursed the Jews and the Christians because they took the graves of their Prophets as places for worship."[55] Aisha observed that had Muhammad not said this, "his grave would have been made conspicuous."[56]

At one point those assembled around his bedside poured medicine into his mouth, ignoring his protesting gestures. When he felt a bit better, he asked them, "Didn't I forbid you to pour medicine in my mouth?" They replied that they thought he was just being a typical patient, expressing a dislike for medicine, but Muhammad was not appeased. He ordered as a punishment that everyone who had been present when he was given the medicine now have medicine poured into his own mouth.[57]

Looking back on his prophetic career, Muhammad remarked: "I have been sent with the shortest expressions bearing the widest meanings, and I have been made victorious with terror (cast in the hearts of the enemy), and while I was sleeping, the keys of the treasures of the world were brought to me and put in my hand."[58] It is one of his most arresting statements. It is true that his Qur'an is quite brief, especially in comparison to the Old and even the New Testaments; whether its contents truly bear the "widest meanings," however, is a matter for the contention of theologians. That he was made "victorious with terror" is undeniable, given the tumultuous history of his prophetic career, with its raids, wars, and assassinations.

Muhammad was referring, of course, not to terror in the modern sense of terrorism but to the terror that Allah would cast into the hearts of unbelievers (cf. Qur'an 3:151; 7:4-5; 8:12; 8:60; etc.)—something akin to what Jews and Christians know as the "fear of God." But for him, that terror was inseparable from the terror his warriors cast into the hearts of their opponents, because for him, they were the instruments of Allah's wrath. And certainly those warriors, and the theology that promised them booty in this world and endless physical pleasures in the next if they but fought for Islam, would put into Muhammad's hand "the keys of the treasures of the world." Those treasures would belong to the Muslims—by means of terror, the terror of Allah.

Finally the end came. Said Aisha: "It was one of the favours of Allah bestowed upon me that Allah's Messenger expired in my house on the day of my turn while he was leaning against my chest, and Allah made my saliva mix with his saliva at his death."[59] She noted that "Allah's Messenger died when he was sixty-three years of age."[60] It was June 8, 632.

Muhammad, the master of Arabia, the founder and Prophet of Islam, left behind very little property. He had expended most of his resources in the cause of jihad. The one thing he most certainly bestowed upon the world was the religion of Islam. And through the centuries, the Muslims who revered him as the most excellent example of conduct would take with utmost seriousness his injunctions to wage warfare on its behalf.

After Muhammad

The Prophet of Islam left no clear successor; his fatal illness apparently came upon him too suddenly. He had daughters, but he had no son: the one boy born to him, Ibrahim, whose mother was Muhammad's concubine Mary the Copt, died at only sixteen months old. ("If Ibrahim had lived," Muhammad declared, "I would have exempted every Copt from poll-tax"—that is, jizya.[61])

According to some traditions, Muhammad appointed Abu Bakr as his successor: Aisha named him as the one Muhammad would have chosen if he had picked someone to succeed him.[62] Significantly, during his final illness Muhammad ordered that Abu Bakr take his place in leading the Muslims in prayer.[63] And indeed, after Muhammad's death Abu Bakr did become the first caliph.

But a faction of the Muslims maintained that Muhammad had actually appointed Ali as his successor. One tradition has Muhammad asking Ali, "Aren't you satisfied with being unto me what Aaron was unto Moses?"[64] This suggests succession, for in the Qur'an Moses says to Aaron, "Take my place among the people" (7:142). However, Aisha scoffed at the idea that Muhammad had chosen Ali to succeed him (perhaps she was still smarting over the cavalier way in which Ali reminded Muhammad that women were plentiful when she was accused of adultery). When some said that Muhammad had willed Ali to be his successor, she responded: "When did he appoint him by will? Verily, when he died he was resting against my chest (or said: in my lap) and he asked for a washbasin and then collapsed while in that state, and I could not even perceive that he had died, so when did he appoint him by will?"[65]

The controversy simmered during the early years of Islam, as Abu Bakr was succeeded by Umar and then Uthman. Each was opposed by a party of Muslims who insisted that the successor of Muhammad should only be someone from Muhammad's own family (Ali was Muhammad's cousin and son-in-law, the husband of his daughter Fatima). Finally he was chosen as the fourth caliph in 656, but was assassinated in 661.

The *Shi'at Ali*, or Party of Ali, known popularly as the Shi'a, did not give up. Their split from the larger group of Muslims widened and became more acrimonious, and continues to this day. Over the centuries Shi'ites evolved expressions of Islamic piety that at times differed quite markedly from the norms of the larger Muslim body, the Sunnis (so called because of their self-proclaimed adherence to the Sunnah, or traditions, of Muhammad).

Shi'a Muslims make up only about 15 percent of the worldwide Muslim community, but with a huge majority in Iran, a majority in Iraq, and significant minorities in other Muslim countries, they remain a force with which the Sunnis must reckon. The Sunni-Shi'ite fault line within Islam has given rise to considerable violence over the centuries, and in the twenty-first century threatens to erupt again into open war in Iraq, Pakistan, and elsewhere.

It is a legacy entirely in keeping with the attitudes and behavior of the Prophet of Islam.

CHAPTER TEN

Muhammad's legacy

◈ Was Muhammad a pedophile?

◈ Was Muhammad a misogynist?

◈ Muhammad's warlike example

◈ Islam's draconian punishments

◈ Is Islam really tolerant of other religions?

◈ Muhammad's gentle side

◈ How jihadists today imitate Muhammad

◈ What is to be done

The War on Terror

WITH THE SEPTEMBER 11, 2001, JIHAD TERROR ATTACKS, Muhammad became more controversial than ever before in the Western world. Numerous analysts and commentators made assertions about him and the religion he founded without ever bothering to investigate the actual record. Since knowledge about Muhammad in the West has always been sketchy, they can be excused; however, many of the questions on which his example was invoked and discussed are still relevant to the War on Terror and the relationship between the Muslim and non-Muslim worlds.

Thus ignorance is increasingly a luxury the West can ill afford. Because jihadists (as well as ordinary Muslims) the world over invoke Muhammad as their example and guide, it is vitally important to know what Muhammad really said and how he lived.

Pedophile prophet?

In 2002, Jerry Vines, former president of the Southern Baptist Convention, said: "Christianity was founded by the virgin-born Jesus Christ. Islam was founded by Mohammed, a demon-possessed pedophile who had twelve wives, and his last one was a nine-year-old girl."[1] Vines's words stirred immense controversy, most of which centered around his alleged "Islamophobia," without examining the factual basis for his words. The Council on American-Islamic Relations called on President Bush and religious leaders to denounce Vines's "reckless, Islamophobic statements."[2]

Yet of these facts there can be little doubt. According to ahadith reported by Bukhari, the Prophet of Islam "married Aisha when she was a girl of six years of age, and he consumed [i.e., consummated] that marriage when she was nine years old."[3] He was at this time in his early fifties. Many Islamic apologists claim—in the teeth of this evidence—that Aisha was actually older. Karen Armstrong asserts that "Tabari says that she was so young that she stayed in her parents' home and the marriage was consummated there later when she had reached puberty."[4] Unfortunately, her readers are unlikely to have volumes of Tabari on hand to check her assertion; contrary to Armstrong's account, the Muslim historian quotes Aisha thusly: "The Messenger of God married me when I was seven; my marriage was consummated when I was nine."[5]

However, other Muslim spokesmen acknowledge what the records say. Islamic scholar Muhammad Ali Al-Hanooti said that Muhammad's marriage to Aisha was the will of Allah, and "Allah usually is not the one who we are allowed to argue with for any ordinance or commandment. The Qur'an says, 'He is not questioned for what He does, but they (people) are questioned for what they do.' Aisha got married when she was nine, when the Prophet (SAAWS) died, she was nineteen.... What is wrong in her marriage of six or nine or whatsoever?"[6]

Child marriages were common in seventh-century Arabia. It is noteworthy that there is no record in the Qur'an or Hadith of Muhammad having to defend his marriage to Aisha—in sharp contrast to his obvious defensiveness over his marriage to his former daughter-in-law, Zaynab bint Jahsh. Moreover, the Qur'an describes a culture in which child marriage is taken for granted. In its directives about the waiting period required in order to determine if one's wife is pregnant before divorcing her, it says: "If you are in doubt concerning those of your wives who have ceased menstruating, know that their waiting period shall be three months. The same shall apply to *those who have not yet menstruated*" (Qur'an 65:4, emphasis added). In this revelation Allah envisions a scenario in which a prepubescent woman is not only married, but also divorced by her husband.

So was Muhammad a pedophile? The concept of pedophilia as a manifestation of deviant sexuality did not exist in the seventh century. In marrying Aisha, Muhammad was doing no more and no less than what was done by many men of his time, and no one thought twice about the matter until much later. From this perspective, Vines's charge is a bit anachronistic. However, in light of Muhammad's status for Muslims as the supreme example of human behavior, his marriage to Aisha becomes more important. Problems arise when an action like this is forcibly removed from its historical context and proposed as a paradigm for human beings of all times and places. Yet this is exactly what has happened in the *umma*. Imitating the Prophet of Islam, many Muslims even in modern times have taken child brides. In some places this even has the blessing of the law: article 1041 of the Civil Code of the Islamic Republic of Iran states that girls can be engaged before the age of nine, and married at nine: "Marriage before puberty (nine full lunar years for girls) is prohibited. Marriage contracted before reaching puberty with the permission of the guardian is valid provided that the interests of the ward are duly observed."[7]

The Ayatollah Khomeini himself married a ten-year-old girl when he was twenty-eight.[8] Khomeini called marriage to a prepubescent girl "a divine blessing," and advised the faithful: "Do your best to ensure that your daughters do not see their first blood in your house."[9]

Time magazine reported in 2001:

> In Iran the legal age for marriage is nine for girls, fourteen for boys. The law has occasionally been exploited by pedophiles, who marry poor young girls from the provinces, use and then abandon them. In 2000 the Iranian Parliament voted to raise the minimum age for girls to fourteen, but this year, a legislative oversight body dominated by traditional clerics vetoed the move. An attempt by conservatives to abolish Yemen's legal minimum age of fifteen for girls failed, but local experts say it is rarely enforced anyway. (The onset of puberty is considered an appropriate time for a marriage to be consummated.)[10]

The United Nations Children's Fund (UNICEF) reports that over half of the girls in Afghanistan and Bangladesh are married before they reach the age of eighteen.[11] In early 2002, researchers in refugee camps in Afghanistan and Pakistan found half the girls married by age thirteen. In an Afghan refugee camp, more than two out of three second-grade girls were either married or engaged, and virtually all the girls who were beyond second grade were already married. One ten-year-old was engaged to a man of sixty.[12]

This is the price that women have paid throughout Islamic history, and continue to pay, for Muhammad's status as "an excellent example of conduct" (Qur'an 33:21).

Misogynist?

Muhammad had many wives; lists vary but usually include eleven to thirteen women. Islamic tradition invests him with superhuman prowess: "Gabriel brought a kettle from which I ate," he says, "and I was given the power of sexual intercourse equal to forty men."[13] Contemporary Islamic apologists assert, in contrast, that his many marriages were matters not of lust but of cementing political alliances. One Muslim biographer of the Prophet of Islam surveys the circumstances of each of his marriages and concludes: "Thus do we see that each of these marriages had some solid reasons behind it; passion and lust were not among them."[14] While it is impossible to determine such a thing, there is no doubt that the laws Muhammad laid down for women have given them numerous disadvantages in Islamic societies to this day.

The Qur'an likens a woman to a field (tilth), to be used by a man as he wills: "Your women are a tilth for you (to cultivate) so go to your tilth as ye will" (2:223). It declares that a woman's testimony is worth half that of a man: "Get two witnesses, out of your own men, and if there are not two men, then a man and two women, such as ye choose, for witnesses, so that if one of them errs, the other can remind her" (2:282). It allows men to marry up to four wives, and have sex with slave girls ("captives that your right hands possess") also: "If ye fear that ye shall not be able to deal justly with the orphans, marry women of your choice, two or three or four; but if ye fear that ye shall not be able to deal justly (with them), then only one, or (a captive) that your right hands possess, that will be more suitable, to prevent you from doing injustice" (4:3).

The Qur'an also rules that a son's inheritance should be twice the size of a daughter's: "Allah (thus) directs you as regards your children's (inheritance): to the male, a portion equal to that of two females" (4:11). Worst of all, it tells husbands to beat their disobedient wives: "Men are in charge of women, because Allah hath made the one of them to excel the other, and because they spend of their property (for the support of women). So good women are the obedient, guarding in secret that which Allah hath guarded. As for those from whom ye fear rebellion, admonish them and banish them to beds apart, and scourge them" (4:34).

Muhammad also says that hell will be filled with more women than men: "O women! Give alms, as I have seen that the majority of the dwellers of Hell-fire were you (women).... You curse frequently and are ungrateful to your husbands. I have not seen anyone more deficient in intelligence and religion than you. A cautious sensible man could be led astray by some of you."[15]

With statements like these from the Qur'an and Muhammad, it is no wonder that women in the Islamic world suffer such inequalities.

Draconian punishments?

Two stiff penalties—stoning for adultery and amputation for theft—define Islamic sharia law for many Westerners, and indeed, they are emblematic of its pre-medieval harshness and unsuitability for the contemporary world. However, making inroads against them as core elements of sharia law will be difficult.

Famously, Muhammad challenged the Jews for concealing the penalty of stoning for adultery in the Torah. Islamic apologists in the West like to point out that the Qur'an does not contain this command. It only commands lashes for stoning: "The woman and the man guilty of adultery or fornication, flog each of them with a hundred stripes. Let not compassion move you in their case, in a matter prescribed by Allah, if ye believe in Allah and the Last Day: and let a party of the Believers witness their punishment" (24:2). Allah also directs that adulterous women be confined to their homes until they die: "If any of your women are guilty of lewdness, take the evidence of four (reliable) witnesses from amongst you against them; and if they testify, confine them to houses until death do claim them, or Allah ordain for them some (other) way" (Qur'an 4:15).

These punishments are harsh enough, but at least they seem to hold out some hope that the traditional Islamic penalty of stoning for adultery, which is still carried out in states that enforce sharia in its fullness, can be mitigated. However, that hope is illusory. The Hadith says that there is more to the story. According to Umar, the Qur'an originally contained a verse enjoining stoning for adultery, but it was inadvertently dropped:

Allah sent Muhammad with the Truth and revealed the Book (the Qur'an) to him, and among what Allah revealed, was the Verse of the *Rajm* (the stoning of married person—male and female) who commits illegal sexual intercourse, and we did recite this Verse and understood and memorized it. Allah's Messenger did carry out the punishment of stoning and so did we after him.

I am afraid that after a long time has passed, somebody will say, "By Allah, we do not find the Verse of the *Rajm* in Allah's Book," and thus they will go astray by leaving an obligation which Allah has revealed. And the punishment of the *Rajm* is to be inflicted to any married person (male and female) who commits illegal sexual intercourse if the required evidence is available or there is conception or confession.[16]

It is difficult, if not impossible, for Islamic reformers to make headway against this when Umar specifically warns against them.

The penalty of amputation for theft is even more strongly attested, by a verse that remains in the Qur'an: "As to the thief, male or female, cut off his or her hands: a punishment by way of example, from Allah, for their crime; and Allah is exalted in power" (5:38). The binding words of Allah, applicable then, now, and forever.

Warrior prophet?

Ibn Ishaq reports that Muhammad participated in twenty-seven battles (the parenthetical material beginning with "T" below refers to Tabari's version of the same material):

> The apostle took part personally in twenty-seven (T. six) raids:
> Waddan which was the raid of al-Abwa'.
> Buwat in the direction of Radwa. 'Ushayra in the valley of Yanbu'.
> The first fight at Badr in pursuit of Kurz b. Jabir.
> The great battle of Badr in which God slew the chiefs of Quraysh (T. and their nobles and captured many).
> Banu Sulaym until he reached al-Kudr.

Al-Sawiq in pursuit of Abu. Sufyan b. Harb (T. until he
reached Qarqara al-Kudr).

Ghatafan (T. towards Najd), which is the raid of Dhu Amarr.
Bahran, a mine in the Hijaz (T. above al-Furu').

Uhud.

Hamra'u'l-Asad.

Banu Nadir.

Dhatu'l-Riqa' of Nakhl.

The last battle of Badr.

Dumatu'l-Jandal.

Al-Khandaq. Banul Qurayza.

Banu Lihyan of Hudhayl. Dhu Qarad. Banu'l-Mustaliq of
Khuza'a.

Al-Hudaybiya not intending to fight where the polytheists
opposed his passage.

Khaybar.

Then he went on the accomplished pilgrimage. The occupation of
Mecca.

Hunayn.

Al-Ta'if.

Tabuk.

Muhammad himself fought in nine engagements: Badr; Uhud; al-
Khandaq; Qurayza; al-Mustaliq; Khaybar; the occupation;
Hunayn; and al-Ta'if.[17]

Here again, Muhammad's example is normative. We have seen how
jihadists today invoke Badr and Khaybar to exhort Muslims to fight according to the example of the Prophet. It is difficult, if not impossible, to maintain that Islam is a religion of peace when warfare and booty were among
the chief preoccupations of the Prophet of Islam. Sincere Islamic reformers should confront these facts, instead of ignoring or glossing over them,

and work to devise ways in which Muslims can retreat from the proposition that Muhammad's example is in all ways normative. If they do not do so, one outcome is certain: bloodshed perpetrated in the name of Islam and in imitation of its prophet will continue.

Islamic tolerance?

The Qur'an says: "Those who believe (in the Qur'an), and those who follow the Jewish (scriptures), and the Christians and the Sabians, any who believe in Allah and the Last Day, and work righteousness, shall have their reward with their Lord; on them shall be no fear, nor shall they grieve" (2:62; cf. 5:69 and 22:17). Muslim spokesmen in the West like to quote such verses and to stress the commonality between Islam and Christianity—and sometimes even between Islam and Judaism. They have painted an irenic picture of Islam's respect for its sister "Abrahamic faiths"—and thereby have given many Jews and Christians confidence that Western countries can accept Muslim immigrants in large numbers without any significant disruptions to their pluralistic societies.

The preponderance of the testimony that the Prophet of Islam left in the Qur'an and Hadith favors not tolerance and harmony between Muslims and non-Muslims, but just the opposite. A fundamental component of the Qur'an's view of non-Muslims is the often repeated and implacable belief in its own absolute truth, admitting of no rival: "The Religion before Allah is Islam" (3:19), or, as another translation has it, "The only true faith in God's sight is Islam." Most Jews and Christians ("People of the Book") are wrongdoers: "If only the People of the Book had faith, it were best for them: among them are some who have faith, but most of them are perverted transgressors" (Qur'an 3:110).

As we have seen, the Qur'an implies that Jews and Christians after the time of Muhammad are renegades who have rejected his prophethood out of corruption and malice. Muhammad weaves his charges against Jews and Christians together by condemning Christians for believing that Jesus was crucified, and Jews for believing that they crucified him: "They said (in boast), 'We killed Christ Jesus the son of Mary, the Messenger of Allah'; but they killed him not, nor crucified him, but so it was made to appear to them, and those who differ therein are full of doubts, with no (certain) knowledge, but only conjecture to follow, for of a surety they killed him not" (Qur'an 4:157).

The idea that Jews and Christians are accursed recurs several times in the Qur'an. Both have rejected Allah and his messenger Muhammad:

> Allah did aforetime take a covenant from the Children of Israel.... But because of their breach of their covenant, We cursed them, and made their hearts grow hard; they change the words from their (right) places and forget a good part of the message that was sent them.... From those, too, who call themselves Christians, We did take a covenant, but they forgot a good part of the message that was sent them: so we estranged them, with enmity and hatred between the one and the other, to the day of judgment. (Qur'an 5:12-16)

So far is the Qur'an from modern notions of tolerance and peaceful coexistence that it even warns Muslims not to befriend Jews and Christians— apparently including those who "feel themselves subdued" and are paying the jiyza: "O ye who believe! Take not the Jews and the Christians for your friends and protectors. They are but friends and protectors to each other. And he amongst you that turns to them (for friendship) is of them. Verily Allah guideth not a people unjust." (5:51).

It is ironic in light of all this that the Qur'an also criticizes Jews and Christians for being *intolerant*. Allah warns Muhammad that "never will the Jews or the Christians be satisfied with thee unless thou follow their form of religion. Say: 'The Guidance of Allah, that is the (only) Guidance.' Wert thou to follow their desires after the knowledge which hath reached thee, then wouldst thou find neither Protector nor helper against Allah" (2:120; cf. 2:135).

A hadith amplifies all this:

On the Day of Resurrection, a call-maker will announce, "Let every nation follow that which they used to worship." Then none of those who used to worship anything other than Allah like idols and other deities but will fall in Hell (Fire), till there will remain none but those who used to worship Allah, both those who were obedient (i.e. good) and those who were disobedient (i.e. bad) and the remaining party of the people of the Scripture. Then the Jews will be called upon and it will be said to them, 'Who do you use to worship?' They will say, 'We used to worship Ezra, the son of Allah.' It will be said to them, 'You are liars, for Allah has never taken anyone as a wife or a son. What do you want now?' They will say, 'O our Lord! We are thirsty, so give us something to drink.' They will be directed and addressed thus, 'Will you drink,' whereupon they will be gathered unto Hell (Fire) which will look like a mirage whose different sides will be destroying each other. Then they will fall into the Fire. Afterwards the Christians will be called upon and it will be said to them, 'Who do you use to worship?' They will say, 'We used to worship Jesus, the son of Allah.' It will be said to them, 'You are liars, for Allah has never taken anyone as a wife or a son,' Then it will be said to them, 'What do you want?' They will say what the former people have said. Then, when there remain (in the gathering) none but those who used to worship Allah (Alone, the real Lord of the Worlds) whether they were obedient or disobedient.[18]

Jesus will set things right at the end of the world. According to Islamic eschatology, He will return to end the dhimmi status of non-Muslims in Islamic societies—not by initiating a new era of equality and harmony, but by abolishing Christianity and imposing Islam upon everyone. As Muhammad explained:

By Him in Whose Hands my soul is, surely (Jesus) the son of Mary will soon descend amongst you and will judge mankind

justly (as a Just Ruler); he will break the Cross and kill the
pigs and there will be no Jizya (i.e. taxation taken from non
Muslims).[19]

Another tradition puts it this way: "He will break the cross, kill swine, and
abolish jizyah. Allah will perish all religions except Islam." And another
hadith has Muhammad saying: "How will you be when the son of Mary
(i.e. Jesus) descends amongst you and he will judge people by the Law of
the Qur'an and not by the law of Gospel."[20]

The Jews, meanwhile, will in the end times fare little better. Muhammad said: "The last hour would not come unless the Muslims will fight
against the Jews and the Muslims would kill them until the Jews would
hide themselves behind a stone or a tree and a stone or a tree would say:
Muslim, or the servant of Allah, there is a Jew behind me; come and kill
him."[21]

Combine this stripping-away of all legitimacy from Judaism and Christianity with Muhammad's exhortations to fight against Jews and Christians,
and it is no wonder that the Islamic world has been at odds with Jews and
Christians through the centuries. As the schools of Islamic jurisprudence
developed, they constructed upon these hadiths and passages of the Qur'an
a legal structure for the treatment of non-Muslims. The features of this
remained remarkably consistent across the centuries, and among all the
legal schools. Consider the contemporary Saudi Sheikh Marzouq Salem
Al-Ghamdi, who several years ago explained in a sermon the terms in
which an Islamic society should tolerate the presence of non-Muslims in
its midst:

If the infidels live among the Muslims, in accordance with the
conditions set out by the Prophet—there is nothing wrong with
it provided they pay Jizya to the Islamic treasury. Other conditions are . . . that they do not renovate a church or a monastery,
do not rebuild ones that were destroyed, that they feed for three
days any Muslim who passes by their homes . . . that they rise

when a Muslim wishes to sit, that they do not imitate Muslims
in dress and speech, nor ride horses, nor own swords, nor arm
themselves with any kind of weapon; that they do not sell wine,
do not show the cross, do not ring church bells, do not raise
their voices during prayer, that they shave their hair in front so
as to make them easily identifiable, do not incite anyone
against the Muslims, and do not strike a Muslim.... If they violate these conditions, they have no protection.[22]

In this the sheikh is merely repeating the classic terms of Islamic jurisprudence for the treatment of non-Muslims in Islamic societies—and he
explicitly links these terms to Muhammad's example. We have already seen
how insistent Muhammad was about the collection of the jizya. Meanwhile, the second-class status for Christians and Jews, mandated by Qur'an
9:29's stipulation that they "feel themselves subdued," was first fully articu-
lated by Muhammad's lieutenant Umar during his caliphate (634 to 644),
in terms strikingly similar to those used by Sheikh Marzouq. The Christians making this pact with Umar pledged:

We made a condition on ourselves that we will neither erect
in our areas a monastery, church, or a sanctuary for a monk,
nor restore any place of worship that needs restoration nor use
any of them for the purpose of enmity against Muslims.... We
will not... prevent any of our fellows from embracing Islam,
if they choose to do so. We will respect Muslims, move from
the places we sit in if they choose to sit in them. We will not
imitate their clothing, caps, turbans, sandals, hairstyles,
speech, nicknames and title names, or ride on saddles, hang
swords on the shoulders, collect weapons of any kind or carry
these weapons.... We will not encrypt our stamps in Arabic,
or sell liquor. We will have the front of our hair cut, wear our
customary clothes wherever we are, wear belts around our
waist, refrain from erecting crosses on the outside of our

churches and demonstrating them and our books in public in Muslim fairways and markets. We will not sound the bells in our churches, except discreetly, or raise our voices while reciting our holy books inside our churches in the presence of Muslims....

After these and other rules are fully laid out, the agreement concludes: "These are the conditions that we set against ourselves and followers of our religion in return for safety and protection. If we break any of these promises that we set for your benefit against ourselves, then our *Dhimmah* (promise of protection) is broken and you are allowed to do with us what you are allowed of people of defiance and rebellion."[23]

Even today, although these laws are not fully in force in most countries in the Islamic world, Christians and other non-Muslims still face widespread discrimination and harassment. Robert Hussein Qambar Ali was a Kuwaiti who converted from Islam to Christianity in the 1990s. He was arrested and tried for apostasy, even though the Kuwaiti Constitution guarantees the freedom of religion and says nothing about the traditional Islamic prohibition on conversion to another faith, which, as we have seen, is rooted in the words and deeds of Muhammad. One of Hussein's prosecutors stated: "With grief I have to say that our criminal law does not include a penalty for apostasy. The fact is that the legislature, in our humble opinion, cannot enforce a penalty for apostasy any more or less than what our Allah and his messenger have decreed. The ones who will make the decision about his apostasy are: our Book, the Sunna, the agreement of the prophets and their legislation given by Allah."[24]

It is nothing short of staggering that the myth of Islamic tolerance could have gained such currency in the teeth of Muhammad's open contempt and hatred for Jews and Christians, incitements of violence against them, and calls that they be converted or subjugated. While human nature is everywhere the same and Muslims can, of course, act as tolerantly as anyone else, the example of Muhammad, the highest model for human behavior, constantly pulls them in a different direction. The fact that Western analysts continue to ignore all this demonstrates the ease with which people can be convinced of something they wish to believe, regardless of overwhelming evidence to the contrary.

A kinder, gentler Muhammad

What are we to make of the Muhammad we saw at the start of this book—the one whose "heart was filled with intense love for all humankind irrespective of caste, creed, or color"?[25] The one who had "the opportunity to strike back at those who attacked him, but refrain[ed] from doing so"?[26] Dr. Mohammad Ahmadullah Siddiqi, a professor of journalism and public relations at Western Illinois University, was the founder of the Students Islamic Movement of India (SIMI), which was implicated in the Mumbai bombings of July 2006. He now repudiates the group's violence, and says that he reminded them that "one of the most noticeable things about the Prophet Mohammed as described by the Koran is that he spoke of mercy for humankind. How can the followers of that faith show a fist and think of violence and things like that?"[27]

This Muhammad is not altogether fictional. One of his companions described him as "neither rough nor harsh. He is neither noisy in the markets nor returns evil for evil, but he forgives and pardons."[28] Another said that Muhammad, improbable as it may seem, was "more bashful than a maiden in her seclusion."[29] He "was not a reviler or a curser nor obscene."[30] One of Muhammad's servants remembered that his master never scolded or rebuked him: "So I served the Prophet at home and on journeys; by Allah, he never said to me for anything which I did: Why have you done this like this or, for anything which I did not do: Why have you not done this like this?"[31]

These elements of Muhammad's personality cannot be denied. After all, he must have had a great deal of personal magnetism, as well as charm, in order to command such fierce loyalty among his followers (though then as now, it cannot be denied that the death penalty for leaving the group was a powerful inducement to remain within it). This charm was generally

reserved for believers only; especially in the Medinan period, when his attitudes hardened toward Jews and Christians, Muhammad generally observed
the sharp demarcation between believers and unbelievers that his Qur'an
emphasizes: "Muhammad is the messenger of Allah. And those with him
are hard against the disbelievers and merciful among themselves" (48:29).

Apologists frequently invoke a tradition in which Muhammad showed
respect for the passing of a Jew. As the funeral procession passed by, the
Prophet of Islam stood up. When his followers told him that the dead man
was a Jew, Muhammad replied, "Was he not a human being or did he not
have a soul?"[32] A beautiful sentiment, but it is not sustained in Islamic tradition. It is not recorded when or where this happened, but it is likely to
date from the early period of Muhammad's prophetic career, when he was
trying to compel the Jews to accept his claim of prophethood. A similar
hadith emphasizes Muhammad's conviction that those who rejected him
would burn in hell. A Muslim recounts that "that the bier of a Jew passed
before the Messenger of Allah (may peace be upon him) and (the members of his family) were wailing over him. Upon this he said: You are wailing and he is being punished."[33]

Islamic apologists who quote instances of the Prophet of Islam being
kind or gentle generally do not mention at all his exhortations to make war
against unbelievers until they are converted or subjugated. They do not
mention his raids, his battles, his joy at the assassinations of his enemies—
assassinations he himself ordered. The Muhammad who emerges from
Islamic tradition was, like all men, multifaceted. He was many things to
many people at many different times. Ignoring the unpleasant elements of
his teachings and actions, however, does not make them go away; jihadists
the world over will still commit violence in emulation of their Prophet.

The veneration of Muhammad

The Qur'an's numerous exhortations to the Muslim faithful to obey and imitate Muhammad became the foundation of an intense effusion of devotion
to the Prophet throughout Islamic history. This devotion was particularly pro-

nounced among the mystically inclined. The Persian Sufi mystic Mansur Al-
Hallaj (858–922), perhaps reasoning from his study of the Qur'an, said that
Allah "has not created anything that is dearer to him than Muhammad and
his family."[34] The renowned Sufi philosopher Abu Hamid Muhammad al-
Ghazali (1058–1111) declared that "the key to happiness is to follow the
sunna and to imitate the Messenger of God in all his coming and going, his
movements and rest, in his way of eating, his attitude, his sleep and his talk."[35]

Sometimes this devotion could not avoid excesses. The Persian poet
Rumi (Jalal al-Din Muhammad Rumi, 1207–1273) said that the scent of
roses was that of the sweat of the Prophet of Islam:

> Root and branch of the roses is
> the lovely sweat of Mustafa [that is, Muhammad],
> And by his power the rose's crescent
> grows now into a full moon.[36]

Likewise a modern Arab writer opined that Allah "created Muhammad's
body in such unsurpassable beauty as had neither before him nor after him
been seen in a human being. If the whole beauty of the Prophet were
unveiled before our eyes, they could not bear its splendor."[37]

This kind of thing is excessive, of course, but it only testifies to the centrality of Muhammad in Islamic piety. The contemporary scholar and mystic Frithjof Schuon (1907–1998) ably summed up this centrality. Speaking
of the virtues inculcated by Islam, he states: "It is inconceivable that these
virtues could have been practiced through the centuries down to our time
if the founder of Islam had not personified them in the highest degree....
For Muslims the moral and spiritual worth of the Prophet is not an abstrac-
tion or a supposition; it is a lived reality."[38]

Imitating Muhammad today

It is certain that mujahedin throughout the world see Muhammad as the per-
sonification of the qualities they are trying to embody. His example cannot

be limited to his kindness to his companions and lack of harshness to his servants. When Muslims look to imitate him, they look to the same sources I have used in this book: the Qur'an, the Hadith, and the Sira. They have provided abundant evidence of this in recent years:

- On March 28, 2003, the Palestinian Sheikh Muhammad Abu Al-Hunud warned in a sermon broadcast over Palestinian Authority television against those who would attempt to "mess with Allah's book, to Americanize the region, Americanize the religion, Americanize the Koran, Americanize Muhammad's message. . . ." Any doubt that he meant by this that the Qur'an and Muhammad's message would be stripped of their violent components were dispelled when he prayed about the Americans in Iraq: "Allah, make their possessions a booty for the Muslims, Allah, annihilate them and their weapons, Allah, make their children orphans and their women widows. . . ."[39]
- On September 5, 2003, Sheikh Ibrahim Mudeiris invoked Muhammad's battles when speaking of the Iraq war in another sermon broadcast by the Palestinian Authority, though his memory of the Battle of Tabuk was a bit faulty: "If we go back in the time tunnel 1400 years, we will find that history repeats itself. . . . Byzantium represents America in the west. . . . America will collapse, as Byzantium collapsed in the west. . . . The Prophet [Muhammad] could, by means of unbroken ranks, conquer Byzantium, the greatest power compared to today's America—and this without a single martyr falling from among the Muslims. . . . The Prophet could, by means of the unity of the Muslim ranks and its awakening, defeat the America of that time. . . . America is our No. 1 enemy, and we see it as our No. 1 enemy as long as we learn from the lessons of the Battle of Tabouk [which took place in

October 630 AD]: 'Make ready for them whatever you can of armed strength and of mounted pickets' [Koran 8:60]. We are prepared and ready, but victory is from Allah...."[40]

◈ On November 21, 2003, Muslims poured out of the Maiduguri Road Central Mosque after Friday prayers in the Nigerian city of Kaduna, demanding the implementation of sharia law and distributing flyers stating: "The only solution is Jihad, the type of jihad put into practise by Prophet Muhammed and exemplified by Shehu Usman Dan Fodio and the late Ayatollah Khomeini of Iran. We Muslims should unite and embrace this concept of jihad that will undoubtedly empower us to destroy oppression and oppressors, and in its place establish Islam."[41]

◈ As late as November 2003, the website of the Islamic Affairs Department (IAD) of the Saudi Arabian embassy in Washington, D.C., contained exhortations to Muslims to wage violent jihad in emulation of Muhammad: "The Muslims are required to raise the banner of Jihad in order to make the Word of Allah supreme in this world, to remove all forms of injustice and oppression, and to defend the Muslims. If Muslims do not take up the sword, the evil tyrants of this earth will be able to continue oppressing the weak and [the] helpless...." It quotes Muhammad delivering Allah's words: "Whoever of My slaves comes out to fight in My way seeking My pleasure, I guarantee him that I will compensate his suffering with reward and booty (during his lifetime) and if he dies, I would forgive him, have mercy on him and let him enter Paradise."[42]

◈ In December 2003, an Iraqi jihad warrior explained why he was fighting against the American troops there: "The religious principle is that we cannot accept to live with infidels. The Prophet Muhammad, peace be on him, said, 'Hit the infidels wherever you find them.'" The man was, of course, quoting not a saying of Muhammad but Qur'an 9:5, the "Verse of the Sword"—but it is easy to see why he would confuse the two.[43]

- Fawwaz bin Muhammad Al-Nashami, the commander of the jihad group that killed twenty-two people in a jihad attack in Khobar, Saudi Arabia, on May 29, 2004, said that he acted in accord with Muhammad's wishes for Arabia: "We are Mujahideen, and we want the Americans. We have not come to aim a weapon at the Muslims, but to purge the Arabian Peninsula, according to the will of our Prophet Muhammad, of the infidels and the polytheists who are killing our brothers in Afghanistan and Iraq....We began to comb the site looking for infidels. We found Filipino Christians. We cut their throats and dedicated them to our brothers the Mujahideen in the Philippines. [Likewise], we found Hindu engineers and we cut their throats too, Allah be praised. That same day, we purged Muhammad's land of many Christians and polytheists."[44]

- In the run-up to the 2004 American presidential election, a Muslim preacher invoked Muhammad to denounce democracy: "Our Prophet did not run for office in any election.... He did not win any political debate. [Instead] he won the war against the infidel."[45]

- A jihadist explaining that the Israeli/Palestinian struggle was more than just a nationalist conflict over land declared: "But all of these people don't realize that our struggle with the Jews goes way back, ever since the first Islamic state was established in Madeenah with Muhammad (SAWS) the Messenger sent to all of mankind, as its leader. Allaah has related to us in the Qur'ân, the reality of the Jews' malice and hatred for the ummah of Islaam and Tawheed, as he says: 'You will

surely find that the people with the most enmity towards the
believers are the Jews and the polytheists.'" (Surah Al-Maa'i-
dah: 82) [Qur'an 5:82].[46]

◈ In October 2004, Sheikh Aamer Bin Abdallah Al-Aamer
wrote this in the Al-Qaeda online journal *Sawt al-Jihad*: "Perform the Jihad against your enemies with your [own two]
hands, sacrifice your souls and your property in fighting your
enemy, as an imitation of [the acts of] your Prophet [Muham-
mad] in the month of Ramadan [and in order to] enrage your
enemies."[47]

◈ The influential American convert to Islam Hamza Yusuf in
November 2004 invoked the Treaty of Hudaybiyya in exhort-
ing Muslims to advance strategically toward their goals.
"There are times when you have to live like a sheep," he
explained, "in order to live in the future like a lion."[48]

◈ In a January 2005 article in *Arab News*, columnist Adil Salahi
reminded his readers that Muhammad never made war on a
people without first inviting them to convert to Islam: "During the Prophet's (peace be upon him) lifetime the Muslim
community had to fight many battles, because there were several sources of danger and many opponents who were keen to
suppress the rising voice of the Islamic message. The Prophet
made sure that in none of these battles the Muslims would
exceed the limits of what is lawful in Islam.... [H]e would not
launch an attack without alerting the enemy and calling on
them to accept Islam and live in peace with the Muslim
state."[49] (In May 2006, President Mahmoud Ahmadinejad of
Iran sent a letter to American president George W. Bush, a
letter which he later explained was a call to Islam: "The letter was an invitation to monotheism and justice, which are
common to all divine prophets. If the call is responded posi-
tively, there will be no more problems to be solved."[50])

◉ London Muslim leader Hani Al-Sibaai in February 2005 justified the slaughters being perpetrated by Al-Zarqawi's mujahedin in Iraq: "Do these people base themselves on Islamic
law or not? They claim that they do, and to support it, they
say that slaughtering appeared in a hadith by the Prophet,
which was pronounces authentic by Sheik Ahmad Shaker.
The Prophet told the Quraysh tribe: 'I have brought slaughter upon you,' making this gesture. But these are religious
issues that may be disputed.... [T]he Prophet drove nails
into and gouged out the eyes of people from the 'Urayna
Tribe. They were merely a group of thieves who stole from
sheep herders, and the Prophet drove nails into them and
threw them into the Al-Hrara area, and left them there to die.
He blinded them and cut off their opposite legs and arms.
This is what the Prophet did on a trifling matter—let alone
in war."[51]

◉ As we saw in chapter eight, in July 2006 a writer on a British
Muslim Internet forum declared: "I'm so fed up with these
dirty, filthy Israeli dogs. May Allah curse them and destroy
them all, and may they face the same fate as Banu
Qurayzah!"[52]

Most Western government and law enforcement officials would dismiss all
this and similar examples as manifestations of the twisting or hijacking of
Islam. But we have seen that all the words and deeds of Muhammad to
which the jihadists refer are amply attested in early Islamic traditions. Nor
is there a wealth of material in those traditions offering a radically different
view of Muhammad.

This explains, of course, why Western officials refer confidently to
mainstream Muslims who abhor terrorism and accept Western pluralism,
but have so much trouble finding reliable spokesmen for this alleged
majority. Such officials often place themselves in the peculiar position of
maintaining that Muslim supporters of terror are only a tiny minority, but

acknowledging at the same time that this tiny minority controls the leadership of virtually every significant Muslim body—and evidently the vast majority that rejects jihad violence can do nothing to dislodge them from these positions of power.

Frightening reality

Of course, many non-Muslims cannot accept the reality of what Muhammad did and taught because its implications are simply too frightening. Many assume that identifying the elements of Islam that today fuel jihad violence and subversive, nonviolent efforts to spread sharia in the West will end up creating a "clash of civilizations" and pitting the West against the entire Islamic world. More than a few analysts believe that if Western governments and media ignore or downplay these facts about Islam, they will be able to head off such a global conflict and empower reformers within the Islamic world.

It should be clear from the above examples that Islamic jihadists are already well aware of the elements of Muhammad's life that they can use to support their actions. They are invoking Muhammad in this way all over the world. It is absurd to think that if Western officials and media outlets refuse to acknowledge that this is being done, it will stop happening. The only way sincere Muslim reformers (as opposed to the many who pose as such but offer only the vaguest condemnations of "terrorism," without even identifying who the terrorists are) can possibly make any headway among Muslims is not by denying that these aspects of Islam even exist—the jihadists know better. Instead, their only hope of succeeding, as slim as it is, is to acknowledge and confront the words and deeds of Muhammad and the doctrines of Islam that teach jihad violence and sharia supremacism, and to construct a case for the rejection of Qur'anic literalism and the definitive discarding of these teachings. But this will, of course, leave them vulnerable to charges from jihadists that they are disloyal to Muhammad and Islam, and that in itself will prevent them from gaining significant ground in the Islamic world.

What is to be done

What, then, can non-Muslim governments do? Many things, including:

- *Stop insisting that Islam is a religion of peace.* This is false, and falsehoods are never productive. There is in fact no need for the president of the United States or the prime minister of Great Britain or any Western leader to make any pronouncements about the nature of Islam at all. They would be much wiser to limit themselves to declaring that their foes wish to impose Islamic sharia rule upon their countries and the world, and that they are going to lead the resistance to that.

- *Initiate a full-scale Manhattan Project to find new energy sources.* During World War II, the United States invested millions and set the brightest scientific minds in the world on the atomic bomb project. A similar effort must be made today to end the Western dependence on oil from the Islamic world — a dependence that deforms the foreign policies of Western nations, preventing them from taking all the steps that they must take in order to defend themselves from the jihad that Muhammad preached.

- *Make Western aid contingent upon renunciation of the jihad ideology.* If Western states acknowledged the existence of a global imperialist Islamic imperative, they could make aid to states like Egypt and Pakistan — in which secular governments generally tolerate the proliferation of jihadist teachings in mosques and Islamic schools — contingent upon the active rejection of those teachings and positive steps against them by the governments of each state. These countries and others profess to reject the contemporary jihad of Osama bin Laden and like-minded mujahedin; let them make good on their rejection, if it is sincere, by developing programs for Islamic schools that explain why Muhammad's exhortations to warfare and supremacism no longer have any merit in today's world or in the future.

◈ *Call upon American Muslim advocacy groups to work against the jihad ideology.* Instead of endorsements of the U.S. Constitution and American values, Islamic institutions in the United States are filled with jihadist propaganda against Jews and Christians. A 2005 report by the Freedom House Center for Religious Freedom found material in American mosques teaching hatred of non-Muslims and stating that apostates from Islam should be killed, in accord with Muhammad's directive.[53] Here again, American Muslim organizations profess to reject the jihad of Osama bin Laden, but have been slow to back up their words with deeds. Five years after September 11 there are still no organized, comprehensive programs in American mosques and schools to teach against the jihad ideology or confront the elements of Muhammad's life that today fuel jihadist violence and subversion. This is not surprising given the pedigrees of such groups (the Council on American-Islamic Relations, for example, emerged from the Islamic Association of Palestine, a Hamas front) and the centrality of jihad in Islamic theology, but government officials and the mainstream media nevertheless generally treat these groups as moderate.[54]

Courageous officials and politicians, if any exist today, should challenge these groups to put up or shut up—to produce genuinely moderate and reformist initiatives that teach against Muhammad's warlike example, or to stop posing as moderate groups. And government and law enforcement officials should accordingly stop regarding these groups as trustworthy, loyal moderates who accept Western pluralism without reservation.

◈ *Revise immigration policies with the jihad ideology in view.* Western nations should develop immigration applications

that ask hard questions about the applicant's views on pluralistic societies, religious freedom, women's rights, and other
features of Western societies challenged by elements of
Muhammad's teachings and Islamic law. Of course, savvy
intelligence officials would not expect honest answers in all
cases, but the very presence of such questions would make it
clear that those who hope ultimately to transform Western
republics into sharia autocracies are not welcome in those
republics, and those who are found in them will be prose-
cuted and expelled. The need for immigration policies with
such a focus has been obscured by fears of "racism," but this
is not a racial issue. Muhammad's teachings are available to
all races, and people of all races adhere to them.

If no Western politicians can be found who are courageous enough to grasp
this nettle, Western countries will eventually pay a stiff price, when the
jihadists they have admitted carry out successful jihad attacks, or inspire
native-born Muslims to do so—or when they advance sharia provisions by
peaceful means, as in the campaign in the United Nations and several
European countries for the adoption of Islamic blasphemy laws in the wake
of the Muhammad cartoon riots.[55]

The words and deeds of Muhammad have been moving Muslims to
commit acts of violence for fourteen hundred years now. They are not
going to disappear in our lifetimes; nor can they be negotiated away. The
best thing that Western governments can do is recognize their character
and move to limit their influence within their countries and around the
world, calling upon Muslims who call themselves moderate to renounce
definitively these elements of Islam, and formulate their policies bearing in
mind that most Muslims will continue to regard Muhammad as "an excellent example of conduct."

The sooner this is done, the safer we all will be. But as long as this man-
ifold problem continues to be ignored, Muhammad will continue to
inspire his followers to wield the sword in his name.

Acknowledgments

There are many people, living and dead, working openly and in hiding, to whom I owe thanks. For a variety of reasons, I am unable to name them here, and must offer instead a "thank you to...you know who you are." To all defenders of civilization against barbarism, however and wherever you are, and however you are contributing to this struggle, my gratitude and thanks.

Notes

Chapter One: Why a biography of Muhammad is relevant today

1. "President Bush Discusses Global War on Terror," White House press release, April 10, 2006.
2. Farida Khanam, "Muhammad's Love and Tolerance for Mankind," IslamOnline, March 15, 2006. Http://muhammad.islamonline.net/English/His_Example/HisQualities/07.shtml. The riots involved cartoons in a Danish newspaper (and republished elsewhere) that depicted the Prophet Muhammad in a comical light. Many of the images circulated in the Islamic world were fakes distributed by Islamic agitators to inflame riots and protests.
3. Carl Ernst, *Following Muhammad*, University of North Carolina Press, 2003, 85.
4. Safi-ur-Rahman al-Mubarakpuri, *Ar-Raheeq Al-Makhtum (The Sealed Nectar)*, Al-Furqan, 1979, 492, 499.
5. http://www.cair.com.
6. Ibrahim Hooper, "What Would Prophet Muhammad (pbuh) Do?," Council on American-Islamic Relations, February 4, 2006. Http://www.islam101.com/rights/wwpMdo.htm.
7. "Cleric calls on Mohammed cartoonist to be executed," *The Telegraph*, February 6, 2006.
8. Saw stands for "Salla Allahu aalayhi Wasallam," which translates as "May the blessing and the peace of Allah be upon him."
9. "Kill those who insult the Prophet Muhammad (saw)," Al-Ghurabaa, http://www.alghurabaa.co.uk/articles/cartoon.htm. The article is quite specific about Muhammad's example: "Ka'ab ibn Ashraf was assassinated by Muhammad ibn Maslamah for harming the Messenger Muhammad (saw) by his words, Abu Raafi' was killed by Abu Ateeq as the Messenger ordered in the most evil of ways for swearing at the prophet, Khalid bin Sufyaan was killed by Abdullah bin Anees who cut off his head and brought it to the prophet for harming the Messenger Muhammad (saw) by his insults, Al-Asmaa bintu Marwaan was killed by Umayr bin Adi' al-Khatmi, a blind man, for writing poetry against the prophet and insulting him in it, Al-Aswad al-Ansi was killed by Fairuz al-Daylami and his family for insulting the Messenger

Muhammad (saw) and claiming to be a prophet himself. This is the judgement of Islam upon those who violate, dishonour and insult the Messenger Muhammad (saw)."

10. "Iraq: Al-Zarqawi Group Boasts Killing Christian," Adnkronos International, April 7, 2006.
11. "Murder 'infidels', Mukhlas urges," *The Australian*, December 18, 2005.
12. Karen Armstrong, *Muhammad: A Biography of the Prophet*, (San Francisco: Harper San Francisco, 1992), 5.
13. "Jihad in Canada," *Ottawa Citizen*, June 5, 2006.
14. "Blair condemns bombers who 'act in name of Islam,'" Reuters, July 7, 2005.
15. Dr. Muqtedar Khan, "The Legacy of Prophet Muhammad and the Issues of Pedophilia and Polygamy," *Ijtihad*, June 9, 2003.
16. See, for example, "Fears as young Muslims 'opt out,'" BBCNews, March 7, 2004.
17. Richard Lowry, "The 'To Hell with Them' Hawks," *National Review*, March 27, 2006.
18. "Gaza EU offices raided by gunmen," BBC News, January 30, 2006.
19. "Gazans burn Danish flags, demand cartoon apology," Reuters, January 31, 2006.
20. "EU Press Reprints Explosive Cartoons," IslamOnline, February 1, 2006.
21. Alan Cowell, "European papers join Danish fray," *New York Times*, February 8, 2006; "Protests Over Muhammad Cartoon Grow," Associated Press, January 30, 2006.
22. "Group stokes cartoon protest," Reuters, February 1, 2006; "Fatwa issued against Danish troops," Agence France Press, February 1, 2006.
23. "Q&A: The Muhammad cartoons row," BBC News, February 7, 2006; "Kashmir shutdown over Quran desecration, Prophet caricature," India-Asia News Service, December 8, 2005; "Cartoons of Mohammed cause death threat," DR Nyheder, December 3, 2005; "Muslim World League calls for UN interventions against disdaining religions," Kuwait News Agency, January 28, 2006.
24. "Clinton warns of rising anti-Islamic feeling," Agence France Presse, January 30, 2006.
25. Hassan M. Fattah, "At Mecca Meeting, Cartoon Outrage Crystallized," *New York Times*, February 9, 2006.
26. "Cartoon Body Count," http://www.cartoonbodycount.com.
27. Toby Sterling, "Dutch Filmmaker Theo Van Gogh Murdered," Associated Press, November 2, 2004.

28. "Everyone Is Afraid to Criticize Islam," interview with Ayaan Hirsi Ali, *Spiegel*, February 6, 2006.

Chapter Two: In search of the historic Muhammad

1. Dr. Muqtedar Khan, "The Legacy of Prophet Muhammad and the Issues of Pedophilia and Polygamy," *Ijtihad*, June 9, 2003.
2. Bukhari, vol. 3, book 46, no. 2468.
3. Maxime Rodinson, *Muhammad*, translated by Anne Carter, Pantheon Books, 1980, 279-283.
4. Bukhari, vol. 7, book 68, no. 5267.
5. Bukhari, vol. 1, book 8, no. 402.
6. Bukhari, vol. 4, book 56, no. 2832.
7. Von Denffer, 18-19.
8. The word *hadith*'s Arabic plural is *ahadith*, and this is found in much English-language Muslim literature. However, to avoid confusing English-speaking readers I have used the English plural form.
9. "Hadith & Sunnah," www.islamonline.net.
10. Abdul Hamid Siddiqi, Introduction to Imam Muslim, *Sahih Muslim*, translated by Abdul Hamid Siddiqi, Kitab Bhavan, revised edition 2000, v.
11. "Ibn Hisham's Notes," in Ibn Ishaq, *The Life of Muhammad: A Translation of Ibn Ishaq's Sirat Rasul Allah*, A. Guillaume, translator, (Oxford University Press, 1955), 691.
12. Ibid., xxxv.
13. Ibid., xxxvii.
14. Ibid., 516.
15. Ibid., 451.
16. My own copy bears the stamp of an Islamic bookstore in Lahore, Pakistan.
17. AH stands for *anno Hegirae*, year of the Hijra, or the number of years after Muhammad fled Mecca for Medina, according to the Islamic lunar calendar.
18. A.I. Akram, *The Sword of Allah: Khalid bin Al-Waleed: His Life and Campaigns* (Feroze Sons Publishers, Lahore, 1969).
19. Javeed Akhter, *The Seven Phases of Prophet Muhammad's Life*, International Strategy and Policy Institute, 2001.
20. PBUH stands for "Peace Be Upon Him."
21. Salah Zaimeche, "A Review on Early Muslim Historians," Foundation for Science Technology and Civilisation, 2001.
22. Yahiya Emerick, *The Life and Work of Muhammad*, Alpha Books, 2002, 311.

23. S. Moinul Haq and H. K. Ghazanfar, "Introduction," in Ibn Sa'd, *Kitab Al-Tabaqat Al-Kabir*, vol. I, S. Moinul Haq and H K. Ghazanfar, translators, Kitab Bhavan, n.d., xxi.
24. Ibn Al-Rawandi, "Origins of Islam: A Critical Look at the Sources," in *The Quest for the Historical Muhammad*, Ibn Warraq, editor, Prometheus Books, 2000, 111.
25. Ibn Sa'd, *Kitab Al-Tabaqat Al-Kabir*, vol. II, 64.
26. See Ignaz Goldhizer, *Muslim Studies*, vol. 2, George Allen & Unwin Ltd., 1971.
27. Itzchak Weismann, "God and the Perfect Man in the Experience of 'Abd al-Qâdir al-Jaza'iri," *Journal of the Muhyiddin Ibn 'Arabi Society*, volume 30, Autumn 2001.

Chapter Three: Muhammad becomes a prophet

1. Ibn Sa'd, *Kitab Al-Tabaqat Al-Kabir*, Vol. I, S. Moinul Haq and H. K. Ghazanfar, translators, Kitab Bhavan, n.d. 111.
2. Ibn Ishaq, 73.
3. Ibn Ishaq, 80.
4. Ibn Sa'd, vol. I, 169.
5. Ibn Ishaq, 80.
6. Ibn Sa'd, vol. I, 177.
7. Ibid., vol. I, 186.
8. Ibid., vol. I, 115.
9. Ibn Ishaq, 82.
10. Ibid., 69.
11. Ibid., 83.
12. Ibid., 93.
13. *The Sealed Nectar*, 493.
14. Ibn Sa'd, vol. I, 491.
15. Muslim, book 30, no. 5776.
16. Ibn Sa'd, vol. I, 489.
17. Ibid., vol. I, 504.
18. Ibid., vol. I, 520.
19. Bukhari, vol. 9, book 91, no. 6982.
20. Ibn Sa'd, vol. I, 220.
21. Bukhari, vol. 9, book 91, no. 6982.
22. Ibn Sa'd, vol. I, 227.
23. Ibn Ishaq, 106.
24. Bukhari, vol. 6, book 65, no. 4953.
25. Ibn Ishaq, 106.
26. Bukhari, vol. 9, book 91, no. 6982.
27. Ibn Ishaq, 107.

28. Bukhari, vol. 1, book 1, no. 3.
29. Ibid.
30. Ibn Ishaq, 107.
31. Ibid., 107.
32. Bukhari, vol. 9, book 91, no. 6982.
33. Bukhari, vol. 4, book 59, no. 3238.
34. Bukhari, vol. 2, book 19, no. 1125.

Chapter Four: Muhammad's revelations and their sources

1. Mishnah Sanhedrin 4:5.
2. Parts of this collection were added later, after the time of Muhammad—but not the section containing the material about Abraham. See Harry Freedman and Maurice Simon, *Bereshit Rabbah*, Soncino, 1961. Vol. 1, xxix.
3. Some may even have tried to fool Muhammad. One man who used to come talk with Muhammad later derided him for perhaps being too credulous in accepting those "tales of the ancients": "Muhammad is all ears: if anyone tells him anything he believes it." Once again Allah answered through the Prophet of Islam: "Among them are men who molest the Prophet and say, 'He is (all) ear.' Say, 'He listens to what is best for you: he believes in Allah, has faith in the Believers, and is a Mercy to those of you who believe.' But those who molest the Messenger will have a grievous penalty" (Qur'an 9:61). The Qur'an also calls down divine woe upon "those who write the Book with their own hands, and then say: 'This is from Allah,' to traffic with it for miserable price! Woe to them for what their hands do write, and for the gain they make thereby" (2:79). And when speaking of the People of the Book, Allah tells Muhammad: "As for those who sell the faith they owe to Allah and their own plighted word for a small price, they shall have no portion in the Hereafter. Nor will Allah (deign to) speak to them or look at them on the Day of Judgment, nor will He cleanse them (of sin). They shall have a grievous penalty. There is among them a section who distort the Book with their tongues: (As they read) you would think it is a part of the Book, but it is no part of the Book; and they say, "That is from Allah," but it is not from Allah: It is they who tell a lie against Allah, and (well) they know it! . . . If anyone desires a religion other than Islam (submission to Allah), never will it be accepted of him; and in the Hereafter he will be in the ranks of those who have lost (all spiritual good). How shall Allah Guide those who reject Faith after they accepted it and bore witness that the Messenger was true and that clear signs had come unto them? But Allah guides not a people unjust" (Qur'an

3:77-78; 85-86). Did some of the Jews mock Muhammad's prophetic pretensions by representing their own writings, or folkloric or apocryphal material, as divine revelation, and selling them to him?

4. Bukhari, vol. 9, book 91, no. 6982.

5. Bukhari, vol. 4, book 61, no. 3617.

6. "The Arabic Gospel of the Infancy of the Savior," 1, Wesley Center for Applied Theology, http://wesley.nnu.edu/biblical_studies/non-canon/gospels/infarab.htm.

7. "The Arabic Gospel of the Infancy of the Savior," 36.

8. Muslim, book 25, no. 5326.

9. "The example of Muslims, Jews and Christians is like the example of a man who employed labourers to work for him from morning till evening. They worked till mid-day and they said, 'We are not in need of your reward.' So the man employed another batch and said to them, 'Complete the rest of the day and yours will be the wages I had fixed (for the first batch).' They worked up till the time of the 'Asr prayer and said, 'Whatever we have done is for you.' He employed another batch. They worked for the rest of the day till sunset, and they received the wages of the two former batches." Bukhari, vol. 1, book 9, no. 558.

10. W. St. Clair Tisdall, "The Sources of Islam," in *The Origins of the Koran: Classic Essays on Islam's Holy Book*, Ibn Warraq, editor, (New York: Prometheus Books, 1998), 281.

11. Bukhari, vol. 1, book 1, no. 2.

12. Ibn Sa'd, vol. I, 228.

13. Imam Muslim, *Sahih Muslim*, Abdul Hamid Siddiqi, trans., Kitab Bhavan, revised edition 2000, book 30, no. 5764.

14. Muslim, book 30, nos. 5766 and 5767.

15. Bukhari, vol. 6, book 66, no. 4985.0

16. Quoted in Ali Dashti, *23 Years: A Study of the Prophetic Career of Mohammed*, F. R. C. Bagley, translator, (Costa Mesa: Mazda Publishers, 1994), 132.

17. Abu Ja'far Muhammad bin Jarir al-Tabari, *The History of al-Tabari*, Volume VIII, *The Victory of Islam*, Michael Fishbein, translator, (New York: State University of New York Press, 1997), 2.

18. Bukhari, vol. 9, book 97, no. 7420.

19. "Behold! Thou didst say to one who had received the grace of Allah and thy favor [Zaid]: 'Retain thou (in wedlock) thy wife, and fear Allah.' But thou didst hide in thy heart that which Allah was about to make manifest: thou didst fear the people, but it is more fitting that thou shouldst fear Allah. Then when Zaid had dissolved (his marriage) with her, with the necessary (formality), We joined her in marriage to thee." Why? "In order that (in future) there may be no

difficulty to the Believers in (the matter of) marriage with the wives of their adopted sons, when the latter have dissolved with the necessary (formality) (their marriage) with them. And Allah's command must be fulfilled."

20. Tabari, vol. 8, 3.
21. Bukhari, vol. 9, book 97, no. 7420.
22. Ibn Kathir, *Tafsir Ibn Kathir* (Abridged), volume 7, Darussalam, 2000, 698.
23. This is a prayer said at a time of distress.
24. Bukhari, vol. 4, book 55, no. 2741.
25. The followers of Muhammad during his lifetime are known as his Companions. The Companions fall into two groups: al-Muhajiroun, or the emigrants from Mecca, and al-Ansar (helpers), the inhabitants of Medina who took in those emigrants after the Muslims' flight (hijra) from Mecca to Medina. The Aws and Khazraj were two Ansari tribes.
26. Bukhari, book 5, vol. 64, no. 4141.
27. Bukhari, vol. 9, book 97, no. 7500.
28. *Zihar* was a pre-Islamic method of divorce, whereby a man would declare that his wife was to him like the back of his mother.
29. See also Bukhari, vol. 3, book 52, no. 2661.
30. Ahmed ibn Naqib al-Misri, *Reliance of the Traveller ['Umdat al-Salik]: A Classic Manual of Islamic Sacred Law,* translated by Nuh Ha Mim Keller. Amana Publications, 1999, o24.8.
31. See Sisters in Islam, "Rape, Zina, and Incest," April 6, 2000, http://www.muslimtents.com/sistersinislam/resources/sdefini.htm.
32. See Stephen Faris, "In Nigeria, A Mother Faces Execution," www.africana.com, January 7, 2002.
33. Emerick, 213.
34. Muhammad Husayn Haykal, *The Life of Muhammad*, Isma'il Razi A. al-Faruqi, translator, 1968. Http://www.witness-pioneer.org/vil/Books/MH_LM/default.htm.
35. Karen Armstrong, *Muhammad: A Biography of the Prophet,* (San Francisco: Harper San Francisco, 1992), 197.
36. Ibid., 202.
37. Bukhari, vol. 7, book 77, no. 5825.

Chapter Five: "A warner in the face of a terrific punishment"

1. Ibn Ishaq, 115.
2. Ibid., 117.
3. Bukhari, vol. 6, book 65, no. 4770.

4. Ibn Ishaq, 118.
5. Muslim, vol. 1, book 1, no. 406.
6. Emerick, 69.
7. *Tafsir Ibn Kathir (Abridged)*, Darussalam, 2000. Vol. 6, 39-40.
8. Ibn Ishaq, 181.
9. Ibn Ishaq, 118; later in his biography Ibn Ishaq relates another tradition that places the killing by Sa'd bin Abu Waqqas shortly after the Hijra.
10. Ibn Sa'd, vol. I, 143.
11. Ibn Ishaq, 130.
12. Ibid., 146.
13. Ibid., 131.
14. Ibid., 199.
15. Ibid., 212-213.
16. Qur'an 22:39-40.
17. Ibn Ishaq, 212-213.
18. Qur'an 2:193, Ibn Ishaq, 212-213.
19. Abu Ja'far Muhammad bin Jarir al-Tabari, *The History of al-Tabari*, Volume VI, *Muhammad at Mecca*, W. Montgomery Watt and M. V. McDonald, translators, (New York: State University of New York Press, 1988), 107.
20. Ibn Ishaq, 165.
21. Ibn Sa'd, vol. I, 237.
22. Ibn Ishaq, 165-166.
23. Ibn Ishaq, 166. The Gharaniq, according to Islamic scholar Alfred Guillaume, were "'Numidian Cranes' which fly at a great height." Muhammad meant that they were near Allah's throne, and that it was legitimate for Muslims to pray to al-Lat, al-'Uzza, and Manat, the three goddesses favored by the pagan Quraysh, as intercessors before Allah.
24. Tabari, vol. vi, 109.
25. Ibid., vol. vi, 111.
26. Ibn Ishaq, 166.
27. Ibid., 166-167.
28. Haykal, "The Story of the Goddesses," in *The Life of Muhammad*.
29. Emerick, 80.
30. Armstrong, 111.
31. Tabari, vol. vi, 107, 108.
32. Ibn Sa'd, vol. I, 236-239.
33. Bukhari, vol. 6, book 65, no. 4863.
34. Ibn Ishaq, 182.
35. Bukhari, vol. 5, book 63, no. 3887.
36. Muslim, book 1, no. 309.
37. Ibn Ishaq, 182.
38. Bukhari, vol. 5, book 63, no. 3887.

39. Bukhari, vol. 4, book 60, no. 3394.
40. Bukhari, vol. 5, book 63, no. 3886.
41. Ibn Sa'd, vol. I, 248.
42. Ibn Ishaq, 183.
43. Ibid.

Chapter Six: Muhammad becomes a warlord

1. Ibn Sa'd, vol. I, 261. This is the conventional dating; however, Ibn Sa'd also records other traditions that differ widely over the length of Muhammad's stay in Mecca.
2. Bukhari, vol. 6, book 65, no. 4492.
3. Ibn Ishaq, 231-233.
4. Ibid., 239.
5. Ibid., 240-241.
6. Bukhari, vol. 6, book 65, no. 4480.
7. Ibn Ishaq, 240-241.
8. Bukhari, vol. 6, book 65, no. 4480.
9. Ibn Ishaq, 240-241.
10. Bukhari, vol. 6, book 65, no. 4480.
11. Ibn Ishaq, 240-241.
12. Ibn Sa'd, vol. I, 188.
13. Ahmad Von Denffer, 'Ulum al-Qur'an: An Introduction to the Sciences of the Qur'an, The Islamic Foundation, 1994, 136.
14. Tafsir Ibn Kathir, vol. 1, 87.
15. Ibn Ishaq, 247.
16. Bukhari, vol. 4, book 56, no. 3012.
17. Ibn Ishaq, 287-288.
18. Ibid., 288.
19. Ibid., 256.
20. Bukhari, vol. 4, book 60, no. 3394.
21. Bukhari, vol. 6, book 65, no. 4493.
22. Ibn Ishaq, 259.
23. Bukhari, vol. 4, book 61, no. 3635.
24. Ibn Ishaq, 267.
25. Bukhari, vol. 4, book 61, no. 3635.

Chapter Seven: "War is deceit"

1. Ibn Sa'd, vol. II, 9.
2. Ibn Ishaq, 294.
3. Ibid., 297.
4. Ibid., 298.

5. For various estimates on the number of Muslim warriors, see Ibn Sa'd, vol. II, 20-21.

6. Ibn Ishaq, 300.

7. Ibid., 300.

8. Ibid., 301.

9. Bukhari, vol. 4, book 58, no. 3185.

10. Bukhari, vol. 1, book 8, no. 520.

11. Ibn Ishaq, 308.

12. Ibid., 304.

13. Bukhari, vol. 4, book 57, no. 3141.

14. Bukhari, vol. 4, book 58, no. 3185.

15. Ibn Ishaq, 306.

16. Steven Stalinsky, "Dealing in Death," *National Review Online*, May 24, 2004.

17. Bukhari, vol. 1, book 8, no. 438.

18. Ibn Ishaq, 308.

19. Ibn Ishaq, 326-327.

20. Ibn Sa'd, vol. II, 40.

21. Abu Ja'far Muhammad bin Jarir al-Tabari, *The History of al-Tabari*, Volume VII, *The Foundation of the Community*, M. V. McDonald, translator, State University of New York Press, 1987, 86.

22. Ibn Ishaq, 363.

23. Tabari, vol. VII, 86.

24. Ibn Ishaq, 363.

25. Ibid., 367.

26. Bukhari, vol. 5, book 64, no. 4037.

27. Ibid.

28. Ibn Ishaq, 367.

29. Bukhari, vol. 5, book 64, no. 4037; Ibn Sa'd, vol. II, 37.

30. Ibn Sa'd, vol. II, 37.

31. Ibn Sa'd, vol. II, 39.

32. Ibn Ishaq, 369; Ibn Sa'd, vol. II, 36.

33. Ibn Ishaq, 369.

34. "Man who knew some plot suspects says Islamic 'anger' prevalent," CBC News, June 16, 2006.

35. Ibn Sa'd, vol. II, 60-61.

36. Ibn Ishaq, 372.

37. Ibid., 381-382.

38. Bukhari, vol. 5, book 64, no. 4065.

39. Ibn Ishaq, 382.

40. Bukhari, vol. 5, book 64, chapter 22.

41. Ibn Ishaq, 386.

42. Ibid., 387.

43. Bukhari, vol. 5, book 64, no. 4072; Ibn Ishaq, 376.
44. Sayyid Qutb, *Social Justice in Islam*, translated by John B. Hardie and Hamid Algar, revised edition, Islamic Publications International, 2000, 19.
45. Tabari, vol. VII, 158.
46. Ibid., 159.
47. Muslim, book 19, no. 4326.
48. Ibn Ishaq, 437.
49. Ibid., 437.
50. Ibn Sa'd, vol. II, 70.
51. Ibn Ishaq, 438.
52. Muslim, book 19, no. 4347.

Chapter Eight: Casting terror into their hearts

1. Ibn Ishaq, 450.
2. Ibid., 452.
3. Abu Ja'far Muhammad bin Jarir al-Tabari, *The History of al-Tabari*, Volume VIII, *The Victory of Islam*, Michael Fishbein, translator, (New York: State University of New York Press, 1997), 11.
4. Ibn Ishaq, 452.
5. Tabari, vol. VIII, 12.
6. Ibn Ishaq, 452.
7. Tabari, vol. VIII, 15.
8. Ibid., 16.
9. Ibn Ishaq, 454.
10. Tabari, vol. VIII, 17-18.
11. Ibn Ishaq, 455.
12. Ibn Ishaq, 458; cf. Bukhari, vol. 4, book 56, no. 3030; Muslim, book 32, no. 6303.
13. Ibn Ishaq, 459.
14. Ibid., 460.
15. Bukhari, vol. 4, book 56, no. 2813.
16. Ibn Ishaq, 461.
17. Ibid.
18. Ibid., 462.
19. Bukhari, vol. 4, book 56, no. 3043.
20. Ibn Sa'd, vol. II, 93; cf. Ibn Ishaq, 464.
21. Ibn Ishaq, 468-469.
22. Abu-Dawud Sulaiman bin Al-Aash'ath Al-Azdi as-Sijistani, *Sunan abu-Dawud*, Ahmad Hasan, translator, Kitab Bhavan, 1990. Book 38, no. 4390.
23. Ibn Ishaq, 464.

24. Ibn Sa'd, vol. II, 93.
25. Ibn Ishaq, 464.
26. Bukhari, vol. 5, book 64, no. 4028.
27. W. N. Arafat, "New Light on the Story of Banu Qurayza and the Jews of Medina," *Journal of the Royal Asiatic Society of Great Britain and Ireland*, 1976, 100-107.
28. Emerick, 226.
29. Armstrong, 207-208.
30. Yaakov Lappin, "UK Islamists: Make Jihad on Israel," YNet News, July 2, 2006.
31. Bukhari, vol. 4, book 57, no. 3128.
32. Ibn Ishaq, 490.
33. Bukhari, vol. 9, book 97, no. 7409.
34. Ahmed ibn Naqib al-Misri, *Reliance of the Traveller ['Umdat al-Salik]: A Classic Manual of Islamic Sacred Law*, translated by Nuh Ha Mim Keller. Amana Publications, 1999, o9.13.
35. Ibn Ishaq, 491.
36. Muslim, book 25, no. 5334. Other ahadith say that another of Muhammad's wives, Zaynab, was the one who was originally named Barra.
37. Ibn Ishaq, 491.
38. Muslim, book 32, no. 6255.
39. Ibn Ishaq, 492.
40. Ibn Ishaq, 492.
41. Muslim, book 38, no. 6680.
42. Muslim, book 38, no. 6681.
43. Emerick, 233.
44. Ibn Ishaq, 504.
45. Ibid., 504.
46. Ibid.
47. Ibn Ishaq, 509.
48. Emerick, 239.
49. Emerick, 240.
50. Ibn Ishaq, 511.
51. Ibid.
52. Ibn Sa'd, vol. II, 132-133.
53. Ibn Ishaq, 515.
54. Ibn Sa'd, vol. II, 136.
55. Ibn Sa'd, vol. II, 137.
56. Bukhari, vol. 4, book 57, no. 3152.
57. Muslim, book 10, no. 3761.
58. Ibn Ishaq, 515.
59. Ibn Sa'd, vol. II, 137.

60. Bukhari, vol. 5, book 64, no. 4200.
61. Ibn Sa'd, vol. II, 142.
62. Ibn Ishaq, 516.
63. Ibn Sa'd, vol. II, 249.
64. Bukhari, vol. 3, book 51, no. 2617.
65. Ibn Ishaq, 516.
66. Bukhari, vol. 5, book 64, no. 4428.
67. Bukhari, vol. 4, book 58, no. 3169; cf. Ibn Sa'd, vol. II, 144.
68. Bukhari, vol. 5, book 64, no. 4242.
69. Bukhari, vol. 1, book 8, no. 371.
70. Muslim, book 8, no. 3329.
71. Muhammad Al-Munajjid, "The true nature of the enmity between the Muslims and the Jews," Al-Minbar.com, http://www.alminbar.com/khutbaheng/9022.htm; Steven Emerson, "Prepared Statement of Steven Emerson Before The Senate Judiciary Committee Subcommittee on Terrorism, Technology and Government Information," February 24, 1998. http://www.geocities.com/CollegePark/6453/emerson.html.

Chapter Nine: Victorious through terror

1. Ibn Ishaq, 544.
2. Ibid., 545.
3. Ibid., 546.
4. Ibid., 547.
5. Ibid.
6. Ibn Sa'd, vol. II, 168.
7. *Sunan Abu-Dawud*, book 38, no. 4346.
8. Bukhari, vol. 7, book 76, no. 5727; cf. online edition, vol. 8, book 82, nos. 794-797. http://www.usc.edu/dept/MSA/fundamentals/hadith-sunnah/bukhari/082.sbt.html.
9. Bukhari, vol. 9, book 87, no. 6878.
10. Bukhari, vol. 9, book 88, no. 6922; cf. vol. 4, book 56, no. 3017.
11. Dr. Ibrahim B. Syed, "Is Killing An Apostate in the Islamic Law?" *The American Muslim*, April 2005. http://theamericanmuslim.org/tam.php/features/articles/shariah_is_killing_an_apostate_in_the_islamic_law/. "Pbuh" stands for "peace be upon him," and is commonly added by pious Muslims after they mention the name of a prophet.
12. Ibn Ishaq, 550-551.
13. Ibid., 552.
14. Ibid., 552-553.
15. Ibid., 554.

16. Ibn Ishaq, 555. It is interesting to note that Emerick renders "The apostle killed men in Mecca" as "the Prophet of God fought in Mecca." See Emerick, 254.

17. Ibn Ishaq, 567.

18. Ibid., 569.

19. Guillaume explains: "*ha'it* means wall and also the garden which it surrounds."

20. Ibn Ishap, 589.

21. Ibn Ishaq, 595-596.

22. Bukhari, vol. 4, book 56, no. 2941.

23. Bukhari, vol. 9, book 93, no. 7196.

24. Ibn Sa'd, vol. I, 306.

25. Bukhari, vol. 5, book 64, no. 4424.

26. Bukhari, vol. 4, book 61, no. 3618.

27. "Fight in the name of Allah and in the way of Allah. Fight against those who disbelieve in Allah. Make a holy war, do not embezzle the spoils; do not break your pledge; and do not mutilate (the dead) bodies; do not kill the children. When you meet your enemies who are polytheists, invite them to three courses of action. If they respond to any one of these, you also accept it and withhold yourself from doing them any harm. Invite them to (accept) Islam; if they respond to you, accept it from them and desist from fighting against them.... If they refuse to accept Islam, demand from them the Jizya. If they agree to pay, accept it from them and hold off your hands. If they refuse to pay the tax, seek Allah's help and fight them." Muslim, book 19, no. 4294.

28. Abu'l Hasan al-Mawardi, *al-Ahkam as-Sultaniyyah (The Laws of Islamic Governance)*, Ta-Ha Publishers, 1996, 28.

29. Ibn Sa'd, vol. I, 310-311.

30. Ibn Ishaq, 602.

31. Ibid., 608.

32. Ibid., 609.

33. Bukhari, vol. 4, book 56, no. 2785.

34. Muslim, book 10, no. 31; cf. Bukhari, vol. 1, book 2, no. 25.

35. Ibn Ishaq, 645-646.

36. Ibid., 643.

37. Muslim, book 19, no. 4366.

38. Ibn Sa'd, vol. I,328.

39. Ibn Sa'd, vol. I,328-329.

40. Bukhari, vol. 4, book 58, no. 3162.

41. Ibn Ishaq, 651.

42. Sita Ram Goel, *The Story of Islamic Imperialism in India*, Voice of India, revised edition 1994, 44.

43. Ibn Ishaq, 675.

44. Ibid., 676.

45. Ibid.

46. Bukhari, vol. 5, book 64, no. 4430.

47. Muslim, book 31, no. 6005.

48. Bukhari, vol. 7, book 75, no. 5666.

49. Bukhari, vol. 5, book 64, no. 4450.

50. Bukhari, vol. 5, book 64, no. 4428.

51. Bukhari, vol. 5, book 64, no. 4439.

52. Bukhari, vol. 5, book 64, no. 4431.

53. Ibn Sa'd, vol. II, 244-245; Bukhari, vol. 7, book 76, no. 5765.

54. Bukhari, vol. 2, book 23, no. 1341.

55. Bukhari, vol. 5, book 64, nos. 4441; vol. 2, book 23, no. 1330.

56. Bukhari, vol. 5, book 64, no. 4441.

57. Bukhari, vol. 5, book 64, no. 4458.

58. Bukhari, vol. 4, book 56, no. 2977.

59. Bukhari, vol. 5, book 64, no. 4449.

60. Bukhari, vol. 5, book 64, no. 4466.

61. Ibn Sa'd, vol. I, 164.

62. Muslim, book 31, no. 5877.

63. Bukhari, vol. 1, book 10, no. 678.

64. Muslim, book 31, no. 5916.

65. Bukhari, vol. 4, book 55, no. 2741.

Chapter Ten: Muhammad's legacy

1. "Vines calls founder of Islam a 'demon-possessed pedophile,'" Biblical Recorder, June 14, 2002.

2. "U.S. Baptist Minister Derogatory Remarks Sparks Anger," IslamOnline, June 15, 2002.

3. Bukhari, vol. 5, book 63, no. 3896; cf. Bukhari, vol. 7, book 67, no. 5158.

4. Armstrong, 157.

5. Tabari, vol. VII, 7.

6. "U.S. Baptist Minister Derogatory Remarks Sparks Anger," IslamOnline, June 15, 2002.

7. Sarvnaz Chitsaz and Soona Samsami, "Iranian Women and Girls: Victims of Exploitation and Violence," in *Making the Harm Visible: Global Sexual Exploitation of Women and Girls*, Donna M. Hughes and Claire M. Roche, editors, The Coalition Against Trafficking in Women, 1999. http://www.uri.edu/artsci/wms/hughes/mhviran.htm.

8. Amir Taheri, *The Spirit of Allah: Khomeini and the Islamic Revolution*, Adler and Adler, 1986, 90-91.

9. Taheri, 35.

10. Lisa Beyer, "The Women of Islam," *Time*, November 25, 2001.
    Reprinted at http://www.time.com/time/world/arti-
    cle/0,8599,185647,00.html.

11. "Child marriage 'violates rights,'" BBC News, March 7, 2001.

12. Andrew Bushell, "Child Marriage in Afghanistan and Pakistan,"
    America, March 11, 2002, p. 12.

13. Ibn Sa'd, vol. I, 439.

14. Syed Saeed Akhtar Rizvi, *The Life of Muhammad the Prophet*, Darul
    Tabligh North America, 1971. http://www.al-islam.org/lifeprophet/.

15. Bukhari, vol. 1, book 6, no. 304.

16. Bukhari, vol. 8, book 86, no. 6830.

17. Ibn Ishaq, 659-660.

18. Bukhari, vol. 6, book 65, no. 4581.

19. Bukhari, vol. 4, book 60, no. 3448.

20. Sunan Abu Dawud, book 37, no. 4310. Bukhari, vol. 4, book 60, no.
    3449.

21. Muslim, book 41, no. 6985.

22. Middle East Media Research Institute (MEMRI), "Friday Sermons
    in Saudi Mosques: Review and Analysis," MEMRI Special Report
    No. 10, September 26, 2002. www.memri.org. This undated sermon
    appeared on the Saudi website www.alminbar.net shortly before the
    MEMRI translation was made.

23. Ibn Kathir, vol. 4, 407.

24. Robert Hussein, *Apostate Son*, Najiba Publishing Company, 1998,
    161.

25. Farida Khanam, "Muhammad's Love and Tolerance for Mankind,"
    IslamOnline, March 15, 2006. http://muhammad.islamonline.net/
    English/His_Example/HisQualities/07.shtml

26. Ibrahim Hooper, "What Would Prophet Muhammad (pbuh) Do?,"
    Council on American Islamic Relations, February 4, 2006.
    http://www.islam101.com/rights/wwpMdo.htm.

27. "The SIMI I founded was completely different," Interview with Dr.
    Mohammad Ahmadullah Siddiqi, Rediff.com, September 2, 2003.
    http://www.rediff.com/news/2003/sep/02inter.htm.

28. Ibn Sa'd, vol. I, 422.

29. Ibid., 432.

30. Ibid., 433.

31. Bukhari, vol. 9, book 87, no. 6911.

32. Muslim, book 4, no. 2098.

33. Muslim, book 4, no. 2026.

34. Annemarie Schimmel, *And Muhammad Is His Messenger: The Ven-
    eration of the Prophet in Islamic Piety*, (Chapel Hill: University of
    North Carolina Press, 1985), 21.

35. Schimmel, 31.

36. Ibid., 35.

37. Ibid.

38. Frithjof Schuon, *Islam and the Perennial Philosophy*, J. Peter Hobson, translator. World of Islam Festival Publishing Company, 1976, 29. Quoted in Schimmel, 29.

39. Steven Stalinsky, "Palestinian Authority Sermons 2000-2003," Middle East Media Research Institute, Special Report No. 24, December 26, 2003.

40. Ibid.

41. Adeyeye Joseph and Agaju Madugba, "Bomb Scare in Lagos," *This Day*, November 22, 2003.

42. Steven Stalinsky, "The 'Islamic Affairs Department' of the Saudi Embassy in Washington, D.C.," Middle East Media Research Institute (MEMRI) Special Dispatch No. 23, November 26, 2003.

43. Ian Fisher, "A Tale of War: Iraqi Describes Battling G.I.'s," *New York Times*, December 5, 2003.

44. "Commander of the Khobar Terrorist Squad Tells the Story of the Operation," Middle East Media Research Institute Special Dispatch Series No. 731, June 15, 2004.

45. Amir Taheri, "Kerry Wins The Arab Vote," *New York Post*, August 18, 2004.

46. "Our Struggle with the Jews is a Struggle for Existence, Not a Struggle for Land," Al-Asaalah Magazine, Issue 30. http://www.allaahuakbar.net/jew/our_struggle_with_the_jews_is_a_struggle_for_existence.htm.

47. "Al-Qa'ida Internet Magazine Sawt Al-Jihad Calls to Intensify Fighting During Ramadan—'the Month of Jihad,'" Middle East Media Research Institute, Special Dispatch No. 804, October 22, 2004.

48. Zaigham Ali Mirza, "Muslim society 'has lost ability to strategise,'" *Khaleej Times*, November 3, 2004.

49. Adil Salahi, "No Fighting Before Explaining Islam," Arab News, January 31, 2005.

50. "President says his letter to President Bush was invitation to Islam," Islamic Republic News Agency, May 11, 2006.

51. "London Islamist Dr. Hani Al-Sibaai Justifies Slaughters in Iraq: The Prophet Muhammad Used to Slaughter As Well," Middle East Media Research Institute (MEMRI) Clip No. 576, February 22, 2005.

52. Yaakov Lappin, "UK Islamists: Make Jihad on Israel," YNet News, July 2, 2006.

53. "New Report On Saudi Government Publications," Center for Religious Freedom, January 28, 2005.

54. Debbie Schlussel, "Bush's scary CAIR friends," WorldNetDaily, October 16, 2001.

55. See, for example, Farahat Al-Abbar, "Norwegian Magazine Apologizes for Cartoons," IslamOnline, February 15, 2006.

Index